# PERSISTENCE

# PERSISTENCE

Evelyn Butts and the African American Quest
for Full Citizenship and Self-Determination

KENNETH COOPER ALEXANDER

ORANGE *frazer* PRESS
*Wilmington, Ohio*

ISBN 978-1949248-371 Softcover
ISBN 978-1949248-388 Hardcover

Published for the copyright holder by:
Orange Frazer Press
37½ West Main St.
P.O. Box 214
Wilmington, OH 45177
For price and shipping information, call: 937.382.3196
Or visit: www.orangefrazer.com

Book and cover design by:
Kelly Schutte and Orange Frazer Press
Cover image credit: *New Journal and Guide*

Library of Congress Cataloging-in-Publication Data

Names: Alexander, Kenneth Cooper, 1966- author.
Title: Persistence : Evelyn Butts and the African American quest for full
    citizenship and self-determination / Kenneth Cooper Alexander.
Description: Wilmington, Ohio : Orange Frazer Press, [2021] | Includes bibliographical
    references and index. | Summary: "Persistence tells the story of Evelyn Thomas Butts
    (1924-1993), an African American civil rights crusader from Norfolk, Virginia, whose
    nontraditional leadership and creative initiatives remain as models for political and social
    change. A courageous, low-income seamstress, Butts is best-known for her 1963 lawsuit
    that resulted in the U.S. Supreme Court's 1966 ruling to ban poll taxes from state and
    local elections. Butts relentlessly encouraged voter-participation and kept marginalized
    citizens connected with the national civil rights movement, which heavily relied on many
    unsung grassroots leaders-especially women-to overthrow America's Jim Crow system
    of segregation and suppression. Standing amid the continuum of Black resistance leaders
    questing for freedom, civil rights, equality, justice, dignity, and self-determination, Butts
    helped reshape the politics of Norfolk, a feat that continues to reverberate today"--
    Provided by publisher.
Identifiers: LCCN 2021005702 | ISBN 9781949248371 (paperback) | ISBN
    9781949248388 (hardcover)
Subjects: LCSH: Butts, Evelyn Thomas, 1924-1993. | African American women
    civil rights workers--Virginia--Norfolk--Biography. | African
    Americans--Civil rights--Virginia--Norfolk--History--20th century. |
    Civil rights movements--Virginia--Norfolk--History--20th century. | Poll
    tax--Law and legislation--United States. | Political
    participation--Virginia--Norfolk--History--20th century. | Norfolk
    (Va.)--Race relations--History--20th century. | Norfolk (Va.)--Politics
    and government--20th century. | Norfolk (Va.)--Biography.
Classification: LCC F234.N8 A45 2021 | DDC 323.092 [B]--dc23
LC record available at https://lccn.loc.gov/2021005702

First Printing

With love to my late parents who made my life possible
and departed too soon:

Ruby Rebecca Cooper (1949–1985)
&
David Alexander (1941–1992)

Blessed memories.
Thank you.

# CONTENTS

# FOREWORD
## *by* Dr. Tommy Bogger

Students and keen observers of American history understand that the system of rights enjoyed by most U.S. citizens is the result of persistent struggle. This system of rights began its evolution in Virginia when the Commonwealth was the setting for many critical actors who shaped the secular democratic ideals that have served as a model for democracies throughout the world. Evelyn Butts was among many Virginians whose work transformed our understanding of rights, specifically voting rights. Through her labor it became universally accepted that participation in elections, which are a cornerstone of democracy, should not be encumbered by taxes or fees on otherwise qualified voters.

The U.S. Supreme Court's decision in *Harper v. Virginia Board of Elections* struck down the imposition of poll taxes in state and local elections. Prior to that decision, this prerequisite for voter registration in Virginia placed an undue financial burden not only on African Americans, but on poor whites as well, significantly skewing Virginia's electorate and the Commonwealth's policy priorities in the process. Evelyn Butts' persistence drove the success of this case and changed the course of history.

In *Persistence*, Dr. Kenneth Alexander brings Mrs. Butts to life. She was a grassroots organizer who not only played a pivotal role in *Harper*, but in the broader modern Civil Rights Movement. News coverage of the movement rarely mentioned Mrs. Butts, and she left no written records. Nevertheless, by extensively mining interviews and employing a multidisciplinary approach along with comprehensive bibliographic research, Dr. Alexander has produced a scholarly study, examining Norfolk's history, the setting for her activism, and the role of women in the modern Civil Rights Movement.

Mrs. Butts not only inspired Dr. Alexander's inquiry, she also inspired his interest in community activism and public service. As an aspiring young politician in Norfolk, he was concerned that neighborhoods requiring the most attention and resources from the city had the lowest level of voter participation. Thus, he chose to analyze the tactics and leadership style of the most influential grassroots organizer who preceded him in Norfolk politics. His decision to focus on an "uncredentialed," Black, female, grassroots leader is very timely. Recently, scholars have begun acknowledging that women, and other marginalized persons, played essential roles in the Civil Rights Movement as well as other crusades. Their stories should be told, too—even though there may be few written records pertaining to them. Because Dr. Alexander has done an outstanding job of researching and telling the story of Evelyn Butts, his examination of her work and achievements should serve as a prototype for the study of other individuals who have been overlooked by history.

The author's extensive bibliography on an assortment of topics central to his study reflects the thoroughness of his research. It includes the relevant books on history and race relations in the South, Virginia, and the Norfolk area, as well as many recently published studies on non-traditional leaders, racism, sexism, and research methodologies. Dr. Alexander faced major challenges in conducting research on a subject who left no written records, was rarely mentioned in news articles, and had few surviving friends and contemporaries. Thus, he had to make the most out of the fragments of information that he uncovered in archives, newspapers, and interviews with the remaining associates of Evelyn Butts who were in good health and willing to share glimpses into her life. In essence, he employed "the methodologies of qualitative research,

historical research, and narrative inquiry with an interdisciplinary
... approach."

In his study of Mrs. Butts, Dr. Alexander provided insight for
answering a significant question that will interest scholars and
general readers alike: How could a low-income African-American
woman—a high school dropout who grew up under a system of Jim
Crow racism—become an accomplished civil rights bridge leader
who helped destroy the oppressive poll tax, inspire thousands of
voters, and change the political landscape of Norfolk, Virginia?
He concludes that Mrs. Butts was influenced by her aunt who read
newspapers and kept up with current events. Also, female activists
in her neighborhood noticed her and invited her to join the local
civic league and the NAACP. In 1954, the decision in *Brown v.
Board of Education* raised her hopes of a better education for her
daughters and she became involved in voter registration. Following
her 1966 poll-tax victory, Mrs. Butts engineered the registration
of almost 3,000 voters within six months, thereby helping her
male allies win election to the Norfolk City Council and the state
legislature.

Dr. Alexander also examines the personal qualities which
enabled Mrs. Butts to emerge as a leader. He details how she
leveraged her stout frame and outgoing personality to be at
times domineering and stubborn, yet also "encouraging ... and
nurturing." Those who worked with her knew that "... she was
genuinely interested in the well-being of her neighbors." She was
also described as an effective communicator, a good organizer, and
a tenacious campaigner.

While Dr. Alexander never met Evelyn Butts, he was mentored
by people she influenced, including his grandmother, Ruby Rose
Cooper. From them, he learned persistence, how to speak up, and
how to organize. By their example, he was shown the value and
importance of getting to know his neighbors and staying connected with them—and ultimately with many other fellow citizens all
across Norfolk. His determination and focus in striving for social

justice and a better world is a direct result of his connection to the Evelyn Butts Way.

*Persistence* is about the "continuum of grassroots African American resistance, resilience, and creative social justice advocacy" and Dr. Alexander has succeeded in bringing to life a complex African American woman who was a major force within that continuum. *Persistence* is a call to future generations. We must discover and acknowledge other grassroots leaders and activists from the era of the Civil Rights Movement and document their stories before it is too late. There is much to learn.

Evelyn Butts, represented by Attorney Joseph Jordan, sued the Governor of Virginia in 1963 to overturn the poll tax. The U.S. Supreme Court voted 6-3 against the poll tax in March 1966. This photo was taken at a Women of Virginia's 3rd Force meeting, where they discussed voter registration. Joe Jordan, Evelyn Butts, Minnie Jordan Brownson and seated is Mrs. Winfield. *Courtesy of Charlene Butts Ligon.*

# PREFACE

Evelyn Thomas Butts, a low-income African American seamstress, learned about voting power—and voter-suppression—during Virginia's Massive Resistance to public school desegregation in the 1950s.

On September 27, 1958, Virginia Governor J. Lindsay Almond Jr. ordered Norfolk's six all-White high schools and junior high schools closed rather than comply with a federal court order to enroll 17 African American students as part of desegregation. The pro-segregation Norfolk City Council scheduled an advisory referendum on November 18 on the question of whether the city should ask the governor to reopen the schools.

The referendum failed, with 12,340 people voting "no" (don't ask the governor to reopen) over 8,712 "yes" votes.[1] Apparently, only 3,500 to 3,700 African Americans participated in the referendum, and contemporary observers blamed Virginia's poll tax and other voter-suppression schemes.[2]

Butts, just emerging as a grassroots civil rights leader, was among those who recognized that the referendum results amounted to more evidence that the lives of Black Americans did not matter to the White-supremacist elites who ran Virginia; that African Americans did not have meaningful and equitable opportunities for political expression in the Old Dominion state; and that their hold on cherished freedoms and civil rights—the ability to fully and equally participate in American society without discrimination—was only tenuous, depending on the whims and say-so of non-Blacks.

Without voting strength, Butts recognized that African Americans could not achieve the full stature of citizenship, which included personal, social, and economic freedoms as well as the political,[3] and that Black communities had little voice in determining their own destinies or the path of their own lives and ambitions.

"We were powerless," Marie G. Young, a close friend of Evelyn Butts, recalled years later.[4]

Although Butts had already become active in her Oakwood neighborhood and in the NAACP, these realizations about civil rights and self-determination seemed to heighten her dedication to the voting-rights struggle—a cause for which she would become locally renown through her voter-participation initiatives and her landmark victory against the poll tax at the U.S. Supreme Court in 1966.

I never met Evelyn Butts, who died in 1993 while I was still feeling my way into neighborhood activism before immersing into Norfolk politics. However, I have come to appreciate her fierce resolve on a range of social justice issues, as well as on Black self-determination, equal citizenship, and especially voting rights and voter engagement. While specific details have changed from Butts' era to ours, the underlying principles that linked through her crusades have largely remained the same in our continuing struggles. They include the demands for fairness, equal opportunity, inclusiveness, and meaningful democratic participation, and to be treated with dignity and respect. Time after time, Butts showed up in the public arena to loudly assert that the lives of her low-income African American neighbors mattered, and so did the lives of other marginalized peoples and of future generations. The 21st century phrase "Black Lives Matter" had not yet been invented; however, Butts lived those words through her actions. She insisted on new textbooks for Black youngsters, not hand-me-downs from White-only schools; she picketed a supermarket for equal pay and working conditions for Black employees; she returned to Norfolk City Council meetings week after week on an assortment of community concerns.

My generation and future generations can learn much from Evelyn Butts about dedication to social justice causes, about determined persistence, and about inspiring leadership that motivates others to join the struggle.

I do not mean to suggest that we should be copycats of Butts' leadership style and techniques. What Butts did as a leader in her grassroots heyday worked for her personality and her times. Also, I believe that Butts recognized and valued the need for different types of leaders and what they could contribute. For example, she and Joseph A. Jordan Jr., who was both her lawyer and close friend, operated in sharp contrast to one another. Butts was boisterous, sprawling, and, at times, intimidating; Jordan, who needed a wheelchair for mobility, was more quiet, scholarly, laser-focused, and adept in political maneuvering. They knew each other's strengths and made for a good team in their common struggle for Black self-determination, full citizenship, inclusiveness, and meaningful participation in elections and government.

In addition, my study of Evelyn Butts has provided me greater insight about the need for continuity, persistence, and helping others develop their leadership abilities. As a result, I now see that Butts' accomplishments left a longer and wider wake, one whose powerful waves continue to roll through our time. Butts not only knocked on doors to encourage people to vote, her initiatives helped open doors for growing numbers of Black and other marginalized citizens stepping forward as emerging leaders.

Butts is best known for initiating the lawsuit that caused the U.S. Supreme Court to abolish poll taxes for state and local elections in 1966. But it was her ceaseless, practical, and well-organized community-based voter-outreach campaigns that helped elect African Americans to political office in Norfolk for the first time since Reconstruction about 80 years before. However, Butts' work as a grassroots civil rights leader and her efforts to advance Black self-determination were never well known outside of Virginia and, these days, are often forgotten within the Old

Dominion state, even in her hometown of Norfolk. As historian Dan Roberts wrote: "The pantheon of civil rights leaders includes obvious names such as Dr. and Mrs. Martin Luther King Jr., Jesse Jackson, Rosa Parks, Thurgood Marshall and Oliver Hill. Few outside Tidewater recall Butts' contributions."[5]

There are several possible reasons for the oversight: the national media during the 1950s and '60s usually focused on charismatic male leaders in the civil rights movement—and many historians initially followed the media's lead; after about 1970, Butts increasingly turned her considerable energies toward formal and partisan politics, and many local and statewide Virginia political hopefuls sought her support; and she declined advice from close friends who suggested she take notes about her civil rights work and accomplishments, excusing herself as too busy to tell her own story.

The few civil rights histories—books, articles, law journals—that include some mention of Evelyn Butts usually explore the legal issues involved in her 1963 poll-tax lawsuit. A more thorough review of her life and advocacy, however, reveals an overarching theme: Butts was not only fighting against the poll tax; she was on a quest to help fellow Black citizens achieve their long-sought goals of attaining full and equal citizenship and self-determination in every arena of their lives, including neighborhood-improvement issues and employment opportunities as well as participation in political decision-making.

My book aims to help remedy the general neglect of Butts' contributions as a grassroots civil rights leader by concentrating mostly on the heyday of her activism, from about 1954 to 1970, including her countless initiatives to increase voter registration, voter education, and voter turnout and to stand up for Black self-determination. There were several major challenges in my study, however. Butts did not leave many personal writings, was rarely quoted in newspapers during her civil rights heyday in the 1950s and '60s, and seemed reluctant—or even terse or self-effacing—when talking about her motivations. Also, she had never been the subject of in-depth scholarly research, and her closest allies and friends were rapidly aging or had already passed from this Earth.

This study of Evelyn Butts evolved from my doctoral dissertation at Antioch University's Graduate School of Leadership and Change. I began my exploration of Butts' life, activism, and grassroots leadership for four main reasons: to educate myself as a community leader in Norfolk; to help fellow citizens and future generations reflect upon their potential roles in civic engagement and social justice advocacy; to anchor Butts' essential place in the civil rights movement; and to consider how her creative leadership activities might teach us how to improve voter participation in general.

Along the way, I discovered a fifth reason: that it is important to collect and preserve the memories of Americans involved in the Civil Rights Movement of the 1940s, '50s, and '60s before it becomes too late to tap into their firsthand stories, experiences, and observations. In proceeding with my study of Evelyn Butts, I found that so many people who knew her well had already passed on or were too frail to participate in research interviews. Fortunately, Butts' last surviving daughter, Charlene Butts Ligon, had produced a self-published memoir of her mother's life, which proved invaluable to my work. I was also blessed to find several longtime Norfolk residents who had been close friends with Butts and participated in many of her voter-outreach campaigns. Their comments, anecdotes, and insights invigorate the story of Evelyn Butts as a flesh-and-blood social justice advocate who accomplished much more than lending her name to a voting-rights lawsuit.

From them I better understood the array of talents, skills, and experiences that equipped Butts for her many crusades and made her a necessary grassroots leader in the modern Civil Rights Movement. Her life story—including family tragedies and setbacks, nourishing moments from relatives and friends, and the ability to persevere and succeed—were representative of the travails, persistence, resilience, and triumphs of Black Americans, especially among women, in their long struggles against the Jim Crow system of apartheid that segregated and suppressed African Americans across the South.

Thus, there is yet another dimension in learning about the life and activism of Evelyn Butts. It adds to our understanding of America's experience with race relations and the keystone roles that Virginia played, right from the start,[6] when the first Africans to be unwillingly transported to British North America arrived in Point Comfort just a few miles from Norfolk in 1619.[7] Also, the Virginia colony was not only among the first to codify slavery between 1662 and 1705, its laws "became the standard that the other colonies followed."[8] This book recounts examples from the continuum of African American resistance to White supremacy's laws and practices, including those in defiance of Virginia's mostly nonviolent and paternalistic yet insidious form of White supremacy known as "The Virginia Way." As the great civil rights leader Ella Baker—also born in Norfolk—once observed about the Black struggle for self-determination and full citizenship, "the freedom movement has been and is as old as the existence of black people on this continent."[9]

It is also important to explore and learn from Evelyn Butts' leadership style to see why she was so effective at the community level. The modern Civil Rights Movement of the 1940s, '50s, and '60s relied heavily on the grassroots leadership and organizational abilities of countless unknown local citizens across the South—especially women usually working behind the scenes—who took it upon themselves to energize and mobilize their neighbors and connect them with the overall struggle to overthrow Jim Crow.

Pulitzer Prize-winning historian David Garrow recognizes that many earlier scholars of the Civil Rights Movement constructed their work on narrow and limited concepts of leadership, usually focusing on those who led or represented the major civil rights organizations.[10] Over the years, I saw that my own understanding of the Civil Rights Movement had been influenced by such a restricted perspective. I began to see that African American women largely had been ignored along with most leaders—male and female—at the grassroots level.

I came to agree with a newer set of scholars, such as Judy A. Alston and Patrice A. McClellan, who write in their 2011 book, *Herstories: Leading With the Lessons of the Lives of Black Women Activists*, that "The exclusion of Black women's roles in leadership literature and the overusage of the 'great man' leadership analysis limits our understanding of leadership as practiced by Black women activists."[11]

And as Joy James explains:

Remembering the contributions of lesser-known women activists and radicals increases understandings of antiracist leadership and progressive change. Male-dominated podiums or pulpits cannot completely hide the democratic agency of grass-roots workers. The majority of these activists were and continue to be women working in churches, schools, neighborhoods, farm fields, and factories, seeking democratic power, liberation, and sustenance.[12]

Sociologist Belinda Robnett also found that Black women in the civil rights struggle were "instrumental as leaders in the recruitment and mobilization process and effective, influential leaders who elicited loyalty from their followers."[13] Echoing Robnett, history professors Bettye Collier-Thomas and V. P. Franklin write in *Sisters in the Struggle: African American Women in the Civil Rights-Black Power Movement* that "Many African American women leaders operated at the local level, establishing the links and connections with grassroots organizations that provided the mass support for civil rights goals and objectives."[14]

Butts was a master at creating and establishing connections between local aspirations for self-determination and the overall movement for civil rights for Black and other marginalized people.

Throughout all her crusades, she continued to have faith in democracy. "The struggle for freedom for black men and black women," she once said, "rests with our right to vote."[15]

Such faith lies at the heart of my study of Evelyn Thomas Butts and contributes to the continuing lesson to which we must rededicate ourselves.

# PERSISTENCE

# SECTION I

*Introduction*

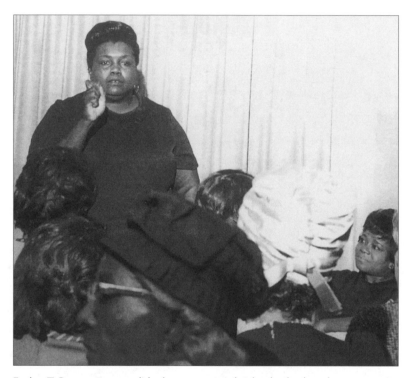

Evelyn T. Butts, an accomplished grassroots civil rights leader, kept her community informed and motivated on a variety of issues and crusades. Here, Butts conducts a meeting of the Women of Virginia's Third Force, an action organization that she led as president. *Courtesy of Charlene Butts Ligon.*

# CHAPTER 1
## Evelyn Butts and Her Quests

On August 28, 1963, an unemployed African American seamstress stood amid some 250,000 people facing the Lincoln Memorial in Washington, D.C., as the Rev. Martin Luther King Jr. boomed out his now-famous "I Have a Dream" speech. That seamstress was Evelyn Thomas Butts, the wife and main caregiver of a disabled World War II veteran and mother of three children. As King intoned his rolling phrases about freedom, citizenship, justice, dignity, and "the promises of democracy," Butts already knew the deep meanings of such words from her experience as a grassroots civil rights leader back in her hometown of Norfolk, Virginia.

Frustrated that Blacks did not have a meaningful voice on many issues directly affecting their lives and communities, Butts would soon catapult herself onto the national stage in pursuit of a dream of her own. She aimed to destroy the last vestiges of the hated poll tax, which had suppressed voting rights for many African Americans and poor whites since the dawn of the Jim Crow era.

The 24th Amendment to the United States Constitution, signed by President Lyndon B. Johnson on February 4, 1964, had abolished poll taxes for federal elections but had left it to individual states to decide the fate of such levies for state and local elections. Alabama, Arkansas, Mississippi, Texas, and Virginia refused to end their fees.

On March 24, 1966, the U.S. Supreme Court gave Butts her victory. By a 6–3 vote, the high court struck down poll taxes for state and local elections in *Harper v. Virginia State Board of Elec-*

*tions,* which had derived from a lawsuit originally filed as *Mrs. Evelyn Butts v. Governor Albertis Harrison et al,* on November 29, 1963.

"I thought it was ridiculous that you had to pay to vote," Butts tersely explained years later about her lawsuit to overthrow Virginia's $1.50 a year poll tax.

Butts, often blunt and to the point, did not spend a lot of time pontificating about democracy. That was never the Evelyn Butts Way for bringing about social justice and political change. She saved her words for door-to-door campaigns to encourage neighbors to register to vote, learn about the candidates, and show up on Election Day, and to keep her community informed and inspired on a variety of civil rights issues. She also never shied from confrontations with the powers-that-be, white or African American.

While she might be best known in history for initiating the successful poll-tax lawsuit, Evelyn Butts' real legacy is that of an accomplished community leader and organizer who quested for African American self-determination and political participation during her grassroots heyday, from the mid-1950s to about 1970.

She aimed her crusades against more than the onerous poll tax or various instances of racial and economic repression. In her overarching struggle, Butts sought to dismantle decades of entrenched White supremacy and Jim Crow apartheid laws and policies embedded into our society and institutions, and often interlocked with gender and class biases.

Throughout her quests, Butts remained unflinching and courageous. "She had more nerves than a red fox," said longtime friend Herbert Smith, who often drove Butts to her activities.[1] Another friend, Alveta V. Green, admired Butts' bravery, especially in filing her poll-tax lawsuit against Virginia Gov. Albertis Harrison, a member of the powerful Harry F. Byrd political machine. "Evelyn wasn't scared of the governor or anyone," Green said. "I can't think of anybody else who would have taken that up because we were afraid of losing our jobs or something like that."[2]

Many of Butts' action campaigns brought results, most notably in politics. After Butts knocked out the poll tax, she stepped up her door-knocking efforts to enlist and motivate voters. The combination of winning at the Supreme Court and expanding the voter-registration rolls parlayed into the election in 1968 of Joseph A. Jordan Jr., the first African American member of the Norfolk City Council in nearly 80 years. Another breakthrough came in 1969 with the election of William P. Robinson Sr., the first Black member of Virginia's House of Delegates from Norfolk, also since the Reconstruction Era.

Black political achievements in Norfolk were more than electoral. Jordan brought to the City Council a more inclusive philosophy about appointments to municipal boards and commissions—non-paid, citizen-based panels that examine various public issues and make recommendations to the council for laws and policy decisions. Jordan demanded greater diversity in the council appointments, not only by race and gender but also by economic and social class. He requested more representation for the "man on the street, the downtrodden, and the lesser citizen."[3]

In 1975, Butts became one of those new representatives as Jordan successfully nominated her to serve on the powerful Board of Commissioners of the Norfolk Redevelopment and Housing Authority, making her the first African American woman in that major policy-making post. Then, in 1982, she earned a gubernatorial appointment to the Virginia Board of Housing and Community Development.

Electoral victories and other governmental achievements also set in motion long-range consequences. Norfolk's African American citizens became more encouraged about political participation, and Norfolk's White political class began showing more respect to requests from the city's Black communities, especially those that flexed their newfound voting power. In addition to the City Council appointing more Black citizens to municipal boards and commissions, the city government began hiring Blacks to key jobs, eventually including city manager, school superintendent, police chief, and planning director.

I am a direct but second-generation beneficiary of Butts' path-clearing work. In my public-service career, I have been appointed to Norfolk's Human Services Commission, Economic Development Authority, and Planning Commission; elected to the Virginia House of Delegates and state Senate; and elected mayor—the first African American to achieve that post in Norfolk—in 2016, which was 50 years after the Supreme Court banned the poll tax for state and local elections, thanks to Evelyn Butts and her lawyers.

Along the way, I have learned from mentors, such as Horace Downing and Dr. Yvonne B. Miller, who were mentored by Evelyn Butts. Downing, a longtime president of the Beacon Light Civic League in Norfolk's Berkley neighborhood, where I grew up, said of Butts when she died in 1993:

> She taught me everything I know about working with the community and politics. I didn't have to go to school. I got a master's degree from her. She taught a whole lot of fellows who now enjoy the benefit of her work.[4]

Among the many lessons Downing taught me were to make myself known to neighbors and continually remind them to vote as Election Day approached, and to be persistent when dealing with City Hall.

Miller, who got her start in politics by helping Butts with voter-registration drives in the 1960s, was elected to Virginia's House of Delegates in 1983 and then the state Senate in 1987, the first African American woman to have those distinctions. She recruited me to run for a delegate seat in 2002.

Although Miller died in 2012, I still remember her words when I was elected: "We are all brothers and sisters, even though we are not always treated that way. So, never forget that we are all equal

Evelyn Butts and Joe Jordan in 1963. Butts sued the governor of Virginia to overturn the poll tax on the grounds that it violated the 14th Amendment. The U.S. Supreme Court voted 6-3 to eliminate the poll tax in March 1966. *Courtesy of Charlene Butts Ligon.*

and don't forget you have a right to be there. Don't be afraid. You don't have to bow down to anybody."

Miller, like Butts and Joseph A. Jordan Jr., thought it important to have more Black voices on our governing bodies and that those African Americans elected or appointed to important positions be well-grounded in their communities. For Miller, the eldest of 13 siblings, whose father was a laborer, rooted her reasons in the spirit of African American self-determination and were remindful of the Black political outlook during the Reconstruction Era. One of my favorite descriptions of the newly enfranchised Black political leaders of the post-Civil War period comes from historian-journalist Lerone Bennett Jr., who writes in *Black Power U.S.A.* that they were "an articulate core of common people who spoke with uncommon authority, not because they had conferred with the people, but because they were the people."[5] In my case, those everyday people were my neighbors in Berkley, a long-overlooked area of Norfolk that has struggled for decades with an array of entrenched urban problems.

Many times, the seeds of social change take time to establish strong roots and grow, but the eventual fruits taste that much sweeter. From my study of Evelyn Butts, especially in the context of the continuity of African American resistance and resilience, my lens into the future now has a sharper resolution. As mayor in 2020, I gave the order for the city government to remove the 80-foot-high "Johnny Reb" Confederate monument from downtown Main Street during the wave of Black Lives Matter protests that swept our nation. I will further elaborate on my decision later in this book, but my reasons included having developed a better understanding of the long struggle against White supremacy by African Americans, especially by Evelyn Butts and her generation.

Much more needs to happen to make Norfolk—and America—truly inclusive, fair, just, and comfortable for all citizens. Understanding history helps to guide us, and that includes learning about Evelyn Butts' struggles for Black self-determination and full citizenship and her achievements.

Struggles and achievements are only part of the story, though. We must also consider how Butts carried forth her social justice advocacy in her grassroots heyday for adaption to our times. The

Evelyn Butts Way of promoting change was not limited to "official" crusades to get out the vote, petition drives, public demonstrations, or speaking out at city council meetings. For Butts, civic activism was very much a lifestyle that she lived and breathed in ordinary places such as her kitchen, neighborhood streets, and her daughter's elementary school. Her activism also entailed a leadership style called "bridge leadership," which sociologist Belinda Robnett contends was critical to the success of the Civil Rights Movement.[6]

Evelyn T. Butts (in back) stands with her husband, Charlie, and their youngest daughter, Charlene, in front of their house at 1070 Kennedy Street in Norfolk, Virginia. This photo was taken in 1968 before this part of the house was enclosed to create Butts' sewing room. *Courtesy of Charlene Butts Ligon.*

# CHAPTER 2
## Life and Leadership

The seeds of change that eventually blossomed into the Evelyn Butts Way of addressing social justice issues were planted during Butts' struggling childhood, nourished by loving family and concerned neighbors, cultivated by a mentor and close friends—but also continuously strengthened by Butts' early lessons about courage and entrepreneurial self-determination. Young Evelyn learned about survival, bravery, and self-reliance in her preteen and teenage years during the Great Depression of the 1930s and then as a young wartime bride in the 1940s, managing her household while her husband served in the U.S. Army thousands of miles away. In these formative years, Butts saw that survival depended on taking action, she grew confident in her leadership abilities, and she recognized that the skills for self-reliance extended from mutual help among family members and neighbors.

Evelyn Thomas Butts was born in Norfolk, Virginia, on May 22, 1924, the third of six children to George and Lottie Thomas. In 1929, George Washington Thomas, a laborer, moved his family to New York City, where he helped build the Empire State Building.[1] The relocation would have life-changing impacts on Evelyn's young life. Her eldest sister, Julia, and then her mother both contracted tuberculosis in New York and soon died.

George Thomas then moved his family back to Norfolk, where Evelyn and the other surviving children would live with their mother's sister, Rosa Lee White, or "Aunt Roz," in Oakwood, a mostly poor, all-Black neighborhood that was not yet absorbed into Norfolk's municipal boundaries. As such, Oakwood residents did not have the benefit of indoor plumbing, sanitary sewers, or paved roads. They traveled on dirt roads or gravel streets, and had to contend with a range of other infrastructure problems.

However, living with Aunt Roz turned into a building block in Evelyn's development because Aunt Roz was a model for entrepreneurship—as a real estate agent and owner of a small corner grocery store—and for paying attention to politics. "She understood the issues, voted in every election, and encouraged her friends and neighbors to do likewise," Evelyn Butts' daughter, Charlene Butts Ligon observed.[2]

While young Evelyn was being exposed to political news and values, she also encountered another set of challenges. She had to step into the role of "female head of the family" as now the eldest girl, even though she was only a 10-year-old fifth-grader.[3]

A few years later, Evelyn faced another personal setback. She became pregnant with Patricia Ann, the first of her three daughters, and dropped out of school in the 10th grade. She never married the young father and did not return to school; yet Evelyn made sure her younger siblings would graduate.

Dramatic changes came again in 1941, when Evelyn met steel-worker Charlie Butts, 17 years her senior, who had returned to Virginia from upstate New York. They married on September 7, 1941, and rented a small house four blocks from her Aunt Roz in Oakwood.

By the end of the year, the United States had entered the con-flagration of World War II. Charlie Butts joined the war effort in 1942, serving in the U.S. Army's 839th Engineering Battalion and operating and maintaining gas- and diesel-powered shovels as well as working with a bridge crane.

With her husband overseas, Evelyn—still a teen and now raising a second baby, Lilly Jeanette—had to find work. Her culinary skills earned her a job as a cook in the Ames & Brownley department store in downtown Norfolk, and she cleaned houses on the side.[4]

Then bad news arrived. Charlie had been severely injured in a blast in New Guinea. He returned to the United States in 1945 with shrapnel wounds in his back and spent seven months in a Kentucky hospital before returning home to Norfolk.[5]

Many young mothers might break down in such trying circumstances, but Evelyn Butts stayed strong. She even became active in the Oakwood Civic League, a community organization that promoted neighborhood improvements. Through the civic league, Butts learned to speak up in front of audiences and to speak out. Her career as a political citizen was just beginning.[6]

Meanwhile, Charlie had recovered enough to work as a civilian employee of the Norfolk Naval Air Station for a few years, and he and Evelyn were able to buy the small house they had been renting. But Charlie was forced to retire early when his disability worsened. Still, he took odd jobs around the neighborhood to supplement his Army pension. The couple's youngest child, Charlene, was born in 1948 in the segregated Norfolk Community Hospital.[7]

Even though Black women like Butts were able to find work—albeit low-paying and out of public view—in downtown Norfolk during and after World War II, the central business district largely did not welcome African Americans as shoppers. "A black woman couldn't try on a hat in many of the department stores," social justice advocate Vivian Carter Mason once angrily reported. "To try on a dress, she had to go into a hidden closet ... so that the other customers would not see that a black person was trying on a dress that they might want to try on."[8]

Evelyn Butts eventually left the downtown department store to do domestic work for two White women, the Lambert sisters, and ironed at home for a "Mrs. Brown." At some point in the early 1950s, Butts decided it would be easier for her to care for her then-100% disabled husband and the children by working at home as a seamstress.[9] "She started staying home and sewing, and sometimes people would bring their laundry and clothes and bedsheets for ironing," Ligon recalled, adding that her mother also

13

made or tailored much of the family's clothing. Also, by working at home, Butts could avoid the indignity of having to ride the local segregated buses and trolleys to jobs in other parts of Norfolk.[10]

Charlie Butts, meanwhile, began receiving a small monthly disability payment from the Army, a source of stability for the Butts family because it "paid the mortgage and the utilities," Ligon said. "My Mom supplemented the disability check with the day's work she did and later by sewing."[11]

Years later, Butts proved to be fearless when challenging Jim Crow, White supremacy and anyone—White or African American—who got in the way of her crusades. But she had forged her resolve and skills during her formative years in the 1930s and '40s, when she overcame the premature deaths of a sister and her mother, survived being a single mother during the Great Depression, and became the key caregiver for her disabled husband. She felt she could face anything else the world would throw at her, including racist oppression. Her attitude became, "I am stronger than you. You can't keep me down."

Ligon has agreed with my assessment. "My momma was strong, and maybe she was because of all the adversity in her young life that she knew she needed to be strong," Ligon told me. "It also meant a lot to her to be able to do things for people."[12]

In the early 1950s, Butts began discovering venues for her gravitation toward social justice and politics. Oakwood neighborhood activism led her to join the Norfolk Branch of the National Association for the Advancement of Colored People (NAACP). Soon, her interest in civil rights further ripened with the Supreme Court's pivotal 1954 *Brown v. Board of Education* decision that declared segregated public schools unconstitutional.[13] At about this time, Butts saw that she needed transportation to her many meetings, forums, rallies, and similar events. Her family did not own a car, but that didn't stop her. Butts began enlisting neighbors to drive her.[14]

Butts was also beginning to apply an entrepreneurial knack to social justice advocacy. She recognized that she could inform neighborhood women about civil rights and politics through get-togethers on household issues and child-rearing.[15] In doing so, Butts transformed her kitchen into an important space for nourishing grassroots activism. Feminist scholars have explained that such intimate gatherings help make "sustained public resistance possible"[16] because everyday life becomes part of the "political struggle," or the "political space."[17]

Years later, Butts would again deploy her ability to combine interests and skills as a matter of economic necessity. In the late 1970s, Evelyn and Charlie Butts learned they were eligible to tap into a Veterans Administration's (VA) grant program as they moved from their old home to a new one, and that the VA money could also be used to add wheelchair access and other features to accommodate disabilities. Unfortunately, Charlie enjoyed the house for only a brief time as he died on November 9, 1979. A year later, however, Evelyn turned the new house into another home-based business, taking in up to three elderly, disabled veterans as boarders for whom she would also provide meals. The arrangement supplemented her seamstress income until the end of her life.[18]

⸺⸺◆⸺⸺

The years immediately after World War II and into the early 1960s made for a heady time for young civil rights activists like Evelyn Butts, who were feeling their way through the world. Challenges to Jim Crow arose on almost all fronts, albeit with serious and deadly threats against the lives of many activists—and even nonactivists. Even professional sports were ending apartheid policies with Jackie Robinson's breakthrough into Major League Baseball in 1947, a beacon that inspired African American baseball fans in Norfolk to boycott the Norfolk Tars minor league team until management agreed to integrate the team and stadium in 1954. On the national scene, the Rev. Martin Luther King Jr. and Rosa Parks were leading the Montgomery Bus Boycott of 1955–56, other bastions were falling, and growing numbers of people, Black and White, organized themselves against segregation, discrimination, and racist brutalities.

As an emerging activist, Butts was developing into a force to be reckoned with, and she stood out from the crowd in both her physicality and demeanor. Family and friends used terms such as the following to describe her: large, loud, gravel-voiced, and, at times, stubborn, domineering and bullheaded.[19] Daughter Charlene Butts Ligon described her 5-foot 7-inch mother as "a big woman ... stout and pillowy, and her size was part of her personality."

In Ligon's words:

> She had a big voice and big laugh to go along with her girth, and under the right circumstances she could come across as intimidating. She knew it, too. She did not mind that people in and outside the family called her bossy.[20]

Her approach could alternate from commanding to encouraging and from blistering to sweet-talking. Said Ligon, "She knew when to be bold and when to be soft. It was a rare gift." To friends and allies, Butts' personality, especially when she was "caring and nurturing" made it hard for them to turn away from her ideas and requests.[21] "She had this way of magnetizing people," said friend Charlie Bryant, while Walter H. Green Sr. observed, "She was the type of person, if she came to your door, you couldn't tell her to go away."[22] State Del. William P. Robinson Jr. characterized Butts as "a woman who didn't know the meaning of the word 'no.'"[23]

As Butts stepped up her community and political activities, she often did so in partnership with Norfolk-based civil rights attorney Joseph A. Jordan Jr., who later represented her in the poll tax lawsuit and would become the first African American elected to the Norfolk City Council since Reconstruction. With Jordan, Butts helped to form or revamp several grassroots political organizations, such as Virginia's Women of the Third Force (sometimes

"3rd Force"), which became her main vehicle for encouraging political citizenship through voter-registration, voter-education, and voter-turnout initiatives. She also spoke out and organized against Norfolk's segregated public schools, and picketed against various instances of discrimination in the community. Butts became an ardent follower of the Rev. Martin Luther King Jr. and served as secretary of Norfolk's chapter of King's Southern Christian Leadership Conference (SCLC).[24]

A problem-solving activist-organizer and civil rights litigant, Butts traveled a pathway pioneered by countless African American women who found ways to stand up against racial and sexual abuses throughout the brutal years of slavery and cruel decades of Jim Crow apartheid.

Described by Norfolk historian Tommy L. Bogger as "a wizard of grassroots organization,"[25] Butts channeled her leadership qualities mostly through three community groups that directly affected the lives of untold thousands of her fellow Norfolk citizens: the Oakwood-Rosemont Civic League, serving as president from 1959 to 1985; Women of Virginia's Third Force, serving as president from 1958 until her death in 1993; and Concerned Citizens for Political Education, for which she was chairperson from 1968 to 1990.

The Concerned Citizens became a sought-after endorsement by candidates until the mid-1980s. Butts and other leaders of the group would interview candidates and then print its endorsements on yellow-colored paper under the title "Goldenrod Ballot." Political scientists Elsie M. Barnes and Ronald E. Proctor observe that, "In its heyday, in the 1970s, it was considered to be the most influential endorsement a candidate in Norfolk could receive. Such an endorsement would reap several thousand black votes."[26]

In the 1970s and '80s, Butts' activities increasingly turned to more formal and partisan politics. She chaired the Second Congressional District Democratic Committee and, from 1980 to 1984, Butts ran three times for the Norfolk City Council—but lost all three hotly contested attempts.

Yet even as her power began to wane, Norfolk politicians—
White as well as African American—knew and respected Butts'
reputation for getting voters to the polls. G. Conoly Phillips, a
White businessman, sought re-election to the City Council in
1986 even though he had lost favor with a politically powerful
group of other White businessmen. Phillips turned to Butts and
beat the odds. "She was able to get me 5,000 Black votes," Phillips said. "If it hadn't been for Evelyn Butts, I would never had
been elected in '86."

About this time, Butts also found herself in bitter leadership
fights, including within the African American community. Weakened physically as well as politically, Butts still maintained a loving
cadre of followers, but she never regained her full stature.

After Butts died on March 11, 1993, mourners recalled Butts'
path-carving energy of her earlier days as a brave and savvy
game-changer. "She single-handedly helped transform the political
process of Norfolk to make it a useful tool for Black empower-
ment," said Paul Riddick, a City Council member and former
Norfolk NAACP president.[28] "No one has or will equal her role
and ability to mobilize the masses to vote and make an impact on
an election."

Yet, her political demise was also noted. Columnist Earl Swift
in *The Virginian-Pilot* regional daily newspaper wrote that Butts
was "an unappreciated heroine" who had "dived from the heights of
power to something very close to irrelevance." He concluded: "History better be kind to this woman. Evelyn Butts was important."[29]

———◆———

As a grassroots civil rights leader, Evelyn Butts was a natural
at earning credibility by serving in the same trenches as her fellow
struggling citizens and doing the same grunt work.

"She wasn't afraid to ask people to do things, and she set the
example by doing those things herself," friend Alveta V. Green

recalled.[30] Former neighbor Andrew Smith, described Butts as "a great role model for us," explaining that "She'd always fight for us. She was right there in the neighborhood doing these things. We could actually see her working. It gave us all a sense that you can fight City Hall and that you can win."[31]

Butts' hands-on efforts often went beyond the call of duty—sometimes resulting in humorous moments that reinforced the loyalty of friends and followers.

A case in point: In May 1968, Butts stepped up when the Southern Christian Leadership Conference sought local volunteers to house and feed out-of-town participants in the upcoming national Poor People's Campaign as they stopped in Norfolk en route to Washington, D.C. Alveta V. Green fed her guest a breakfast of cereal and fruit before driving to pick up the young man who stayed at Butts' home and take both visitors to the campaign's local meetup point. "Evelyn had a spread for her guest that put my breakfast to shame. I felt so bad, I asked, 'Evelyn, can we have some of that too?'" Green said. Butts, who loved combining her culinary talents with social justice activities, cheerfully agreed. "We laughed about that for a while," Green said.

While Butts could be a joyful warrior, most of her advocacy activities for political inclusion and self-determination did not end so mirthfully. Still, her friends and allies found it a treat to watch Butts in action, from confronting the politically powerful, to going door to door to rally neighbors, to encouraging neighborhood schoolchildren. Butts relished all opportunities.

Norfolk City Council sessions turned into frequent speaking platforms for Butts. There, she would lecture the council for 15 to 20 minutes about one issue or another, yet she would not get angry if the council members rejected her plea. "She just told them, 'I'll see you again next week,'" said friend Herbert Smith, who drove Butts to the meetings.[32]

Butts also proved to be a tenacious fighter against perceived injustices.

Driving home from work one winter day, Smith noticed a family being evicted from an apartment building in the nearby Chesapeake Gardens community—with snow falling on all their belongings. Minutes later, Smith said, he told Butts what he had witnessed and she said, "Take me over there." Butts marched up to the apartment employees and a deputy sheriff who were carrying out the eviction and "told them 'you can't put people out like this,'" Smith recalled.[33]

"Whatever else she said, it looked like she [had] scared them to death," Smith continued. "The deputy sheriff turned those guys around and made them put all that furniture back in the house."[34]

Such incidents helped Butts gain local fame as "the voice of the poor and disenfranchised," as she is characterized in a history of Norfolk's African American community.[35] Watching Butts stick up for poor and marginalized people also inspired Herbert Smith to assist Butts on many of her missions, usually by driving her to meetings and events even after he had just come home from a long, hard day of labor as a brick mason.[36]

Butts could also be as unrelenting with neighbors as she was with local authorities. If Green mentioned to Butts that a neighbor would not sign a political petition on some issue, Butts would respond: "Give me that petition. I'm going to get her to sign." Green added, "And that's what she did."[37]

She also frequently prodded neighbors to pay their poll taxes so they could vote. "She would check with you, 'Did you pay it?' And, if not, she'd be 'Get down there and get it done! Thank you!'" said Herbert Smith.[38]

Butts was also unafraid to take on African American institutions. Marie G. Young, a close friend and her chief lieutenant in Women of Virginia's Third Force, told a news reporter that the organization, under Butts' leadership, once picketed the Black-owned *Journal and Guide* newspaper after disagreeing with a political endorsement.[39]

"Evelyn was fearless," Green repeated to me several times in interviews for this book.[40]

Butts would naturally command attention when she led a neighborhood meeting or a gathering of the Women of Virginia's Third Force. "I can always remember her gesturing with her right hand and arm while talking," said Charlene Butts Ligon. "And no matter what topic, she would always get in something about voting because she said that was the way for us to have our voice heard."[41]

She also had an aptitude for rousing audience members into action. "When anything came up, she had somebody, some man with a car, one of her drivers, and she could say, 'Go take this petition and that one,' and she knew it would get done. We were like her army," Green noted.[42]

Creative and entrepreneurial like her Aunt Roz, Butts possessed a knack for combining her talents in ways that helped other citizens connect with both her and community issues. Annette Bryant told a news reporter that Butts was always available to help with a question about cooking or sewing—just as Oakwood neighborhood women had assisted a younger Butts years earlier. Butts would then use such opportunities to pass on information about civil rights or politics. "And we always got a good laugh out of her. She was an all-around person. She loved her family, loved her neighborhood and, oh yeah, she could cook!" Bryant said.[43]

In effect, Butts built upon the community esprit de corps that she had learned years earlier from her Aunt Roz and other Oakwood women who assisted her as a single mother and then a young bride whose Army husband had gone off to war. In giving back to her neighborhood through homemaking tips, Butts demonstrated an effective grassroots leadership technique of using "community mothering" to motivate "political agency."[44]

Butts conceived of another motivational opportunity in her leadership of the Parent Teacher Association (PTA) at daughter Charlene's elementary school, especially in voter-participation advocacy work. One year, Butts installed a large cardboard chart in the school and listed the names of all the parents—with a star next to each one who was registered to vote. She envisioned this display as a way to motivate other parents to register and had cleared the arrangement with the school's principal. However, the principal then removed the chart either on direct orders from Norfolk's school superintendent or in fear of losing his job.[45]

Alveta V. Green witnessed Butts' leadership and organizational abilities at many events. For example, Butts helped launch Joseph A. Jordan Jr.'s successful candidacy for the Norfolk City Council with a meeting of dozens of women in Green's living room in late 1967. Butts told the gathering that Jordan needed to collect a certain threshold of voter signatures to properly file as a candidate, and she explained to the women how to collect the signatures and make sure the signers were registered voters in Norfolk and had clearly printed their addresses. "This happened right over there, and we set up folding chairs all over the room," Green told me on a visit to her home. "Evelyn gave them a real good pep talk about going out and getting this petition signed."[46]

In most of her grassroots activities—especially with the Oakwood-Rosemont Civic League, Women of Virginia's Third Force, and Concerned Citizens for Political Education—Butts applied similar methods of leadership. They included hours of personal outreach through door-to-door canvassing and telephone calls, organizing carpools or van rides for dozens of people to attend local government meetings and other events, carefully maintaining rosters of registered voters, and mentoring other African Americans with leadership abilities.

In Butts' heyday, the small house where she raised three children, cared for her disabled husband, and worked as a seamstress, also served as her command headquarters for organizing neighborhood, civil rights, and political action. "I remember her having her legal pads with lists of people she had to coordinate," Ligon said. "And if they were doing something for Election Day, she had to make sure they all had their lunches."[47]

Family and friends say she was also so prepared with handwritten lists of neighbors and other Norfolk residents that she could quickly determine who she needed to reach out to and either call that person, knock on their door, or send a volunteer with a car to give the person a ride.

"I do my homework. And nobody knows how that homework gets done," Butts once told a newspaper reporter on an election day.[48]

Butts would use the same process over and over for a variety of issues or when trying to make sure that everyone she knew voted on Election Day.

"I can still hear [Butts] with her megaphone riding down our street ... calling my mother and grandmother by name, reminding them and the entire neighborhood to get out and vote," Melony Spratley remembered.[49]

Ligon recalled a typical Election Day scenario. Her mother would arrive at her precinct polling place at 6 a.m., toting lunch with her because she planned to be there all day. She also had either a handwritten list of everyone registered to vote in her precinct or computer printout in later years, and arranged to have "four cars and drivers on hand."[50] "She knew everyone in the community, and as they came to vote, she marked them on the list," Ligon said. "But if they didn't vote by a certain time," then Butts would send one of the drivers to the person's home and expect the person to show up at the polls.[51]

Herbert Smith, Butts' reliable driver for so many activities, was always among the drivers on Election Day, too, and said he sometimes would carry "four or five voters at a time."[52]

As the years went by, the primary changes in Butts' outreach techniques entailed learning how to drive herself and using computer-generated voter lists.[53]

Whether it was politics or civil rights, Butts always tried to help others around her gain greater insight and access to the political process—the opposite of what most Black Virginians at the time experienced under the domination of White political elites. She was even able to procure a voting machine, which she carried to various community meetings for confidence-building demonstrations. "She would go around to the neighborhoods to educate the people with it and then encourage them to go register to vote," said Alveta V. Green. "Evelyn would tell them, 'You don't need to be afraid to go and vote. This is how you vote on the machine.'"[54]

Butts was so passionate about voting power that whenever she met newcomers to Norfolk, she made sure to ask about their voter-registration status, Green also recalled.[55]

Political candidates also got to know Butts up close as she hosted many gatherings where voters could meet the candidates. Some such events became legendary. In 1977, President Lyndon B. Johnson's son-in-law, Charles S. "Chuck" Robb, stayed overnight in Butts' home while successfully campaigning for lieutenant governor of Virginia and held a press conference there. Robb's visit generated some humor in the Butts family as a niece, Roxanne, teased her Aunt Evelyn: "He don't have enough money to stay at a hotel? Dude must be hard up if the best he can do is stay in Oakwood." Butts replied curtly, "It's politics."[56]

Visits from out-of-town and state-level politicians created a buzz in the Oakwood neighborhood. "You could tell when people like that came to her house," recalled Rachel Smith, daughter of Herbert Smith. "There were police cars or state troopers or something, so everybody would be going, 'Who's at Ms. Evelyn's house today?' And you went by to see what's going on."[57]

Butts also seemed popular with Oakwood neighborhood children, Rachel Smith said. Butts frequently engaged with children playing outdoors, asking about their well-being and their parents. Invariably, she also inquired about their grades in school, reminded them that they were the future generation, and fussed at them if she caught them playing hooky. "She really pushed education. One of the things she'd say was 'Your moment is going to come, but you got to be ready for it. That's why you go to school and go to college so you'll be ready for a different day. You got to be ready,'" Rachel Smith said.[58]

Her talks with children weren't always about school. She loved watching them play, and many times gave youngsters a little money to run errands for her. As the children grew, Butts told them she would provide them with job references. "If we had a question about something and she didn't know, she said she'd look into it. And she did," Rachel Smith said. "That's how the kids grew to love her because she was a woman of her word."[59]

"Ms. Evelyn was the go-to person to get stuff done in Oakwood, and you saw every day she was doing something," Rachel Smith added.[60]

Some youngsters were so impressed with Butts that they chose to write essays about her for Black History Month.

"I didn't know Booker T. Washington," Rachel Smith said. "But I knew Evelyn Butts."[61]

———— ◆ ————

**Leadership Style:** Two scholars of leadership, Richard A. Couto and Belinda Robnett, provide keys to interpreting Butts' leadership abilities, style, and techniques. Couto's work in analyzing "citizen leaders" serves as a backdrop to Robnett's more specific depiction of what she has termed "bridge leaders."

To Couto, grassroots citizen leaders are vital to a democracy but are not often appreciated, especially early on in their efforts. Couto observes that there were two competing forces: All political systems erect barriers to change, while the work of citizen leaders inherently means trying to reduce or remove those obstacles to enable broader citizen participation and allow new issues to surface for serious consideration.

Couto ascribes several characteristics to grassroots citizen leaders, including that they organize action to improve life in low-income communities; work to elevate conditions for all people instead of further enable a chosen few; step forward when there is a need for sustained leadership; recognize and respect existing communities; have simple motives; and base their actions on a belief that society is responsible for conditions that impair human dignity.

Such citizen leaders, Couto says, are essential to a movement despite a general tendency in the public, news media, and academia to ignore them for not fitting within traditional definitions of leadership or not holding formal titles and not being a part of established institutions and businesses.

Couto asks, "What sets these largely ignored leaders apart?"[62] The answer, he says, includes their ability to "facilitate organized action to improve conditions of people in low-income communities and to address other basic needs of society at the local level. Their goal is to raise the floor beneath all members of society, rather than to enable a few to touch its vaulted ceiling."[63] These citizen leaders, he adds, are often "transforming leaders who engage others in efforts to reach higher levels of human awareness and relationships."[64]

But perhaps their truest "distinguishing characteristic of leadership," Couto says, is the "gift of trust" that has been bestowed upon them by the people "with whom they work"[65] or work for. Continuing, he writes that "citizen leaders act from fairly simple motives" and they speak in simple terms about the basic dignity of every human being. They act from the conviction that we, as a society, are responsible for redressing the conditions that undermine and understate the human dignity of any of its members.[66]

Those who knew Butts as a grassroots civil rights leader described her in similar terms to those used by Couto, including with many expressions about how deeply they trusted her.

Robnett, in her 1997 book, *How Long? How Long? African-American Women in the Struggle for Civil Rights*, defined a particular category of grassroots leaders, whom she calls "bridge leaders." She devised the concept of bridge leader to explain the important roles of grassroots leaders—usually women, but sometimes men—who were "not simply organizers within the civil rights movement" but "critical mobilizers of civil rights activities."[67] As such, they were often women and men who were not necessarily in the formal hierarchy of a civil rights organization but trusted and relied upon by fellow citizens for problem-solving, information, and emotional support. Bridge leaders, according to Robnett, created and maintained linkages between a local community and a larger social movement and helped fellow citizens connect their lives with the larger civil rights effort.

The Civil Rights Movement, Robnett contends, could not have been as effective as it was without bridge leaders, especially those women in informal leadership roles whose "activities ... were the stepping stones necessary for potential constituents and adherents to cross formidable barriers between their personal lives and the political life of civil rights movement activities."[68] Bridge leaders, Robnett writes, operated "through one-on-one, community-based interaction,"[69] and that mobilization in the Civil Rights Movement "could not have succeeded without the efforts of indigenous bridge leaders, who facilitated the connection between these [local] communities and movement organizations."[70]

Robnett discusses characteristics and behaviors of bridge leaders, including the ability to "foster ties between the social movement and the community" and to "cross the boundaries between the public life of a movement organization and the private spheres of adherents and potential constituents."[71]

Like Couto, Robnett suggests that bridge leaders share some key characteristics. They include being adept at one-on-one contact for recruitment and mobilization; tending to advocate nontraditional or even more radical tactics than formal leaders of older, established organizations; being initiators of new organizations or impromptu crusades; and operating in the Civil Rights Movement's informal or "free spaces," which were defined as niches "not directly controlled by formal leaders or those in their inner circle."[72] Some bridge leaders also held formal positions in civil rights entities, Robnett says, noting that being a bridge leader and an organizational officer were not mutually exclusive.[73]

27

The descriptions provided by Robnett certainly resemble Butts' multiple roles and activities in civil rights. Butts excelled at one-on-one interaction with neighbors and other fellow citizens, and served as a flesh-and-blood bridge between them and the activities of formal organizations such as the NAACP or in mobilizing them for various crusades, including voter participation. Butts, at times, wore multiple hats, including secretary for the local NAACP and SCLC chapters, while also leading the Women of Virginia's Third Force, Oakwood-Rosemont Civic League, and various ad hoc activities, such as picketing against job discrimination and segregated schools. Established leadership of the Norfolk NAACP called her a radical and militant when she challenged them.

Butts enjoyed the flexibility of operating within free spaces, and she did so with both creative flair and the instinct of a protective mother, sometimes in combination.

I believe that Butts was a bridge leader in more ways than contemplated by Robnett. Butts certainly connected her neighbors to the Civil Rights Movement and political issues, but she also served as a bridge between her neighborhood and the Norfolk city government and as a builder of bridges to the future.

There are many examples of how Butts bridged the gap between struggling low-income Black neighborhoods and the operations of Norfolk City Hall. She attended and spoke out at City Council and School Board meetings—and returned home with information; she learned the rules of voter registration—and gave confidence to thousands of first-time voters, even traveling around with a voter machine to demonstrate how to use it; she brought political candidates, African American and White, to her home for meals—showing neighbors that these local politicians needed them as much as they needed the ear of City Hall.

Butts encouraged neighbors and mentored others to join with her when she crossed bridges—and then, like abolitionist hero Harriet Tubman, she returned time and time again to pull more people over the bridges with her.

As Butts built bridges to City Hall and to other neighborhoods, she also helped Oakwood children build bridges to their future by encouraging them to do well in school, behave in the community, and use her name as a reference when looking for jobs. Friends knew that Butts was helping to build a different type of future for Norfolk's African Americans than they could hope for under Jim Crow domination.

A few years after she died, when the City Council named a street after Evelyn Butts, longtime friend Alveta V. Green recited a poem at the ceremony. The poem, entitled "The Bridge Builder," by Will Allen Dromgoole, was about an old man who crossed a deep, wide river but turned around to build a bridge back to the other side. Asked why, the old man explained that he did so to help young people cross safely.

"Evelyn was always thinking this way," Green told me.[74]

I have some ideas on how Evelyn Butts developed her leadership creativity and her abilities to promote African American self-determination. Her first lessons in self-determination came in family settings soon after her widowed father arranged for her and her siblings to live with their entrepreneurial and politically minded Aunt Roz. Such a household made conditions ripe for Evelyn to draw connections between self-determination and politics.

As an adult, Butts maintained her ability to perceive connections—and to act upon them—in quite a different way. In essence, Butts often operated as a "bridge" in helping neighbors in her poor Oakwood neighborhood and other marginalized citizens in Norfolk see the linkages between their struggles and political solutions.

While I did not know Evelyn Butts, I have come to appreciate her grassroots organizing abilities as well as the insights about citizen leadership from Couto and bridge leadership from Robnett. This study also gave me a new perspective of the leadership activities I observed while growing up in Norfolk's Berkley neighborhood, especially the neighbor-to-neighbor community roles performed by elders such as Horace Downing, George Banks, and Minnie Madrey, and my grandmother, Ruby Rose Cooper, in whose household I lived for most of my childhood.

Both Evelyn Butts and my grandmother were reputed to know everyone in their respective neighborhoods, were adept at enlisting neighbors in various community improvement efforts, and carried out many of their initiatives by going door to door or by telephone. My grandmother, however, was a much quieter person than Evelyn Butts. Both women, though, had something else in common: They appreciated the value of education and strove mightily for the educational advancement of the children they raised.

Here is what my aunt, Shirley Maxine Whitley, recalled about my grandmother, who was her mother:

> She always told us to participate in elections when we grew up. Even when we were not old enough, she carried us to go work the polls. She told us it makes a difference, that "we are going to have to fight for what we get in life."[75]

Like Evelyn Butts, my grandmother also reached out to neighborhood children. My neighbor, Bernard "Pee Wee" Thompson, a longtime community activist, told me this:

> I was 15 or 16, and she was like an anchor lady for us, not just in politics but in life. She would call me and say, "I got some flyers. Can you help get them out?" Then she'd talk about the unborn generations, like "think about the future of your unborn children." She emphasized politics and education, and if she saw someone not in school during the day, she would get you a ride or make someone give you a ride.[76]

Looking back, I see that my grandmother and Evelyn Butts had other commonalities when it came to political participation.

During local elections, candidates would visit my grandmother at home or at her job as secretary for 50 years of Antioch Missionary Baptist Church in our neighborhood. My grandmother also walked door to door to help introduce candidates to neighbors and assigned me to distribute flyers. Over the years, I learned that these activities were among the basic touchstones for motivating people to vote. I also observed that it was important to provide rides to the polls on Election Day.

My grandmother did not drive, but she was frequently seen walking everywhere throughout Berkley. She was a relentless gatherer of neighborhood intelligence, knowing the names and addresses of nearly everyone and their children. She put this information to great use, including when she needed help with church projects or matters that concerned the greater community, such as petition drives in support of political candidates.

And while she did not drive, I noticed that my grandmother was involved in coordinating rides to the polls on Election Day, helping to make sure that anybody who needed a ride got one. So, sure enough, when I got older, one of my frequent Election Day volunteer jobs became driving people to the polls.

My grandmother, who died in 1995, drummed into me one other important lesson about how to bring about change. She said, quite often, "you've got to show up." It's a motto that I repeat now to my own children and to many fellow citizens who want to help improve our communities. "You've got to show up"—especially on Election Day.

The Rev. Martin Luther King Jr., long a hero of Evelyn Butts, spoke in the Norfolk area on June 28, 1963, and asserted that "the Negro wants all the privileges of citizenship—now." In this photo, King is holding a press conference at the Golden Triangle Motor Hotel in downtown Norfolk before leading a rally at Peanut Park in Suffolk. © *Virginian Pilot All rights reserved. Distributed by Tribune Content Agency, LLC.*

# CHAPTER 3
## Political Citizenship and Self-Determination

From her years as a young adult through the rest of her life, Evelyn Butts blended her advocacy for political citizenship with her quest for self-determination for African Americans and other marginalized citizens. Butts never used such terms—political citizenship and self-determination—but "that's what she meant, that's what she was all about," said daughter Charlene Butts Ligon.[1] "Her actions spoke for her."

For example, in a 1960 letter to fellow members of the Norfolk Branch of the NAACP, Butts wrote: "Is it radical to dream of and work for a City where Negroes are citizens, free and proud, living peacefully and in prosperity, in good times and bad times, and participating in every area of life? Are these things radical?"[2]

While Butts did not voice the phrase "political citizenship," the term characterizes much of Butts' activism as she relentlessly encouraged fellow citizens to register to vote, learn about the candidates and issues, turn out on Election Day, and help others get to the polls. The concept of political citizenship was popularized in the 1950s by British sociologist T. H. Marshall, who analyzed citizenship as having three components—civil, political, and social[3]—and defined the political as "the right to participate in the exercise of political power as a member of a body invested with political authority or as an elector of the members of such a body."[4]

While Marshall mostly wrote about Great Britain, the idea of political citizenship equated to what many American civil rights activists promoted in their advocacy: the right to fully participate in the political decision-making of their localities, states, and nation. Political historian Eric Foner for example, uses a more common American phrase, "the right to participate in public affairs," in his analysis of concepts of freedom in the United States.[5]

In the Civil Rights Movement of the 1940s, '50s and '60s, the political imagination of African American activists—often fired up by Black veterans of World War II who fought for democracy overseas—combined in powerful ways with the long yearning of Black communities for self-determination, the opportunity to frame and direct their own lives and ambitions, including and beyond political citizenship. Countless statements by African Americans over the decades expressed their desire for "full citizenship" or "first-class citizenship" that they believed voting rights could help bring about. A flyer produced by the Richmond Crusade for Voters exemplifies the voting-freedom-citizenship equation with a depiction of a mallet (labeled with the word "VOTE") breaking a heavy chain and slogans such as "Votes mean FREEDOM," "Votes mean EQUALITY," and "Votes mean first-class citizenship."[6]

Just as importantly, in addition to suffrage, African Americans sought to extinguish the ceaseless fire of humiliations and intimidations and to be treated as equals to Whites in all regards.

Longtime civil rights leader Roy Wilkins once described some of the indignities heaped upon Blacks:

> We have been subject to the whims and fancies of white persons, individually and collectively. We went to back doors ... we stepped off sidewalks and removed our hats and said "Sir" to all and sundry, if they were white ... we could not vote. Our health and our recreation were of little or no concern to the responsible officials of government. In time of war we were called to serve, but were insulted, degraded and mistreated.[7]

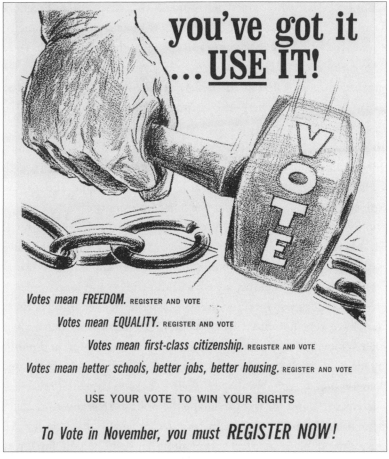

Throughout the decades, African Americans expressed their desire for "full citizenship" or "first-class Citizenship" in countless ways. They believed that voting rights would help them achieve that goal as illustrated in this 1950s flyer from the Richmond Crusade for Voters, with slogans such as "Votes mean FREEDOM," "Votes mean Equality," and "Votes mean first-class citizenship." *Courtesy of Special Collections and Archives, Virginia Commonwealth University Libraries.*

And Mississippi civil rights activist and community organizer Fannie Lou Hamer famously described how blacks felt about such abuse in a 1964 speech: "I am sick and tired of being sick and tired, and we want a change."[8]

In her quest for change, Hamer organized voter-registration campaigns among fellow poor African Americans in Sunflower

County, Mississippi, and co-founded the Mississippi Freedom Democratic Party and the National Women's Political Caucus. From studying Hamer's community, civil rights historian J. Todd Moye observes, "True *movements* occurred when the people of a given community found in themselves—both as individuals and as members of a group—the courage and strength to define the obstacles they faced in an inherently unequal society and began to propose solutions that would allow them to overcome."[9] Thus, Moye importantly contends that the essence of the modern civil rights crusade was akin to a human rights struggle and rooted "preeminently as a movement for self-determination."[10]

Evelyn Butts probably did not read academic discourses by T. H. Marshall, Eric Foner, or J. Todd Moye. But she might have gathered her notions about political citizenship and self-determination much closer to home, albeit without the formal labels.

An avid newspaper and news magazine reader, Evelyn Butts may have kept up with a weekly column, "Rights and Duties in a Democracy," that African American historian, educator, and public intellectual Luther P. Jackson wrote for Norfolk's black-owned *Journal and Guide* newspaper. There, Jackson urged fellow black citizens to "claim the right to shape the policies that govern them"[11] by making America a "participatory democracy"[12] that "challenged the axiom of black political submission that sustained the Jim Crow order,"[13] says historian and Jackson biographer Michael Dennis.

Jackson, a major voice in African American opposition to Virginia's poll tax, died prematurely in 1950. However, he wrote his political citizenship columns in the 1940s, when Butts and her future lawyer, Joseph A. Jordan Jr., were just beginning their activism.

Along with other civil rights activists of his generation, Jackson "imagined racial justice ... in terms of political inclusion along the lines guaranteed by the Constitution," says Dennis.[14] Such faith was also often articulated by Jordan's father, Joseph A. Jordan Sr., and inspired Jordan Jr.'s decision to become a lawyer. The younger Jordan would quote his father's words: "[If] you look at the Constitution, you'll see that it is an umbrella which can bring us all into the mainstream equally."[15]

The importance of inclusionary political citizenship based on the Constitution became a key concept in Butts' 1963 poll-tax lawsuit, which asserted that "Denying the right to vote by requiring the payment of a poll tax deprives citizens of their First Amendment rights to petition the government and to freedom of speech."[16] It is clear that Butts realized that the poll tax restricted the ability of many African Americans to participate fully as political citizens: this, in a country where the opening words of the U.S. Constitution—"We the people"—idealizes citizens as the basic building block of our democracy.

As for the push for self-determination, Moye suggests that grassroots struggles for basic freedoms and human rights often motivate and undergird what emerges as a movement for civil rights.[17] He writes, "it seems so natural that a father whose children are being educated at a substandard school would start advocating for better educational opportunities for his children."[18] But Moye asks: Why do only some parents of children deprived of equal educational opportunities take the risky step of turning into activists and then learn how to organize with others?[19]

The towering monument to General Robert E. Lee in Richmond, Virginia, was installed in 1890 to help perpetuate the so-called noble cause of the Confederacy, but many African Americans regarded it as an offensive reminder of oppression and White supremacy. *Courtesy of Sargeant Memorial Collection, Norfolk Public Library.*

# CHAPTER 4
## The Virginia Way

Because Evelyn Butts lived in Virginia, it is important to note that the course of White supremacy and Black suppression in 20th century Virginia diverged in some key aspects from racist practices more prevalent in other Southern states. During the first quarter of the 1900s, leaders of Virginia's all-White dominant political class began to promulgate a genteel form of segregation and racial oppression that did not rely on physical brutality against African Americans. These White oligarchs believed—or tried to make Black Virginians believe—that blacks were willing partners in a system of "separation by consent."[1]

White elites referred to this self-ordained paternalism as "the Virginia Way" of managing race relations, a term attributed to segregationist Douglas Southall Freeman, a powerful aristocratic editor of the *Richmond News Leader* newspaper in Virginia's capital city and prize-winning biographer of Confederate General Robert E. Lee.[2] Freeman, who grew up watching his father, Walker Freeman, participate in parades and reunions of Confederate war veterans, was known to give a daily salute to Richmond's statue of General Lee.[3]

Freeman "considered himself liberal" and "a friend of blacks," but as Hall points out, he was part of Virginia's White "ruling elite." Says Hall, "He supported segregation, opposed interracial marriage, and accepted the disenfranchisement of blacks that resulted from the 1902 state constitution."[4]

White Virginia Way patricians allowed African Americans little room for succeeding in their collective quests for political citizenship and self-determination. "White elites styled themselves the 'patrons' and 'guardians' of the state's Black population, appropriating the right to determine when and where uplift should be championed and when Black aspirations should be squelched," writes historian Jill Ogline Titus.[5] "Casting themselves as benefactors, White leaders demanded that Blacks approach them as suppliants grateful for the patronage of their 'betters.'"

Sociologist and civil rights activist Edward Harden Peeples Jr. characterizes the nonviolent Virginia Way paternalism as "a dignified way to be racist." The arrangement, as imposed by White elites, Peeples says, worked in this way:

> You can believe in white supremacy but you don't have to hurt anybody to do it. You don't have to restrain them with shackles. All you do is control their mind in such a way that they will appreciate the fact that what you do is good for them ... When you hand out the dollars or you hand out the jobs or whatever, then people will be docile—and with no labor protection laws and things like that, it just worked.[6]

The nonviolent Virginia Way, however, was devastating in itself to Virginia's African American citizens and communities in so many other regards, such as by allocating only meager resources for education and health care. "Virginia government was renowned for its gentility because its leaders couched vile policies in soft language," writes Jeff Thomas in his political analysis, *The Virginia Way: Democracy and Power After 2016.*[7]

Under the Virginia Way of White supremacy, Blacks were expected to know their "place," be deferential to Whites and trust their word, and not push too hard for change, which well-bred Whites promised would eventually come when Virginia society "was ready." As newspaper editor Freeman counseled, "The first law of the South—that a white man is a white man and must be treated as such regardless of his station."[8]

In return, White political and business leaders felt empowered to make major decisions about the destiny of African American communities, education and enterprises. As Rebecca Candace Epps-Robertson writes, "maintaining the 'Virginia Way' meant that Whites saw themselves as distributors of rights for Blacks."[9]

Whites also expected—even instructed—Blacks to stay out of electoral politics, a disabling mandate that was spoken and demonstrated time and time again as well as enforced through poll taxes and other legalized voter-suppression schemes. "White elites demanded complete deference and expected blacks to seek redress of their grievances only through channels deemed appropriate by whites," J. D. Smith writes.[10]

In 1914, for example, Virginia Governor Henry Carter Stuart made clear his expectations about Black self-determination in a speech to African Americans at Richmond's Fifth Street Baptist Church in Richmond. "I am in favor of your people having all of your rights, with the understanding that you have no part in the government of this country," he said, adding. "This is the view of the people of the South."[11] The dangerous hollowness and cruelty of White Virginia's paternalism toward Blacks is also apparent in another quotation ascribed to Stuart: "I have never seen any good resulting from educating the negro."[12]

Stuart's reputed words proved more than prophetic. Effectively disenfranchised, Black Virginians had no meaningful voice in how White-dominated state and local governments allocated public resources, especially for education. By 1919, Virginia had only three fully accredited high schools for African Americans—in Norfolk, Portsmouth, and Richmond.[13] Paternalistic Whites continued to tell Black citizens to trust them, but Virginia Way promises repeatedly proved hollow. The number of Black high schools increased to eight by 1928 while there were about 400 White-only high schools across the state, according to a study by the O'Shea Commission, a committee of out-of-state educators empaneled by the General Assembly. The commission "blamed Virginia's pathetic inattention

to public education in general, and to black education in particular, on an unwillingness, not an inability, to provide adequate
facilities," writes historian J. D. Smith.[14]

With Black Virginians politically toothless, governing bodies
enacted even more laws to reinforce Jim Crow apartheid and racial
stereotypes. In 1922, the General Assembly created a State Board
of Censors to scrutinize and license every movie before allowing
its showing in Virginia. Race was not expressly listed as a factor
in the act, but the three board members were aware that their job
included making sure "Virginians saw only stereotypical images of
blacks on the screen: the faithful servant, the ignorant child, and
the loathsome criminal" and not "educated persons who did not
relate to whites in a servile capacity," writes J. D. Smith.[15]

In 1924, the year Evelyn Butts was born, the General Assembly
passed the Racial Integrity Act to make racial lines more rigid and en-
snaring by defining "white" as someone with no "black blood" and no
more than one-sixteenth of Native American "blood." The legislation
reinforced prohibitions against racial intermarriage previously enacted
in 1873, which then had made Virginia the third Southern state with
such a law.[16] The intermarriage prohibition lasted another 43 years
until the U.S. Supreme Court declared this law unconstitutional in
the famous *Loving v. Virginia* case of 1967.[17]

The Racial Integrity Act was followed, in 1926, by the Separation of Races law, also known as the Public Assemblages Act,
which made Virginia the first and only state to mandate segregated
seating at all venues for entertainment and public meetings.[18] The
Public Assemblages Act, advocated by members of the White-supremacist Anglo-Saxon Clubs, was heavily pushed by Walter Scott
Copeland, editor of Newport News *Daily Press*, and his wife,
Grace B. Copeland, who were aghast to find themselves seated
next to African Americans while attending a dance recital at the
Hampton Institute (now Hampton University) in February 1925.[19]

In his newspaper editorials, Copeland alleged that the auditori-
um's mixed seating suggested that education at Hampton Institute

was moving too far from manual and vocational training to help Blacks fulfill their designated role in American society and that students were being "taught that the Negro race is in all respects the equal of the white race and that no racial distinctions should be made either in law or society," an attitude that would lead to racial "amalgamation"—in other words, intermarriage.[20]

While the Virginia Way suppressed African Americans in nonlethal ways, the state's ruling White elites did not see a need to intervene in racial mob violence until the mid-1920s during a resurgent phase of the Ku Klux Klan and similar terrorist groups. In August 1926, White-owned newspapers editorialized against White racial violence after a masked mob in Wytheville murdered and then mangled the body of a Black man awaiting trial for allegedly assaulting two girls. The *Richmond News Leader* asserted "it was not the 'Virginia Way.'"[21]

Governor Harry F. Byrd was initially reluctant to pursue anti-lynching legislation, but by 1928 he had become convinced by crusading newspaper editorial writers, such as Louis I. Jaffe of *The Virginian-Pilot*, with whom he carried on a private correspondence. In addition to coaxing from Jaffe and editorials by the Black-owned *Journal and Guide* newspaper in Norfolk, Byrd also realized that negative national news about lynchings was tarnishing Virginia's "genteel" and pro-business image.[22] In January 1928, Byrd asked the state legislature to pass an anti-lynching law and signed it, making Virginia the first state to designate lynching as a crime.[23] Byrd went on to serve in the U.S. Senate for 32 years and also headed a statewide Democratic political monopoly known as the Byrd Organization and also called the Byrd Machine. But for decades, he continued to cite his signing of Virginia's anti-lynching legislation[24] as evidence of his respect for Blacks even as he remained an avowed segregationist and defender of the oppressive poll tax.

In public pronouncements, Byrd was also usually careful not to use inflammatory racial language,[25] unlike his father, Richard

E. Byrd II, who, as speaker of the Virginia House of Delegates in 1907, declared: "the negro must be placed in a condition of absolute and unquestioned subordination. The subordination must pertain to every point of contact with the white race. This is not only essential to the stability and prosperity of society, but it is essential not only to the well being but the very continued existence of the black race."[26]

Instead, Harry F. Byrd's public manner and policies were those aligned with the Virginia Way—as a White political oligarch who characterized segregation as "essential to the maintenance of peaceful and friendly relationships between the races"[27] and who anointed himself with the power to determine "the proper interests of the Negro citizens of Virginia."[28]

With or without the velvet glove of paternalism, the resulting public policy continued to subordinate African Americans. Early in his political career—1919—Harry F. Byrd wrote "where the negro predominates in number, it would certainly be a most dangerous thing to permit them to vote without restrictions—either the male or the female."[29] He continued to support the poll tax as a "safeguard against the negro vote" because "one-third of our population is negro."[30]

Byrd's advocacy for Virginia's poll taxes for state and local elections continued up until their demise, when the U.S. Supreme Court declared the levy unconstitutional in 1966 in the *Harper* case initiated by Evelyn Butts.[31]

Meanwhile, Byrd's tamping down on racial violence in Virginia contrasted with the approach of some politicians in other Southern states who threatened violence in their rhetoric. Mississippi Governor James K. Vardaman, for example, proclaimed in the early 1900s: "If it is necessary every Negro in the state will be lynched; it will be done to maintain white supremacy."[32]

Virginia's approach may have been the reason that Virginia had the lowest number of known racial-terror lynchings among 12 Southern states between the end of Reconstruction in 1877

Longtime Virginia political boss and U.S. Senator Harry F. Byrd Sr. was usually careful not to use inflammatory racial language, but he was an entrenched segregationist who asserted that separation was "essential to the maintenance of peaceful and friendly relationships between the races." He also fought to retain poll taxes as a means to "safeguard against the negro vote." This photo shows Byrd outside the old Cavalier Hotel in Virginia Beach in 1938. *Photo courtesy of Sargeant Memorial Collection, Norfolk Public Library.*

and 1950 as compiled in a 2015 study conducted by the nonprofit Equal Justice Initiative. According to the report, the 12 states saw 4,084 lynchings, including 84 in Virginia, while Mississippi had the most at 654.[33] Nonetheless, NAACP Executive Secretary Walter White came to regard Byrd as more dangerous than some other White-supremacist political leaders in the Southern states because he was "more sophisticated" in his policies and pronouncements, especially in trying to cast his segregationist rhetoric in the guise of states' rights instead of overt racial terms.[34]

Under Byrd's domination, the Virginia Way's suppressive paternalism continued for decades, even into and beyond the 1950s when federal courts ordered the end of segregated public schools and other so-called separate-but-equal facilities. As J. D. Smith observes, the White governing powers of Virginia slowly allowed integration "in order to protect the state's reputation for continued industrial development—rather than out of any commitment to justice for African Americans."[35]

Historians and authors do not agree on when the Virginia Way style of managing race relations began to unravel—and some, such as Jeff Thomas, contend that its purpose and practice continues into the 21st century after evolving from blatant racial suppression to protecting the economic power of political and business elites.[36] A *New York Times* article adds that "This anything goes culture is rooted at least in part in Virginia's idea of itself, or what is sometimes referred to there as 'the Virginia Way,'" which included being soft on ethical standards for state leaders "who were unrepresentative of the population at large."[37]

J. Douglas Smith suggests that cracks in the Virginia Way edifice began as early as the 1920s during public-issue debates between hardline White supremacists and those who were more practical. Other historians cite the late 1930s when innovative NAACP attorneys began their string of court victories against Jim Crow or the end of World War II when Black military veterans returned home determined to fight for a more equitable democracy in America after helping to save freedom in other countries. By-and-by, new generations of African Americans became inspired and willing to step forward to challenge Virginia's old order.

Verbal dust-ups over the Virginia Way certainly became more frequent and public in the 1930s and '40s as African American leaders talked about asserting full citizenship and angry White-supremacist elites accused Blacks of not being grateful enough.

In 1939, for example, NAACP chief counsel Charles Hamilton Houston encouraged more fellow African Americans to apply to White-only graduate and professional schools. "It is not a question of wanting to sit in the same classroom with white students. It is a question of vindicating one's citizenship," Houston told an audience in Richmond.[38] His comments angered Virginius Dabney, editor of the influential *Richmond Times-Dispatch*, who responded that Blacks were being unreasonable.

Roy Wilkins of the NAACP's national office followed up on Houston's comments by proclaiming that Blacks should be on the same "plane of absolute political and social equality" with Whites.[39] That made Dabney shed his gentility, at least momentarily, as he warned that Black agitation, lawsuits, and "insistence upon complete equality in the South would result in a racial war in which blacks were bound to be losers"[40] and bring about the "worst internal clashes since Reconstruction, with hundreds, if not thousands, killed and amicable race relations set back for decades."[41]

The newspaper editor's intimation of violence infuriated many Black Virginians, including the often-cautious P. B. Young Sr., publisher of the influential *Journal and Guide* newspaper in Norfolk. Young shot back at Dabney that he was just as oppressive as the worst White Southern brutes.

"While your language is always cultured and your attitude dignified," Young wrote, "the result is the same."[42]

The worn-out racist phrases and paternalistic promises continued for decades but were losing their magic.

In Norfolk, World War II veteran Victor J. Ashe, who held a law degree from Howard University, campaigned for a City Council seat in 1946, the first time an African American had tried since Reconstruction. His energetic campaign included a huge parade with floats and four bands.[43] White politicians did not seem to know how to respond. Addressing a Black audience, White incumbent City Council member Richard W. Ruffin declared that "the time has not come for Norfolk to elect a Negro to the council." He went on to say that Ashe was "a credit to his race and the city, but … his election would be injurious to his race as well as to the white population."[44]

Although Ashe lost, finishing seventh among eight candidates, his ability to draw votes from every one of Norfolk's 37 precincts, including White districts, kept incumbent Ruffin from winning another term.[45]

More than 20 years later, Norfolk's dominant White politicians apparently still did not feel that their city was ready for a Black City Council member—unless it was one of their choosing. This time, the leading African American candidate was Joseph A. Jordan Jr., who, like Ashe, was an attorney and World War II veteran and whose key supporters included Evelyn Butts. Mayor Roy B. Martin Jr., a White politician who supported public school integration only a few years earlier, now racialized the 1968 council campaign by noting that Jordan's election would mean that a Black man would replace one of the White incumbents.

Martin said of the White incumbents: "I don't think one of these men ought to be turned out just because of the color of his skin. It would be a blight on the city of Norfolk if one is turned out just because we should have a colored man on the council." Meanwhile, Albert Teich Jr., a White lawyer who co-chaired the Citizens for Jordan Committee, suggested that Martin preferred to handpick a Black for a City Council seat.[46]

Years later, Walter H. Green Sr., husband of Butts' friend Alveta V. Green, explained that White business and political leaders had hoped to recruit a "qualified … competent" black, "someone they could control" and "That meant they did not want Joe Jordan."[47]

Nevertheless, Jordan beat the Virginia Way system in 1968 and earned the honor of being the first African American elected to the Norfolk City Council since 1889. Even one of Jordan's defeated White opponents, incumbent Paul Schweitzer, conceded that Jordan's victory represented "a new era that we're coming into."[48]

Evelyn Butts was already very much a part of this new era. Since her emergence as a grassroots civil rights leader in the mid-1950s, she had witnessed many other examples of the Virginia Way's suppressive paternalism among Norfolk's dominant White elites. Examples, which later chapters will discuss, include:

- The city's powerful Norfolk Redevelopment and Housing Authority designating Butts' Oakwood neighborhood and nearby Rosemont and Lincoln Park for massive clearance—without consulting the residents in advance.
- The Norfolk School Board requiring Black students to undergo psychological examinations if they wished to transfer from all-Black schools to all-White schools under court-ordered desegregation, often citing the need to protect the emotional health and physical safety of the Black children.

Throughout her heyday as a grassroots civil rights leader, Butts persisted in educating and encouraging thousands of new African American voters in Norfolk. The community learned that the Virginia Way need not be the only manner of race relations. Other options included the Evelyn Butts Way.

# SECTION II

## *The World That Evelyn Butts Inherited*

When Evelyn T. Butts was born in 1924, the White supremacist Ku Klux Klan organization was at the height of its popularity in Virginia. In the top photo, a Norfolk women's
contingent of the KKK parades along East Main Street in downtown Norfolk. The
bottom photo, taken from the intersection of Granby and Plume streets, shows scores
of Klan members marching along downtown Granby Street. *Both Photos Courtesy of
Sargeant Memorial Collection, Norfolk Public Library.*

# CHAPTER 5
## Born in Virginia

Friends and family recall Evelyn Thomas Butts as a force to be reckoned with when it came to protecting her family and neighborhood as well as for advancing the civil and political rights of African Americans in their quest for self-determination. Undoubtedly, she had to be strong and resilient during the upheavals of the 1940s, '50s, and '60s, a span that encompassed World War II, the beginning of the modern Civil Rights Movement, and the tumultuous 1960s. Like many African American women, she had to swim through both the stormy waters of White supremacy and the fresh but uncertain tides of hope in the struggle to overthrow America's Jim Crow system of apartheid. At the same time, Butts had to be careful to not fall victim to the perpetual undertows of racism, sexism, and poverty.

Like many African American activists of the era, especially in the South, Butts was not only struggling to overthrow the Jim Crow apartheid of her era but to also address centuries of oppressive White-supremacist political and social structures that had accumulated since the Colonial era of the 1600s and that had become embedded deep within American society from top to bottom.

The interlocking mechanisms of White supremacy and the repression of African Americans were continually reinforced, even through tax-supported public education systems and policies, including at the university level, as well as through racist pronouncements of White political leaders and influential educators along with myths, distortions, and stereotypes promulgated in textbooks.

As a backdrop to studying Evelyn Butts' efforts to gain political citizenship and self-determination for fellow African Americans, it is helpful to understand some of the roots and practices of American White supremacism from their beginnings in Colonial Virginia through the suppression of African Americans during the Jim Crow era, including the paternalistic genteel racism of the so-called Virginia Way of the 20th century and beyond. Indeed, the events and policies of 17th century Virginia became the toxic foundation of the various forms of racism that Evelyn Butts encountered in her life and activism. These historic insights help to better understand the society that Evelyn Butts was born into as well as the frustrations and aspirations that shaped her emerging generation.

A study of the modern Civil Rights Movement should include the pre-1950s because so much of the White supremacy of the previous three centuries still influenced race relations at the 20th century's midpoint. For example, White Southern political leaders who opposed the great Voting Rights Act of 1965 relied upon many of the same arguments dragged out by Southern politicians to undermine Reconstruction in the 1870s and 1880s and to launch the reign of Jim Crow apartheid that soon began. Historian Allan J. Lichtman, in *The Embattled Vote in America: From the Founding to the Present,* drew up a list that includes assertions about states' rights against the alleged tyranny of the federal government and the teaching and reinforcing of myths about Black inferiority and corruptibility.[1]

The year 1619 was a watershed for setting the courses for politics and race relations in Virginia and North America. The first English settlers in Colonial Virginia began establishing racial and class divisions by suppressing Native Americans, importing Africans against their will and turning them into an enslaved workforce, and imposing restrictions on who could possess political power through voting rights and holding elective office, according to Brent Tarter's insightful *The Grandees of Government: The Origins and Persistence of Undemocratic Politics in*

*Virginia* and James Horn's revealing *1619: Jamestown and the Forging of American Democracy.* Historian Jon Meacham makes similar observations in *The Soul of America: The Battle for Our Better Angels* as he noted that the events of the early 17th century had deep and long-lasting effects. Meacham writes: "While whites built and dreamed, people of color were subjugated and exploited by a rising nation that prided itself on the expansion of liberty. Those twin tragedies shaped us then and ever after."[2]

In his *The Grandees of Government,* Tarter defines the "grandees" as "the richest white men ... who ran the plantations and governed Virginia" by pursuing "their personal ambitions and acquisition of wealth and individual freedom in ways that led them to deprive other people of their freedom."[3] The grandees' style of governance, as well as racism, continued to manifest itself well into the 20th century.

In July 1619, Virginia's House of Burgesses—predecessor of today's Virginia General Assembly (state legislature)—came into being. Virginia boasts of having the "oldest continuous law-making body in the New World,"[4] but the creation of the legislature and its early activities helped launch America's dichotomous politics and culture.[5] As Tarter wrote, "The men who made the first laws and established representative government in Virginia also took the first steps toward creating a system of slavery."[6]

This first foray into representative government also did not allow for equality among White settlers. Only White male property owners held the right to vote and to serve as elected leaders.[7] Virginia's colonial government even involved itself in dictating what people should wear. "Men who violated standards of proper apparel for their stations of life—standards that the assembly's law did not specify—were to be assessed a penalty," according to Tarter.[8] As Tarter explains, "All men were not equal and they were not to appear dressed in such manner as to give a false appearance about their rank in society."[8] Thus, government and culture in Virginia were entwined from the beginning, and as Tarter observes, what this first legislature "did and how they did it influenced the whole future of Virginia's history and the history of the United States."[9]

The colony's influence on Black-White race relations began in August of that same year, 1619, when "20 and odd" Africans—possibly the first in Virginia—arrived unwillingly aboard the White Lion, an English privateer, which had pirated the enslaved Africans from a Portuguese slave ship headed to Mexico. The White Lion landed in Point Comfort (now part of Hampton, Virginia, just a few miles from Norfolk) and traded the Africans for food. Scholars believe this group of Africans and others soon to come, along with many of their immediate offspring, were put to work as indentured servants alongside poor Whites from England in accord with the traditions of the time.[10]

Already concerned with establishing and preserving a class hierarchy, the legislature began taking steps to consign the first Africans, their offspring, and additional African arrivals to "one new lower level to the social ranks,"[11] a status "degraded far below the most contemptible servant or Indian."[12] For example, one early law, in 1662, established that slave status was inheritable through the mother,[13] and another, in 1669 automatically exonerated a slave owner or his employee from beating a slave to death for insubordination based on the assumption that a man would never willingly "destroy his own estate."[14] By 1705, Virginia had enacted a comprehensive array of slavery laws that "became the standard that the other colonies followed,"[15] or as Tarter describes it, "a whole new body of law that permitted masters to rule their new laboring force more violently than their indentured servants, not a contractual law of master and servant but a brutal law of master and slave."[16]

This brief summary from the 1600s illustrates Virginia's prominent role in the codification and proliferation of slavery and the evolution of White supremacy culture. As Tarter observes, "White people, most of them men, made those laws, and the laws that they made reflected common and persistent attitudes that white people in Virginia and elsewhere in the United States held about black people."[17]

Those "attitudes," according to examples from numerous scholars, such as C. Vann Woodward in his 1955 classic *The Strange Career of Jim Crow*, have included the notions that Blacks were an inferior breed of people, incapable of being completely civilized, tending toward violence and out-of-control sexual lust, lazy workers, untrustworthy, created to serve White people, that they actually benefited from slavery and second-class citizenship, and that they were impudent if they did not accept their inferiority and other forms of White domination.[18] A president of Virginia's prestigious state-run Longwood College, Dabney S. Lancaster, even proclaimed that Black children were happier in separate, albeit inferior, public schools "due to the fact that the Negro race has a fine sense of humor."[19]

At times, Southern Whites seemed to acknowledge that Blacks could be capable and intelligent citizens, especially in the antebellum decades long before the Civil War. However, political leaders sought to suppress the expression of free Blacks and restrict Black access to learning to read and write. In the early 19th century, the Virginia General Assembly required Blacks to leave the state if they gained freedom after 1806[20] as well as enacted laws governing the teaching of reading and writing to slaves. According to historian Antonio Bly, "Elite whites worried that slaves who could read and write could travel through white society more easily and be exposed to ideas of freedom, making them more inclined to rebel."[21]

While Virginia did not specifically ban the education of slaves, the state passed laws to thwart educational opportunities for Black people, beginning with a network of oppressive laws aimed at both the enslaved and the free in antebellum times. For example, the General Assembly crafted and tightened laws that prohibited slave gatherings at meetinghouses and schools.[22] Technically, slaveholders could take it upon themselves to teach reading and writing to the enslaved, according to Bly, who explains in Encyclopedia Virginia:

> While many white Virginians believed that literacy was necessary for the religious conversion of slaves, they also feared the consequences of such an education. For one, a slave's ability to read and write contradicted one of the ideological foundations of slavery—the idea that Africans and African Americans were intellectually and morally inferior and, therefore, in need of guidance by white men. For another, the education of slaves risked exposing them to ideas of human equality that circulated during the American Revolution. Virginia slaveholders worried that their slaves, armed with such ideas, might rebel.[23]

In 1831, the General Assembly extended the ban on educational gatherings to "free negroes or mulattoes," Bly adds.[24]

White-supremacist attitudes were so widespread and deeply ingrained among many White Americans that they were voiced publicly, blatantly, and without shame at even the highest levels of government. U.S. Supreme Court Chief Justice Roger B. Taney wrote the majority opinion in the infamous Dred Scott decision of 1857, which ruled that enslaved African Americans could not sue for freedom, even when taken to a free state, because they were not American citizens and had no standing in legal proceedings.[25] Taney also described African Americans as "a subordinate and inferior class of beings, who had been subjugated by the dominant race" and as "beings of an inferior order, and altogether unfit to associate with the white race, either in social or political relations; and so far inferior, that they had no rights which the white man was bound to respect."[26]

During the post-Civil War Reconstruction era, from 1865 to 1877, the U.S. government officially recognized African Americans as citizens and required the 11 Southern and two border states that made up the Confederacy to adopt new state constitutions that guaranteed voting rights for Black men. The federal government sought to guarantee citizenship and voting rights with the 14th Amendment, which included birthright citizenship and equal protection of the law, and the 15th Amendment, which prohibited states from denying voting rights based on race.[27]

However, deep-seated racism across the region could not be dislodged and White-supremacist organizations sprang up to undermine Black political, economic, and social rights.[28] Most notable among them was the Ku Klux Klan, created in 1866 by former Confederate army officers who wore white robes to simulate—in the words of an original member—"the ghosts of the Confederate dead, who had risen from their graves in order to wreak vengeance."[29] Such terrorists even had undue influence on White political leaders. Virginia Governor Frederick William Mackey Holliday, for instance, allowed the Ku Klux Klan to decorate the parlors and halls of the governor's mansion for his inauguration reception in 1878.[30]

Anti-Black public expressions of all types were common throughout Virginia during the Jim Crow era. A Danville, Virginia, newspaper in 1880 referred to "the viper of negroism,"[31] and *The Richmond Times* in Virginia's capital city demanded strict segregation in 1900 because "God Almighty drew the color line and it cannot be obliterated."[32]

Meanwhile, prominent White Southern intellectuals and politicians reframed the Confederacy's losing war effort in a "strategy to bring victory out of defeat."[33] The early luminaries of this movement included journalist Edward Alfred Pollard, a longtime defender of slavery best known for his 1866 book, *The Lost Cause: A New Southern History of the War of the Confederates,* and his 1868 sequel, *The Lost Cause Regained.* Describing *The Lost Cause* as "a bold call to fight on in the face of loss,"[34] Meacham notes that Pollard encouraged a long counter siege by waging a holy war of ideas in which the South reasserts the concepts of states' rights, White supremacy, and the illegitimacy of a strong, centralized national government. Examples of reshaping history included the work of Jubal A. Early, a former Confederate general who became president of the Southern Historical Society. From that perch, Early promoted the life and career of Confederate General Robert E. Lee "as a model of virtue,"[35] and generations of Americans, not just Southerners, grew up believing that Lee was a noble and upstanding foe. In reality, Lee came from a family of slaveholders and believed in White supremacy as evidenced by this quote: "The negroes have neither the intelligence nor the qualifications which are necessary to make them safe depositories of political power."[36]

By 1877, White-supremacist terrorism and the cultural war waged by ex-Confederates began to show their effects. The North gave up on Reconstruction, and the federal government withdrew its troops from the former Confederate states under a political deal engineered to win the presidency for Rutherford B. Hayes.[37]

Then, from 1890 to 1910, the Southern states replaced their Reconstruction constitutions with constitutions that largely disenfranchised African Americans by punching so many loopholes in the 14th and 15th amendments that these amendments became "dead letters" for Southern African Americans.[38] Common initiatives included enacting poll taxes that had to be paid months before an election. Virginia's poll tax stayed in effect until the U.S. Supreme Court invalidated it in 1966 in the landmark *Harper v. Virginia State Board of Elections* (1966) decision that had originated with the 1963 lawsuit, *Mrs. Evelyn Butts v. Governor Albertis Harrison et al.*

Virginia and the other former Confederate states also established literacy tests, written voter-applications, and "understanding clauses" that allowed local voter-registration officials to quiz voter-applicants on their knowledge of government—all subject to the interpretations of voter-registration officials who were White and politically connected.[39]

Alfred P. Thom, one of Norfolk's delegates to Virginia's 1901–02 Constitutional Convention, explained to that gathering how he expected local voter-registration boards to work in executing the understanding clause:

> I expect the examination with which the black man will be confronted, to be inspired by the same spirit that inspires every man upon this floor and in this convention. I would not expect an impartial administration of the clause. I would not expect for the white man a rigid examination. The people of Virginia do not stand impartially between the suffrage of the white man and the suffrage of the black man.[40]

Poor and illiterate Whites were also hit but not as hard as Blacks because Southern states had enacted so-called "grandfather clauses" that exempted Civil War veterans and also excused a man from poll taxes and tests if he, his father, or grandfather had voted before 1867.[41]

Many important White political leaders were unabashed in their supremacist comments even as they rose in power on the national stage. Glass, who was elected to the U.S. House of Representatives in 1902 and went on to serve as United States secretary of the treasury under President Woodrow Wilson and then as a U.S. senator, famously declared in a national news interview that "people of the original thirteen Southern States (in the Confederacy) curse and deride and spit upon the 15th amendment—and have no intention of letting the Negro vote."[42] Referring to the accomplishments of the 1901–1902 Virginia Constitutional Convention, Glass boasted that:

> We obey the letter of the [14th and 15th] amendments and the Federal statutes, but we frankly evade the spirit thereof—and purport to continue doing so. White supremacy is

too precious a thing to surrender for the sake of a theoretical justice that would let a brutish African deem himself the equal of white men and women in Dixie.[43]

Notions about White supremacy and Black inferiority were also promoted through Virginia's educational system, including in textbooks, while powerful and respected professors continued the racist onslaught at the university level, thereby influencing generations of white Virginians.[44] Historian Charles E. Wynes reports in *Race Relations in Virginia 1870–1902* that Dr. Paul B. Barringer, chairman of the faculty of the University of Virginia in 1900 (then equivalent to university president), characterized Black people as "naturally a savage in whom the discipline of slavery had produced temporary elevation."[45] A physician, Barringer spread his beliefs through medical curriculum and medical societies.[46] He later became president of Virginia Tech.

Virginius Dabney, a well-known Virginia patrician and editor of a Richmond daily newspaper in the mid-20th century, acknowledged how he and other White Virginians had grown up learning "that the white race not only is superior to the black race, but that every individual white is superior to every individual black."[47] Smith continues: "This lesson was taught, learned, and reinforced in homes, schools, and churches throughout Virginia."[48]

Even White children felt empowered to display their so-called superiority, as the great civil rights organizer Ella Baker recalled about her childhood in Norfolk, Virginia. Walking with her father through downtown Norfolk during one Christmas season, Baker was confronted by a young White boy taunting her with N-word epithets.[49] She punched the boy before her father could stop her.

Indeed, White and Black children of both sexes usually grew up learning different dos and don'ts about interracial etiquette in the South, according to Tarter. Whites, especially the middle to upper classes:

Almost never accorded courtesy titles of Mr. or Mrs. or Miss to black men or women of any social rank, including educators, bankers, or attorneys. Conversely, the racial etiquette that white people created for the segregated South required that black people of every class address white people of any class with courtesy titles appropriate to their status.[50]

Whites and Blacks also had different interpretations of social equality. For Whites, the notion of Black social equality meant "interracial social mingling,"[51] an unthinkable concept that many Southern Whites feared would lead to intermarriage and "'mongrelization' of the races."[52] For Blacks, social equality meant equal access to public accommodations, such as hotels, restaurants, theaters, mass transit, and to be accorded equal respect in these places.[53] In some ways, social equality to Blacks also meant equal pay for the same work.[54]

Yet, as Wynes notes, no matter how many times African Americans explained their definition of social equality, White segregationists maintained their different interpretation, a matter that Wynes suggests became susceptible to willful political manipulation to keep "the Negro in an inferior position."[55]

Jim Crow also held forth outside the political arena. In 1905, the Rev. Thomas Dixon Jr. published *The Clansman*, a romance novel that glorified the Ku Klux Klan, and also presented it as a live stage play with the same name that year, premiering in Norfolk.[56] The book-turned-play showed up again in 1915 as the infamous White supremacy movie, *The Birth of a Nation*.

Virile White supremacism had pushed its way into the spotlight in many localities and venues. The rejuvenated Ku Klux Klan terrorist organization openly spread hatred and fear across the land—and the Norfolk area was one of the Klan's hot spots in Virginia.

Promoting itself as patriotic, the KKK organized Independence Day rallies at Norfolk's Fairmount Park fairgrounds, complete with picnic lunches, sports activities, concerts, fireworks, White supremacist speakers and evening cross burnings. A year after Evelyn Butts was born, some 35,000 people showed up for the KKK's 1925 Fourth of July event, where the Klan swore in nearly 1,000 new members.[57] Then, on September 1, 1926, hooded Klan terrorists kidnapped a White Catholic priest, Father Vincent B. Warren, apparently because he taught African American children at the mostly Black St. Joseph's Catholic Church and School in downtown Norfolk.[58]

White supremacism was so entrenched and widespread that some of the ugliest nonviolent racism even surfaced in consumer-oriented marketing of household products and family games that featured distorted facial and body features of African Americans. Some merchandise even invoked the N-word. In 2017, the Norfolk Public Library hosted an exhibition to educate people about artifacts of racism. The display, "Relics of Racism: A Historical Portrayal of African Americans in Advertising," was organized by Therbia Parker Sr., an African American collector based in Suffolk, Virginia. Parker's items included "Darkie Toothpaste," a "Little Black Casper the Friendly Spook" wall clock, "Coon Chicken Inn" restaurant souvenirs, a can opener shaped like an alligator swallowing a Negro boy, a game called "Darkies in the Melon Patch," a "Jolly Darkie Target Game," and a toy-sized model of an obese black woman sitting on a toilet to promote laxatives.

Other forms of rampant racism in the private sector hit African Americans in their wallets.[59] Kluger notes that insurance companies charged higher premiums to Black customers than to Whites and that banks discriminated against African Americans when issuing mortgages.

Virginia's African Americans rarely gained attention from most of the state's White-owned newspapers, even when it came to routine news about accomplishments and human-interest stories. "Daily newspapers gave little coverage of the events in the black communities," notes historian Terry L. Jones.[60] "About the only time most Southern newspapers carried news about blacks was when one was involved in a crime."

As a result, "This condition tended to foster and continue stereotypes," Jones writes.[61] John Hope Franklin, who pioneered studies of African American history, makes a similar point in observing that "this ignorance should soon breed contempt and later hatred."[62]

Racial stereotypes and misconceptions during the Jim Crow era proved consequential in public policy, especially when it came to public education for African Americans and voting rights. Robert Lewis Dabney, former chief of staff to Confederate General Thomas "Stonewall" Jackson and a persuasive theologian, used the bible to defend slavery and opined while Reconstruction was being dismantled that "the Negro does not need (education) to fit him for the right of suffrage, since the Negro will soon be stripped of that 'right.'"[63] Another influential Dabney—Richard Heath Dabney, a professor of history at the University of Virginia and father of the powerful journalist Virginius Dabney—proclaimed that "All lawful measures should be taken to remove any removable cause of economic, social, or political competition between the races."[64]

The White supremacy that fed into public decision-making often returned with even more vehemence, making Southern Blacks feel they were caught in an endless loop. Some scholars have even labeled the all-encompassing Jim Crow political, economic, and social systems as "totalitarian," a term Americans usually reserve for Joseph Stalin's Soviet Union and Adolf Hitler's Nazi Germany. Steve Martinot, an author specializing on racialization and Whiteness, points out in an essay on fascism that "The Jim Crow era was characterized by an intricate, universal, and totalitarian system of segregation and disenfranchisement of black people."[65] Patricia Michelle Buzard-Boyett, in her study of the Black freedom struggle in Mississippi, writes that:

> Blacks were turned into noncitizens divested of suffrage, civil liberties, and judicial protections. They had no right to

protest their oppression or petition their government. The white patriarchs perpetuated a free society of whites who accepted the system and a totalitarian society for blacks by separating the races through segregation laws and customs.[66]

Although historian Brent Tarter also does not use the word "totalitarian," he explains some of the factors that led to White-supremacist cultural control as he writes: "Even though the Confederacy had certainly lost the Civil War, its white Southern interpreters and their sympathizers won the history, and with that victory the right to regulate race relations as they pleased."[67] And Kluger writes of the panoramic intolerance, noting that, "Stripping the African American of his civil rights ... was not enough ... . Restaurants and saloons and boardinghouses throughout the South soon sprouted signs declaring which race they served."[68] Separated public washrooms and water fountains soon followed.

White supremacists found support for their apartheid policies in many courtrooms. The 1896 *Plessy v. Ferguson* decision by the U.S. Supreme Court was the most well-known and far-reaching decision. The high court validated the state of Louisiana's 1890 law that required Blacks and Whites to sit in "separate-but-equal" railroad cars and asserted that the equal protection clause of the 14th Amendment did not apply.[69]

The Plessy decision emboldened White-supremacist state and local governments to codify Jim Crow seating in other forms of mass transit, such as streetcars and later with buses. African Americans saw such forms of segregation as "as emblem of social retrogression"[70] and "the very symbol of the system"[71] because it meant they would face daily humiliation in a very public setting that they had to use for traveling to work.

The allegedly separate-but-equal standard stimulated the enactment of even more laws promoting segregation across the South. The movement snowballed after a 1908 Supreme Court ruling required separate educational facilities for Black and White

The former Market Square that once existed in the heart of downtown Norfolk included an auction site where enslaved people of African descent stood to be inspected by potential buyers before being sold off. This 1845 engraving depicts just part of Norfolk's significant role in the slave trade until Union forces took over the city in 1862. *Courtesy of Sargeant Memorial Collection, Norfolk Public Library.*

students at Berea College in Kentucky. Kluger writes that the Berea decision "flashed the green light" for the enactment of Jim Crow laws and policies, thereby ending any last vestiges of "biracial attendance in barbershops and baseball parks, in auditoriums and pool halls, at circuses and domino matches."[72]

In Norfolk, for example, laws requiring segregation in transportation and restaurants proliferated in the first quarter of the 20th century along with a residential segregation ordinance passed on August 25, 1925.[73]

The lack of meaningful political voice also underscored the lie in so-called separate-but-equal schools for African Americans. According to Kluger, 11 Southern states in 1910 "spent an average of $9.45 on each white child enrolled in their public schools and $2.90 on each black child"[74] and the gap continued to widen. In 1916, Kluger writes, the states expended an average of $10.32 per white schoolchild and $2.89 for each Black school child.[75] Huge disparities were also common in teacher pay throughout the South, with White public school teachers often earning about twice the salary of a Black teacher.[76] In Norfolk, in 1939, the White janitor at the Black Booker T. Washington High School earned more than the Black principal or Black teachers.[77]

Virginia, under the political machine of Harry Flood Byrd Sr., held the purse strings tightly when it came to funding education and programs important to the state's poorest populations, including African Americans. In the mid-1940s, Virginia was ranked 44th of the then-48 states for percentage of state income spent on education, 44th in the percentage of people receiving assistance through welfare, and 48th in assistance to the elderly.[78]

Racist beliefs were reinforced even through the work of nonprofit and tourism organizations that promoted Southern history, such as the Association for the Preservation of Virginia Antiquities,[79] which once limited African American visits to historic Jamestown Island to just two days per year, and then only in coordination with activities involving the Hampton Institute (now Hampton University).[80] Such discrimination was ironic because Colonial Jamestown had played such an important role in the importation of slaves and the enactment of laws that governed them. However, the association, founded in 1889, then considered its mission was to reinterpret Virginia's history as glorious and progressive and "to win through monuments and pamphlets what [Confederate General Robert E.] Lee had lost at Appomattox."[81] Lindgren, writes, "Virginia inspired a mythology all its own within the complex mythology of the states of the defeated Confederacy."[82]

Byrd held similar ambitions for Virginia's roadside historical markers, the first in the nation, when his gubernatorial administration created that ongoing commemoration program in 1926 to boost tourism.[83] Tarter writes that the highway markers, combined with the dedication of many monuments and statues honoring Virginia's Confederates, "made the landscape itself a powerful educational text."[84] Joseph Bayless elaborates on this point, noting that the historical marker program, which became a national model, emphasized "Colonial, Revolutionary, and Civil War history to promote the popular conception of the past (as it also) blotted out histories relating to African American and Native American history,"[85] adding that "The lack of commemoration for African Americans was illustrative of the restrictions on black franchise and dominant class of whites in power."[86]

Overall, as historian Larissa M. Smith observes, Virginia's organized historical homage initiatives encouraged its 20th century White citizens to:

> Take pride in upholding "the Virginia tradition." This tradition meant sustaining what was believed to be the values of the eighteenth-century elite—gentility, respectability, and moderation. Moreover, the code of gentility included a sense of paternalism and *noblesse oblige* to poorer whites and African Americans. A thick veneer of politeness often coated the racism of white Virginians.[87]

Virginia's White political structure found ways to embed White supremacy and racism into public school textbooks. In 1950, the General Assembly formalized the effort by establishing the seven-member—all-White—Virginia History and Government Textbook Commission, which hired and supervised textbook writers. Three new books were published and disseminated to fourth, seventh, and 11th graders across the commonwealth.[88]

Through these books, for example, fourth-graders learned, that "Life among the Negroes of Virginia in slavery times was generally happy. The Negroes went about in a cheerful manner making a living for themselves and for those for whom they worked.[89] The seventh-grade *History, Government, Geography* textbook included a half-page color drawing of a well-dressed Black family newly arrived from Africa, holding their luggage while being warmly welcomed on the deck of a sailing boat by a distinguished-looking

White slaveowner.[90] Meanwhile, the 11th-grade textbook taught that enslaved African Americans "did not work so hard as the average free laborer, since he did not have to worry about losing his job. In fact, the slave enjoyed what we might call comprehensive social security. Generally speaking, his food was plentiful, his cabin warm, his health protected and his leisure carefree." This high school book also instructed that slaves and masters "understood that bondage as they knew it was not totally evil; both realized that enslavement in a civilized world had been better in many respects for the Negro than the barbarities he might have suffered in Africa."[91]

The results of such nonviolent oppression in Virginia were still so brutal and comprehensive that historians provide depressing characterizations, including this from Wynes: "For the Virginia Negro there was truly no hiding place and no refuge from the long arm of white supremacy."[92]

Reactionary forces also took root in Virginia's academic world, even in prestigious institutes of higher learning. In one instance, a perceived threat to White supremacy even caused the removal of a College of William and Mary student editor from her campus newspaper position. The student, Marilyn Kaemmerle from Michigan, commemorated the February 12, 1945, anniversary of Abraham Lincoln's birthday by writing that "Negroes should be recognized as equals in our minds and hearts"[93] and urged educating "ourselves away from the idea of White Supremacy, for this belief is as groundless as Hitler's Nordic Supremacy nonsense."[94] What apparently infuriated the campus, community, board of trustees, and politicians the most was Kaemmerle's opinion that "Negroes should attend William and Mary; they should go to our classes, participate in college functions, join the same clubs, be our roommates, pin the same classmates, and marry among us."[95] Those who took issue with her, focused the most on her suggestion of the freedom to intermarry, says J. D. Smith.[96] The college president not only yanked Kaemmerle from her editing position, he required faculty supervision of all future student publications.[97]

The prospect of desegregated public education (the focus of Chapter 9) became a major arena for reactionary rhetoric and racist backlash in the 1950s across the South, throughout Virginia, and in the schools and neighborhoods of Norfolk. Virginia's political leaders pledged "massive resistance" to court-ordered desegregation and enacted sweeping laws that stymied thousands of parents. Evelyn Butts was among them when she attempted to transfer her daughter, Charlene, from an all-Black school to one that had been all-White.

The Great Depression of the 1930s took a greater toll on Norfolk-area Blacks than on Whites. African Americans were frequently the first to lose their jobs or were laid off and replaced by Whites. When Blacks found work, the jobs were often the lowest-paying and involved hard physical toils. A federal Works Progress Administration grant of $76,278 in 1938 enabled the Norfolk government to hire 220 African Americans—200 women and 20 men—to begin developing Azalea Garden (pictured here, now Norfolk Botanical Garden) as a tourist attraction. The harsh work, which paid 25 cents an hour, involved clearing trees, stumps, and dense vegetation in an environment infested with snakes, ticks, and poison ivy. The women and men also had to carry the equivalent of 150 truckloads of dirt to build a levee for the garden's lake. *Courtesy of Sargeant Memorial Collection, Norfolk Public Library.*

# CHAPTER 6
## Let the Men Lead

A March 1960 courtroom tiff involving Evelyn Butts included a type of public insult long endured by Black women, one that was reminiscent of the indignities that the famous abolitionist and voting-rights advocate Sojourner Truth complained about in her legendary "Ain't I A Woman" speech in 1851. Speaking at the Women's Rights Convention in Ohio, Sojourner Truth had reportedly proclaimed:

> *That* man over there says that women need to be helped into carriages, and lifted over ditches, and to have the best place everywhere. Nobody ever helps me into carriages, or over mud-puddles, or gives me any best place! And ain't I a woman?[1]

Evelyn Butts was not delivering a dramatic speech but testifying in Norfolk Circuit Court about her role in organizing a picketing demonstration against discriminatory hiring and pay practices at a local Be-Lo supermarket. A lawyer for Be-Lo (identified only as "A. Howard" in news reports) kept referring to Evelyn Butts by her last name only—"Butts." Butts' attorney, Edward A. Dawley, told the judge that Howard was being purposely disrespectful to a Black woman and asked that his client be called "Mrs. Butts" during the proceedings. Howard then switched to calling her "Evelyn Butts," a seeming refusal to use the courtesy title of "Mrs." even though Howard referred to a White female witness as "Mrs. Schwartz."[2]

Unequal etiquette in addressing Black and White women may have been treated as a relatively minor issue during the era of the Civil Rights Movement, but it represented an entrenched pattern of racial, sexual, and class humiliations and abuse that African American women had encountered in their daily lives since Colonial days.

Sexist discrimination was only part of the problem. The abuse consisted of powerful combinations of racial and sexual hatred and bullying, sexual oppression and sexualized abuse, demagoguery and political suppression, myths based on ignorance and purposeful lies about their gender and their abilities, and misconceptions about their contributions to society—all these not only in the attitudes and behavior of White men but also from White women and even from many Black male civil rights leaders.[3]

Many times, this deep-rooted animosity, often seething and malicious, intersected with racism and class issues as well as with an odd fear among many White Southerners that African Americans—both male and female—had long-range designs on intermarrying with Whites in order to destroy the White "Christian civilization."

"Constantly, the [N]egro will be endeavoring to usurp every right and privilege which will lead to intermarriage," declared Mississippi judge Thomas Pickens Brady.[4]

Virginia Governor J. Lindsay Almond Jr. was more graphic as he denounced court-ordered desegregation of schools in 1959. He warned statewide television and radio audiences that integration would bring "the livid stench of sadism, sex immorality, and juvenile pregnancy" to Virginia just as it had infested "the mixed schools of the District of Columbia and elsewhere."[5]

Jim Crow treatment of African American women had its roots in the legacy of sexual assaults during the slavery era, brutality that was used to remind Black women of the power of white male supremacy.[6] Such assaults against Black female slaves were widespread, according to scholar-activist Angela Y. Davis, who writes in *Women, Race & Class*, that slave owner rapes of enslaved Black females had less to do with "excessive sex urges"[7] and more to do with "ruthless economic exploitation."[8] Davis observes:

> Slave women were inherently vulnerable to all forms of sexual coercion. If the most violent punishments of men consisted in floggings and mutilations, women were flogged and mutilated, as well as raped. Rape ... was an uncamou-flaged expression of the slaveholder's economic mastery and the overseer's control over Black women as workers.[9]

Davis adds, "The right claimed by slave owners and their agents over the bodies of female slaves was a direct expression of their presumed property rights over Black people as a whole"[10] and this "pattern of institutionalized sexual abuse of Black women became so powerful that it managed to survive the abolition of slavery."[11]

Thus, the raping of Black women by White men continued for decades during the post-slavery Jim Crow era. According to historian Danielle L. McGuire in her pioneering study, *At the Dark End of the Street: Black Women, Rape, and Resistance—a New History of the Civil Rights Movement from Rosa Parks to the Civil Rights Movement*, reasons for the assaults included Southern White men using rape as "a form of retribution [for the defeat of the Confederacy or other alleged affronts to Southern or White male pride] or to enforce rules of racial and economic hierarchy."[12] And, as Hale writes, White men who sexually exploited Black women, including by rape, could usually do so "with little fear" of legal consequences.[13] If White men happened to be arrested for rape, they would frequently offer the excuse that "the women were asking for it," according to Olson,[14] who explains that "The flagrant humiliation of Black women was tied to the widespread belief, stemming from the days of slavery, that they did not deserve respect or consideration, because they were sexual wantons who led men astray."[15]

Black women as jezebels who invited rape with their allegedly loose morals and impudence was a common myth held by many White supremacists. Another myth portrayed the Black woman as a contented mammy, an all-purpose domestic worker who happily put the needs of White people before hers or her own family's.[16] The mammy was often conceived as a desexualized large-bodied, very dark Black woman with a big round face and deep laugh, who had an "implicit understanding and acceptance of her inferiority and her devotion to whites."[17] African American women who did not approximate the deferential qualities of the legendary mammy could be considered untrustworthy or uppity by Whites.

The so-called genteel racists of The Virginia Way also relied upon the "beloved mammy" stereotype as they professed their respect for Black women and concern for their well-being. Walter Scott Copeland, the newspaper editor who advocated for the rigid racial separation in the 1926 Public Assemblages Act, presented himself as a friend to Blacks "and cited as proof the love and respect he felt for his mammy," writes J. D. Smith.[18]

As in other racial relationships imposed one-sidedly, affluent Norfolk residents in 1917 pined for the happy, hardworking "antebellum auntie" (mammy) who had become hard to find in the 20th century; yet, at the same time, the Whites did not want to pay such valued help what they were really worth.[19] Almost 82% of working Black women in Norfolk at the time were employed as domestics or personal servants, and there was a movement afoot to enroll them in a labor union. That October, the organized domestics threatened to strike for wages of $1 per day, but the local police department broke up the initiative before it could start.

Whites labeled the Black women involved as insolent, and one Norfolk resident reported his cook to federal agents because she "had recently been indulging in frequent and lengthy dissertations on the great injustice done the negroes by the whites."[20]

At the same time, paternalistic affluent White women "envisioned themselves ... as capable of providing the necessary guidance for black uplift and advancement," especially in being role models to their low-paid maids.[21] In return, the Black domestic service workers were expected "to be honest, to be truthful, to be polite, to be cleanly, to be on time in performing her tasks"[22] or risk having part of their pay withheld.

White fear, ignorance, and stereotypes of African Americans, as well as condescending attitudes of superiority and perhaps guilt for abusing Black people, fed into rumor-mongering about how African American domestic workers intended to change their relationships with the White families that employed them. Howard W. Odum, one of the nation's leading sociologists at the time, was so concerned about the potential impact of these and other racial rumors on America's democracy and military efforts during World War II that he put together a compendium, *Race and Rumors of Race: Challenge to American Crisis*. The widespread rumor about domestic workers, reported in many Southern localities, including Norfolk, was that the African American maids and cooks were forming "Eleanor Clubs," named in honor of the progressive-minded First Lady Eleanor Roosevelt. Various versions of this rumor had Black maids planning massive strikes that went beyond demands for higher wages and shorter work weeks. Goals would include entering the White employee's home by the front door instead of the back, requirements that maids be addressed as "Miss" or "Mrs." and not by first names, a place at the family dining table to share meals with the employers, tolerance when refusing to serve anyone who insults the maid or other African Americans, and respect for the purported club motto: "A white woman in her own kitchen by Christmas."[23]

The steady flow of these rumors apparently caused so much political agitation that the White House directed the FBI to investigate. Even though the agency was headed by J. Edgar Hoover, who was not friendly to Black civil rights initiatives and disliked Eleanor Roosevelt, the FBI's extensive examination found the rumors to be just that—baseless fiction.[24]

While many Southern White households were frightened or angered by the purported Eleanor Clubs, African American women who depended on domestic jobs were being further marginalized by high-level political deals that excluded low-paid maids, nannies, cooks, farm workers and similar employees from the protections of federal labor laws for wages, overtime pay, and collective bargaining.[25] Meaghan Winter, for example, notes that President Franklin D. Roosevelt agreed to Southern political demands for such exemptions because he needed the votes of Southern senators and representatives in order for his Fair Labor Standards Act of 1938 to win congressional approval.[26]

White-supremacist Southerners were also in the driver's seat, both figuratively and literally, when it came to devising and enforcing Jim Crow laws and policies for local mass transit and inter-city transportation. Low-paid Black women—again, mostly domestic workers who needed these forms of transportation to travel to their jobs—faced daily real-life humiliation because of segregated seating arrangements in streetcars, buses, railroad cars, and ferry boats, as well as in train, bus, and ferry stations.[27] Many Southern states and localities empowered bus drivers to enforce Jim Crow in whatever form they interpreted—and at gunpoint.

Many times, public humiliation went far beyond enforcing the segregated seating. Bus drivers boarded White people before Blacks, directed Black riders to climb in through the back door, made Blacks give up their seats for Whites even in Black sections of a bus, sometimes drove away after taking a fare and refused to stop when a Black rider wanted to get off, and called Black women racially and sexually offensive names.[28] There were even instances of sexual abuse. A Black woman named Ferdie Walker in Fort Worth, Texas, said White bus drivers would expose themselves to her while she stood at a bus stop waiting to get on.[29]

Although she lived in Montgomery, Alabama, civil rights icon Rosa Parks summed up the frustrations for low-paid Black women throughout the South, explaining "You spend your whole lifetime in your occupation ... making life clever, easy and convenient for white people, but when you have to get transportation home, you are denied equal accommodation."[30] Throughout the Jim Crow era, the manner in which Black women were treated on buses and streetcars became "a particularly powerful and symbolic issue for African American women," Ransby says.[31]

Montgomery's domestic service workers thus became the core group among the thousands of African Americans who made the 1955–56 boycott a success by walking miles to work every day rather than ride the Jim Crow buses. Olson, who calls the maids and other low-paid women "the true heroines," recounts how these domestic workers would also participate in the boycott's weekly mass meetings and talk about their experiences, including being fired for joining the boycott. "For women who had spent all their lives being told they were inferior because of their race, sex, and social status, challenging the authority of those who had forced them into submission was a heady, if frightening, experience," Olson writes.[32]

Combinations of race, gender, and class biases or oppression frustrated many more African American women in the workforce all over the country, including teachers in Norfolk.

In the 1930s, "Salary differentials based on race, sex, and educational level existed in the Norfolk school system," Lewis notes,[33] adding that White teachers generally earned more than Black teachers and men were paid more than women. For example, he says, a starting Black female teacher at the secondary level "earned 72.1 percent of the salary earned by a similarly educated white female teacher."[34]

In Norfolk's private sector, Black women, as a group, "had the highest female labor force participation levels in the country, although most were mired in low-paying, domestic service jobs," Lewis writes.[35] New opportunities came with the start of World War II but with mixed results. Says Lewis, "When men left for the war, black women stepped in to fill the void. Their presence was not always wanted or accepted, but they were not deterred."[36]

Lewis notes that Black women applied for many war-related industrial jobs but were often rebuffed by hiring managers who said that employment sites or job-training programs could not accommodate Black women.[37] "Despite a desperate need for war workers," Lewis observes, "it seemed that a reservoir of labor would go untapped. Across the nation, black women were equally victimized by racism and sexism."[38]

Sexist beliefs and practices thwarted all women who desired voting rights and political inclusion, but especially African American women.

From Colonial times, many men had insisted that women were too delicate to withstand the burden of decision-making required for elections.[39] During the adoption of the U.S. Constitution and Bill of Rights, most men regarded women as childlike dependents "outside the political community."[40] By the early 1800s, opponents to women's suffrage often argued that women "lacked the independence and strength of mind and body to cast a responsible vote" and that nastiness in politics would "corrupt women," thereby harming home and family values.[41]

This attitude continued throughout the 1800s. As Collier writes:

As late as the late-nineteenth century it was believed by many—that is, many *men*—that contemplation of matters political—as with contemplation of any abstract field such as mathematics—would overtax the female intelligence and drive the adventuresome lady into the insane asylum.[42]

For example, during debates in 1887 over a proposed constitutional amendment to give voting rights to women, U.S. Senator George G. Vest of Missouri said women were too emotional as well as susceptible to corruption. He added that women's voting rights would undermine families by disrupting God's arrangement of the sexes.[43] Other politicians opposed to women's suffrage made similar assertions in the last quarter of the 19th century and even up to ratification of the 19th Amendment that granted women's suffrage in 1920.[44]

Virginia's history regarding voting rights for women was among the most stubborn. The 19th amendment to the U.S. Constitution, giving women the right to vote, was ratified by the required 36 states between June 10, 1919, and August 18, 1920. Virginia was not among them.

Instead, Virginia joined with seven other Southern states to withhold ratification until decades later, with Virginia signing off in 1952, 32 years after women's voting rights was already the law of the land.[45] The delay in Virginia did not deprive women from voting or running for office in that state, but it reinforced Virginia's reputation for foot-dragging and tepid endorsements of expanded suffrage.

The suffrage debate in Virginia was also infused with racism. White women opposed to women's voting rights often injected racial themes into their arguments in the years just before national ratification of the 19th Amendment. An anti-suffrage White women's group in Virginia warned:

> Every argument for sexual equality in politics is, and must be, an argument also for racial equality. ... If the white woman is entitled to vote because she bears, has borne, or might have borne children, the Negro women is entitled to the same right for the same reason.[46]

Meanwhile, Southern White male political leaders worried that suffrage for women would inspire African American women to be more aggressive and resourceful in overcoming various voter-suppression schemes that had disenfranchised Black men so effectively. Keyssar quotes a Mississippi senator as saying, "We are not afraid to maul a black man over the head if he dares to vote, but we can't treat women, even black women, that way."[47] And the Virginia Association Opposed to Woman's Suffrage warned that allowing voting rights for African American women would eventually lead to social equality for all Blacks and intermarriage between Blacks and Whites.[48]

Anti-suffragists also tried to incite racial fear in efforts to stop momentum toward the 19th Amendment. "Providing women the vote, they argued, meant providing African American women the vote. This, in turn, would as much as double the total African American vote and lead to black control at the polls," according to McDaid.[49]

The women's suffrage movement, however, had its own problems with racism and class discrimination, a split that dated back to post-Civil War efforts to approve voting rights for Black men via the 15th Amendment. Elizabeth Cady Stanton, a White woman long active in the abolitionist movement, lashed out against the idea that Black men would gain suffrage before White women. She demanded to know why White women, especially those who are educated and affluent, should "stand aside and see 'Sambo' walk into the kingdom first?"[50]

Racialized divisions among women suffragists would continue for decades, even up to and beyond passage of the 19th Amendment. Lichtman notes a 1906 statement by the Conference of Southern Women Suffragists that said, "We ask for the ballot as a solution of the race problem. There are over 600,000 more white women in the southern states than all the negro men and women combined."[51] The meaning was clear: that if women gained voting rights, then a male-female White voting bloc would be too great an obstacle for the combined forces of Black men and women to overcome. Terborg-Penn writes about White supremacy as an important factor in suffragist strategy to make inroads among Southern White women.[52] Terborg-Penn and Hale provides a blatant example from a 1907 letter from Kate Gordon, a Louisiana suffragist, to Laura Kay, a Kentucky women's voting-rights advocate, noting that White men who opposed women's suffrage "would gladly welcome us as a measure to insure white supremacy."[53]

Southern White-supremacist politicians feared voting rights for Black women, according to Olson, who reports that South Carolina Senator Ben Tillman said:

> Experience has taught us that Negro women are much more aggressive in asserting the "rights of the race" than the Negro men are, and that Mississippi Senator James K. Vardaman said "The Negro woman will be ... more difficult to handle at the polls than the Negro man."[54]

White women in Virginia's suffrage movement, however, gave assurances that White voting strength would also be protected by Virginia's poll taxes, literacy tests, and other devices that thwarted the vote of Black men.[55] Indeed, as it became apparent in 1920 that the 19th Amendment would be approved, Virginia's white male political establishment pondered how to stymie Black women who wanted to vote. U.S. Representative Henry Flood, an uncle of future political boss Harry F. Byrd Sr., declared that it was "of paramount importance to protect the electorate from the colored female voters."[56] Flood recommended another safeguard: that the state devise additional laws in the vein and spirit of discriminatory literacy tests, residency requirements, property qualifications, and the understanding clause.[57]

Despite ratification of the 19th Amendment in 1920, "racism continued to block black women's political aspiration," writes historian Martha S. Jones.[58] Across Virginia, local voter-registration officials, already holding power to discriminate among voter-applicants, knew what they had to do.[59] Newspapers in Richmond reported in 1920 that White women applying to vote for the first time were quickly accommodated by the registrar's office on the main floor of city hall, while Black women were sent to register in the basement and were often challenged or left in line without being served.[60] In Hampton, home to many African Americans associated with Hampton Institute (now Hampton University),

Black women who sought to register felt humiliated by the delaying tactics, including being forced to stand in line all day and then told to come back the next day, while White women were registered first and within a few minutes. Also, Black women reported being asked impossible questions such as, "How many people does it take to make a county?" and "What is the maximum and minimum number of section districts in the State of Virginia?"[61]

At the same time, White political leaders such as John M. Purcell, chairman of the Richmond Democratic Committee, were imploring White women to pay their poll taxes and register if they agreed that "the domination of the white race (was) essential to the welfare of the Southland."[62]

White-supremacist politicians were also known to inject offensive language into their political campaigns—and with African American women serving as the unwitting foil. One of the most egregious occurred during the 1938 congressional elections when the campaign of Norfolk's Colgate W. Darden Jr. produced a flyer that labeled his opponent, Norman R. Hamilton, a "nigger lover" because he set up a campaign office in Portsmouth's Black district and hired young Black women to work there.[63] Darden's staff sent photographers to capture the scene and circulated copies with captions that read, "Look Hamilton's a nigger lover!" "See the niggers are set up better than your own people by him," and "If you vote for Hamilton, niggers will be teaching your children soon!"[64] At the same time, Darden made his own duplicitous pitch for African American votes by contending he would be a stronger advocate of national anti-lynching legislation than Hamilton. Meanwhile, at least two influential Black voters reported that Darden supporters were offering payments to help campaign for Darden.[65] Darden won by 1,547 votes.

African American women also struggled against discrimination within civil rights organizations and were given little encouragement for leadership positions. The now-revered Ella Baker toiled for years for the national office of the NAACP but had to work extra-hard for her ideas to be considered by the male-dominated leadership.

"Women were indispensable but underappreciated," Ransby writes. "The (NAACP) had never elected a woman as its executive secretary, and women were often excluded from the informal inner circle of decision makers" despite serving as "the backbone of many of the most active local branches, as well as of the national office staff itself."[66]

Baker persisted, even changing the minds of a few African American men. In the 1940s, the national NAACP sent the Norfolk-born Baker to help with branch organizational work in Richmond. She arrived to discover that John M. Tinsley, the Richmond branch president and state chairman, strongly preferred a man. According to historian Barbara Ransby, Baker endured and, after 11 days, shattered Tinsley's "sexist assumptions about a woman's limited capabilities."[67]

However, Baker continued to face sexism in the civil rights movement for the rest of her career. She felt her work was not even fully appreciated by the African American male leaders of the SCLC, mostly clergymen, including its first president, the Rev. Martin Luther King Jr. Baker helped organize important voter-registration drives for the SCLC, but as Ransby tells it, "She became especially annoyed that many SCLC ministers viewed her as a glorified secretary who was there to simply 'carry out King's orders.' Although the SCLC needed Baker's skills, it was not willing to recognize or affirm her leadership."[68]

Because Ella Baker and many other talented women in the civil rights movement were rarely recognized, the general public still carries a misconception about the movement's leadership. "They think it was all men. Even now," says Judy Richardson, a former staff member of the Student Nonviolent Coordinating Committee.[69]

Actions of Black male leaders of the civil rights movement as well as the news media contributed to this misconception. A now well-known behind-the-scene story about the famous 1963 March on Washington, where Martin Luther King Jr. gave his "I Have a Dream" speech, exemplifies what happened. Key organizers of the march—all men—mostly excluded women in the leadership committee or did not let women share the speaker's rostrum in any meaningful way. Only one woman, Anna Arnold Hedgeman, from the Commission on Religion and Race of the National Council of Churches, was a member of the march's administrative committee. After Hedgeman and other women privately protested the exclusion of women as speakers, several women were added to the program as part of an almost separate "Tribute to Negro Women Fighters for Freedom."[70] "For many Black women who were actively involved in the civil rights movement, especially those in leadership positions, the blatantly insensitive treatment of Black women leaders was a new awakening," Dorothy I. Height, president of the National Council of Negro Women, later wrote.[71]

Historians of the civil rights movement attribute the discrimination against women to an overlapping of self-perpetuating factors that often reinforced each other. For example, African American churches held great sway in the struggle for civil rights, and most of the pastors were men. Also, the hierarchy of church structures was often gendered, with men in more publicly visible leadership roles and women assigned to positions in the choirs and social functions as well as serving as secretaries. Then, as Black ministers stepped into the spotlight of the civil rights movement through organizations such as the influential SCLC, these men transferred their concepts about leadership to movement activities.[72] When the news media covered an event or needed spokespersons, male leaders seemed to be the most readily available.[73]

Even the most prominent women in the Civil Rights Movement, such as Rosa Parks and Coretta Scott King, could not break the cycle because, according to historian Jeanne Theoharis, the civil rights leadership, the media, and the public all seemed to desire certain characteristics in their female crusaders. Both Rosa Parks and Coretta Scott King "were framed as having fought for justice sweetly and demurely" despite long histories of strident activism, Theoharis writes,[74] adding that "Parks and King were celebrated for their modesty and respectability, Parks for being quiet and never raising her voice, and King for being gentle and beautiful."[75] As a result, other female African American civil rights leaders were overlooked as not being worthy of national attention, especially if they were too "outspoken and outraged, for being poor or overweight or loud and angry."[76]

———•———

In Evelyn Butts' life, there is only a scant public record of her encountering overt sexism and other forms of gender bias or gender abuse aimed at her individually—and Butts usually did not characterize her struggles with powerful men in terms of sexism.

Similarly, there is no record of Butts specifically advocating for equal rights for women apart from crusading for civil rights and voting rights for all African Americans and poor people. However, throughout her many years of activism, there is ample evidence that Butts strongly encouraged African American women to participate in the civil rights struggle and in politics. She devoted countless hours to informing women about civil rights and political issues and helping them attain access to the political process.

As noted in Chapter 2, Butts combined the sharing of homemaking tips with her Oakwood neighbors with the opportunity to dispense information about civil rights, voting rights, and politics.[77] She also led the Women of Virginia's Third Force organization on annual visits to Virginia's General Assembly.[78]

While Butts' friends and allies, characterized her as courageous and the heroic leader of an "army" of civil rights activists,[79] some journalists applied more traditional feminine terms, even in Norfolk's Black press. In an otherwise laudatory opinion piece in the *Journal and Guide*, an influential local columnist thanked civil rights attorney Joseph A. Jordan Jr. and Butts for toppling Virginia's

In addition to questing for voting rights, African Americans sought to extinguish the endless humiliations and intimidations that spewed from White supremacists. Mississippi civil rights activist and community organizer Fannie Lou Hamer once famously described how Blacks felt about being subjected to such all-encompassing abuse, declaring: "I am sick and tired of being sick and tired, and we want a change." *Courtesy of the United States Library of Congress Prints and Photographs division.*

poll tax in 1966 but referred to Butts as "the housewife"[80]—even though Butts already had a long track record as a leader in several civil rights, voting rights, and political organizations and provided for her family as a skilled seamstress.

The sparse contemporaneous records of Butts' encounters with overt sexism or of crusading specifically for women's rights does not necessarily mean that Butts did not experience or observe sexism in Norfolk; in fact, there is evidence that Butts encountered sexism (as well as class bias) in the actions of several African American men, including the Rev. Jesse Jackson Sr., although Butts may not have described these events as sexist at the time.

Also, the absence of Butts' comments about feminism also does not mean that Butts was dismissive about women's rights. It may mean that the news media never reported on Butts' position on sexism and equality for women, or it may be a reflection of the times, as she belonged to a generation of Black women who felt it more important to focus on the civil rights of African Americans in general.[81] Meanwhile, several incidents in Butts' life show she was not afraid to stand up to politically powerful or otherwise domineering men or go counter to their wishes as well as examples of when Butts helped African American women connect with civil rights and with the political system.

While Butts sometimes was described as stubborn and bull-headed,[82] longtime friend and political ally Alveta V. Green, a retired educator, disagrees with that assessment. Green suggests that such terms could be based in sexism because most male activists were not accustomed to working with strong, outspoken women. "She might have been aggressive for the times," Green says.[83] "But that's what she needed to be to get the job done."

"Looking back on it," Green adds, "she was also a Black woman breaking some barriers."[84]

Herbert Smith, a retired brick mason and also a longtime friend who drove Butts to many meetings and events, concurred with Green, saying that some men, including several African American ministers, did not respect Butts' leadership abilities because she was a woman.[85]

One example of Butts defying the wishes of a Black male authority figure occurred during the 1959-60 picketing of the Be-Lo supermarket and follow-up injunction trial. An African American minister, the Rev. John B. Gray of the nearby Mount Gilead Missionary Baptist Church, told Butts and her fellow picketers, and later testified in Circuit Court, that his entire community-based congregation of 700 members did not approve of the picketing.[86] Butts and her allies continued to picket, and at least two church members, Ruth Whitney and Willie A. Minggia, testified in the trial that they supported the picketing and their pastor was wrong about the entire congregation being against the protest.

The Be-Lo picketing apparently also became a factor when Butts and several allies challenged the leadership of Robert D. Robertson, the longtime president of the Norfolk Branch of the NAACP, later in 1960. The local NAACP leadership did not support the protest activity against the supermarket, according to the *Journal and Guide* newspaper.[87] The newspaper reported that branch leadership believed that residents living near the store were already negotiating with Be-Lo management about hiring more African Americans and that picketers were "outsiders" even though at least Butts and Walter H. Green Sr. lived only a few blocks away.[88]

The Norfolk NAACP Branch had been led since at least 1953 by Robertson, a former steelworker, stevedore, and longshoreman who had also worked as a labor union organizer.[89] Butts and her allies, though, found him to be too moderate, accommodating, and slow to respond to White authorities when it came to civil rights issues. Indeed, the *Journal and Guide* noted Robertson's reputation for purposeful avoidance of "needless agitation" and his "policy of desegregation by negotiation wherever possible."[90]

Butts and her allies also charged that Robertson and his forces had scheduled a branch election for December 1960 without informing all members. Butts and her group notified the national NAACP, which then invalidated the branch election and arranged a new vote for March 13, 1961, with Butts running for president against Robertson.[91] In response, Robertson labeled Butts and her allies as militants, dissidents, and radicals, which prompted Butts to send a letter to branch members in which she characterized Robertson as "dictatorial."[92]

Continuing in her letter, Butts accused Robertson of not being vigorous in challenging racial discrimination but then taking credit for the civil rights accomplishments of others. "We admit that we are militant in fighting for the civil rights of Negro citizens. The NAACP is supposed to be a militant organization. It was founded for this purpose," Butts wrote,[93] adding: "because many of us, on account of our jobs, our families, or other reasons, cannot be militant, the NAACP was established to be militant for us."

With the Norfolk NAACP election scheduled for March 13, 1961, Butts and her slate of challengers to Robertson's team withdrew their candidacies a day before. Butts contended that Robertson was being given "improper and unfair" advantage[94] by "unprecedented meddling in local affairs" from the national and state NAACP organizations.[95] "We cannot accept a situation in which we must tolerate a dictatorship which is allegedly fighting for democracy and justice, regardless of what national or state official intervenes," Butts huffed to a reporter.[96] The Norfolk Branch proceeded with the election anyway, and Robertson "won a smashing victory" with 361 votes against 45 for Butts.[97] However, Butts and her slate did not quit the NAACP but continued to participate, even riding on buses that the branch chartered to the March on Washington in August 1963.[98]

Perhaps the most significant of Butts' public disagreements with politically powerful African American men came in the 1980s after Butts had deepened her involvement in partisan politics. The story of her political fights with a man named Bishop Levi E. Willis Sr. involves the fast-changing alliances of Norfolk's complicated local political scene of the 1980s and occurred after Butts' heyday as a grassroots civil rights leader. The example is included here only to help illustrate Butts' encounters with sexism.

In amassing her political power, Butts chaired the Concerned Citizens for Political Education, which endorsed candidates for the Norfolk City Council and candidates for General Assembly seats from Norfolk. She also rose in the Democratic Party to chair of the Second Congressional District Democratic Committee. Willis, meanwhile, was a charismatic preacher who had been born in poverty but had become a shrewd and wealthy owner of a network of radio stations and a funeral home and held an ownership stake in a local bank. He then set his sights on political power and out-flanked Butts in her activities.

In 1983, Willis brought the famous Rev. Jesse Jackson Sr. to Norfolk for a protest march with 6,000 people and then created a local Rainbow Coalition, borrowing the name from a national organization headed by Jackson. Jackson, at the time, was preparing to seek the Democratic nomination for president in the 1984 election.

Butts was among 225 people invited to a breakfast meeting with Jackson, but it was clear that Willis had Jackson's ear. As Butts' daughter Charlene tells it, Butts later confided to her three daughters that Jackson had pulled her aside to tell her that as a woman she needed to step aside and allow men to take the political lead in Norfolk. Butts felt insulted.[99]

Within months, Willis had engineered the ouster of Butts from her leadership position in in the Second Congressional District Democratic Committee and dramatically weakened the effectiveness of the Concerned Citizens.[100]

A few years later, Willis' financial empire began to unravel. His downward spiral included actions from the Internal Revenue Service and federal banking regulators, the arrest of his daughter for embezzling, liens and lawsuits against his radio stations, and a federal felony conviction for mishandling a loan repayment. In 1989, Willis no longer held his political leadership positions.[101] By the late 1980s, however, Butts' health was in decline and she was stepping away from her remaining civic and political activities.[102]

There is one other aspect to Butts' fearlessness in standing up against the political tides on gender-related issues; there is evidence that Butts spoke in favor of gay rights long before even most liberal politicians would add their public support. In 1984, while seeking election to the Norfolk City Council, Butts participated in a candidates' forum sponsored by the Tidewater Chapter of the Virginia Gay Alliance. Each of the eight candidates who attended were asked:

Would you be willing to introduce or support a city ordinance which would prohibit discrimination in city and
private employment, housing, and public accommodations
based on race, color, religion, sex, creed, age, national or-
igin, physical handicap, marital status, sexual orientation,
or any other non-merit factor?[103]

Butts was one of only two candidates to voice unqualified
support, saying she wanted "equal rights for everybody."[104]

Colonial-era plantation owners like William Byrd II, pictured in 1718, boasted of their "in-dependence," but their wealth often depended in great measure on the African American men and women they enslaved. *Courtesy of Virginia Museum of History & Culture*

# CHAPTER 7

## Class—and No Class

As with racism and White supremacy, issues related to class in the United States have their American roots in Colonial Virginia and the region that encompasses present-day Norfolk. American concepts about the allocation of voting rights also had their beginnings in Colonial times and then carried over into how our democracy evolved.

Among these early strictures was that wealth was a determinant for voting rights, a prerequisite that surfaced in various forms over the decades but was not eliminated until March 24, 1966, when the U.S. Supreme Court ruled state and local poll taxes unconstitutional in the *Annie E. Harper vs. Virginia State Board of Elections* decision, the same case that began as *Evelyn Butts vs. Albertis Harrison, Governor.*[1]

During the period when Africans arrived in Virginia in 1619 and entered servitude, the colony was developing a caste system for political participation and social status.[2] At first, the English colonists proclaimed voting rights for White male landowners. But they quickly made an exception for Eastern European artisans and skilled laborers who launched the first labor strike in British North America in protest against being excluded.[3]

For the most part, though, suffrage was limited to only the "better" elements of society, which in Virginia meant White Protestant men who owned property, known as "freeholders."[4]

Around the same time, these early English colonists began a political and economic culture of deference that would grow and

influence White-supremacist attitudes into the mid-20<sup>th</sup> century. As
Rogers notes, "Extremely important also was the political custom of
'deference,' where potential voters of the middling and lower social
orders deferred to the authority of their social betters."[5] Collier
expands on this aspect of social deference, explaining that colonists
accepted a "a hierarchical society which was divided between the
better sort, the middling sort, and the lower orders" and that:

> The last of these were not eligible to vote, and the middling
> tended to let neighbor George do the voting when George
> was wealthy or enjoyed some other evidence of accom-
> plishment or status. Those who came to the polls voted
> for their betters.[6]

As tobacco plantations grew in importance in Virginia's econ-
omy, the colony's political system became essentially, in Tarter's
words, "a government of the tobacco planters, by the tobacco
planters, and for the tobacco planters"[7] with slavery as its under-
pinning. The system was so entrenched by 1772, the eve of the
American Revolution, that Richard Bland, a powerful lawyer and
longtime member of the House of Burgesses, explained that "societies of men could not subsist unless there were a subordination of
one to another, and that from the highest to lowest degree."[8]

Plantation owners behaved as European aristocrats and considered themselves entitled to the bounties of Colonial culture, including
its riches and unchallenged political power. William Byrd II, an an-
cestor of 20<sup>th</sup> century political boss Harry Flood Byrd Sr., boasted to
an English earl that "Like one of the patriarchs, I have my flocks and
my herds, my bond-men, and bond-women ... so that I live in kind
of an independence (sic)."[9] Yet, as Tarter observes, Byrd, and wealthy
planters like him, were "utterly dependent on (their) bondsmen and
bondswomen for (their) economic security and (their) social eminence.
Without enslaved laborers there would have been no liberty or independence"[10] in the ways they had become so accustomed.

The rhetoric of the American Revolution led political leaders to consider expanding voting rights to men who were not property owners.[11] Popular phrases, such as "no taxation without representation" and "consent of the governed," made it difficult for elites to continue denying voting rights to men who did not own property or were otherwise poor.[12] However, voting-eligibility rules varied from state to state and even among same-state localities, and they often involved requirements for paying certain state or local taxes.[13]

Leaving it up to each state to determine who gets to vote was a critical mistake by the delegates to the Constitutional Convention of 1787, according to political scholars such as Michael Waldman and Allan Lichtman.

The absence of a national standard for voting rights had "lasting consequences" ... for "one of the most basic elements of national citizenship," Waldman writes in *The Fight to Vote*,[14] continuing: "[It] set the stage for continued conflict, when national effort was required to forcefully advance democracy." Lichtman, in *The Embattled Vote in America: From the Founding to the Present*, adds that the suffrage omission in the Constitution contributed to endless voting-rights disputes that continue "to rage in the halls of Congress and in the courtrooms of federal judges."[15] In addition, as Lichtman observes, generations of American political leadership have "considered suffrage not a natural right but a privilege bestowed by government on a political community restricted by considerations of wealth, sex, race, residence, literacy, criminal conviction, and citizenship."[16]

The lack of national standards for suffrage has meant that the evolution of American democracy has been marked by countervailing trends of expansion and contraction, and inclusion and exclusion, according to scholars such as Alexander Keyssar[17] and Hanes Walton Jr.[18] Furthermore, Walton et al.[19] point out that the ever-changing fate of African American suffrage has been a major storyline in examining voting-rights trends.

Class tension has been a significant ingredient in the cycles of expanded and contracted voting rights, says Keyssar, who hastens to add that a "nuanced interpretation" of voting-rights history must recognize that "race, class, gender, and ethnicity ... have always been overlapping, dynamic, intertwined dimensions" when examining American suffrage,[20] especially in the imposition of financial requirements such as the poll taxes that African Americans struggled against.[21]

Free African Americans generally had a mixed experience with voting rights in Northern states, including encountering years of discriminatory restrictions according to Foner.[22] For example, New York's Constitutional Convention of 1821 eliminated the property-ownership requirement for White men but increased mandates that Black men own at least $250 worth of property, which was beyond the means of most of New York's Black population.[23] Peter Jay, a delegate to the New York Constitutional Convention and an opponent to this new restriction on Black voting, asserted that the provision was an act of White supremacy, saying that Whites were so "accustomed to look upon black men with contempt...that they ought not to vote with us."[24] In 1837, Pennsylvania went even further by eliminating Black voting rights all together.[25] The nationwide spread of such constraints on African Americans, Foner writes, indicated that race had "supplanted class as the major line of division between those who could vote and those who could not."[26]

Virginia, however, continued to officially overlap race and class restrictions on suffrage until 1850, making it the last state to require voters to own property, albeit in a modified form.[27] That change came after years of petitioning by White non-property owners (non-freeholders) who had pleaded their cause to Virginia's planter aristocracy in terms of social deference—even while turning their own backs on other groups that did not have voting rights. For example, in an 1829 petition, non-freeholders said they concurred with the upper classes that the right to vote was not a "natural right" but a "social right" that "must of necessity be regulated by society" and that women, children, foreigners and slaves should be excluded from voting.[28] As Pole sagely observes, "Equality would not spring from inequality."[29]

Slaveowners, though, successfully fought against giving voting rights to non-freeholders during Virginia's 1829–30 Constitutional Convention out of fear that any sharing of political power eventually would be too democratizing and thereby "undermine slavery itself."[30] Eerily, the phrases that "The right of suffrage is not a natural right. ... It is a social right and must necessarily be regulated by society" would be repeated by John Goode, a former member of both the Confederate Congress and the U.S. House of Representatives, as he presided over the Virginia 1901–02 state Constitutional Convention that largely disenfranchised Virginia's Black citizens.[31]

Other Southern states during the 1820s and '30s expanded voting rights to all White men, including the poor, as a means of motivating them to serve in militias that guarded against slave rebellions.[32] For Virginia, though, the antebellum pattern of intertwining race and class biases was a precursor of what was to come in post-Civil War struggles over voting rights.

Soon after the Civil War, Congress enabled African American men to vote (only men had voting rights under the laws of the time) by ratifying the 15th Amendment to the U.S. Constitution in 1870. Congress also required the former Confederate states to add Black voting rights provisions to their state constitutions in order to be readmitted to the Union. Almost immediately, Keyssar notes, the Ku Klux Klan and similar White-supremacist terrorist groups initiated "violent campaigns against blacks who sought to vote or hold office."[33]

Nevertheless, Black men enthusiastically embraced their voting rights, and the Southern states elected 22 African American congressmen and 600 state legislators during the Reconstruction period of 1865 to 1877.[34]

Yet, even before Reconstruction's end in 1877, Southern states were already developing ways to constrain the African American vote and, as in Keyssar's words, to return Blacks to "their place."[35]

Keyssar asserts that there were "important class dimensions to this political and racial agenda," explaining that "emancipation and Reconstruction threatened white control over needed black labor," therefore revealing that White Southern resistance "to black voting was rooted in class conflict as well as racial antagonism."[36]

Voting, though, was not the only arena for conflict involving the overlap of class and race. The combination showed up in how white Virginians still expected social deference when crossing paths with Black men and women in public settings. Whites felt Black people were insolent when not stepping out of the way of White people or ignoring them, and these brief encounters sometimes led to physical fighting on the streets.[37]

Whites sometimes recognized their class bias, but they usually explained it as part of the natural order. An exception was Lewis H. Blair, a Richmond-based businessman and economics expert, whose 1889 book, *Prosperity of the South Dependent Upon the Elevation of the Negro*, warned fellow White Southerners that their system of "oligarchy, caste, (and) vassalage" would be disastrous to the economic advancement of the region.[38] Blair also urged an end to segregated schools because educated African Americans would be more "useful and valuable citizens."[39]

A more common White political practice was to shortchange education for African Americans out of fear that educated Blacks would use their knowledge on Election Day. Wynes quotes Virginian Walter A. Watson as being horrified that Blacks were receiving too much education and that Black schools were "turning out your voters by the thousands."[40] Denying African Americans the same quality of education that White children were receiving would soon go hand in hand with taking away Black voting rights.

Systematic efforts to comprehensively disenfranchise African Americans began in 1890 with Mississippi rewriting its constitution to add a $2 poll tax and literacy tests that made would-be voters show they understood the U.S. Constitution or state constitution.[41] Mississippi also made its residency requirement more stringent, with the state attorney general rendering an opinion that said "the negro is ... a nomadic tribe" and therefore did not have a permanent residence.[42]

The intersection of class and race also played out in the operation of mass transit in both law and deference. Not only were Blacks required to sit toward the back of a bus behind Whites, but in many localities it became the custom for African Americans to continue waiting at a bus stop until Whites climbed aboard first. In addition, historian Henry Lewis Suggs reports in his biography of the Norfolk Black newspaper publisher P. B. Young Sr., *P. B. Young Newspaperman: Race, Politics and Journalism in the New South 1910–62*, that White female passengers often complained about getting their clothing "dirtied" by Black workingmen passing through the bus aisle to get to the vehicle's rearward seating.[43]

African Americans who lived in other parts of the country often were not accustomed to the rigidity of Southern White supremacism they encountered in public settings. In 1946, boxing champion Joe Louis, for example, did not realize he had crossed a color line when he went into a White waiting area to buy magazines while waiting to board an Elizabeth River ferry to travel from Portsmouth to Norfolk. A White employee scolded him.[44]

Class issues rose, too, among African Americans. Ella Baker, who traveled alone through the South to organize or bolster NAACP branches for the organization's national office, told friends that she found class hierarchy in some Black communities to be a large impediment to overthrowing Jim Crow and that some branches operated like social clubs.[45]

Evelyn Butts voiced a similar concern about the Norfolk Branch when her slate of candidates ran against the local Black establishment in March 1961. She wrote to fellow members: "If the NAACP is not going to be militant, why do we need it? We already have peaceful social clubs, card clubs and fraternal organizations. ... We ask you to support the Militant Candidates who, when elected, will remain your servants and militant warriors in the cause of freedom."[46]

## Colored Personal Head Tax.

### FIRST WARD.

ALEXANDER, JOHN
BRIDGEFORTH, SOLOMON

BOULDING, B. R.
WALTERS, MILES.

### SECOND WARD.

.............. .................. ...

### THIRD WARD.

BAGNALL, T. S.
BRIGHT, L. W.
BROWN, D. D.
BUTT, HENRY
CARTER, JAMES P.
CROMWELL, J. H.
COLLINS, J. M.
DAVENPORT, GEO. W.
DELOACH, INO. H.
ELEY, ROBERT
FEREBEE, EDWIN
GRANDY, CHARLES
GIBBS, JNO. L.
HALL, JOSEPH, S.
HARRISON, W. H.
ISBELL, MARCELLUS
JOHNSON, J. H.
KELLUM, ROBERT
KEELING, JEFF.
LANGLEY, ST. PAUL

LAND, W. H.
LAYCOCK, J. Z.
MILLS, W. H.
MOSS, W. M.
MULLEN, HENRY
PARKER, W. H.
PERRY ANDREW
PORTLOCK, ROBERT
PUGH, JOHN
PURYEAR, F. E.
RANSOM, WESLEY
REYNOLDS, L. H.
RUFFIN, PETER
SPARROW, W. H.
TABB, W. H.
THOROWGOOD, WM.
WARREN, JACOB
WEBB, RICHARD
WILLIS, W. L.

### FOURTH WARD.

ALLEN, BOSTON
ANDERSON, HEZEKIAH
ANDERSON, EUGENE
ARMISTEAD, WM.
ALSTON, LOUIS
BRADLEY, JACOB
BENSON, ANDREW
BRICKHOUSE, DANIEL
BRIDGES, EDWARD
BRIGHT, J. EDWARD
BROWN, WM.

BROWN, WM. A. H.
BOWE, JOSHUA
BOWEN, G. J.
BUTT, CHARLES
BUTLER, P. A.
CARR, WM. H.
CRAIG, HORACE
CANADY, E. M.
COLLINS, S. S.
CUSTARD, F. R.
CURRY, EDWARD

76

A page from the 1903 Norfolk City Poll Tax list shows the names of African American men who qualified to vote by paying the $1.50 annual poll tax that the Virginia constitutional convention of 1901-02 imposed as part of a package of voter-suppression provisions. Other former Confederate states adopted similar measures between 1890 and 1910. The $1.50 tax in the early 1900s equates to $44.72 in 2020 U.S. dollars. The levy was so burdensome that the number of Black voters in Norfolk decreased from 1,826 before the convention to 504 by 1904. *Courtesy of Sargeant Memorial Collection, Norfolk Public Library*

# CHAPTER 8
# Voting Rights—and Wrongs—in Our Democracy

On January 26, 1966, Evelyn Butts watched from the spectator seats at the U.S. Supreme Court as her lawyer, Joseph A. Jordan Jr., summarized how Virginia's imposition of the poll tax in 1902 shut African Americans out of representative democracy.

"Almost like a magic wand, after the passage of ... these poll tax laws, not a single Negro has sat in the Virginia General Assembly, and not a single Negro has held a state office in the state of Virginia. We say that the evil intent was accomplished in direct confrontation to the Fifteenth Amendment," Jordan, sitting in his wheelchair, told the nine justices.[1]

The Virginia constitutional convention of 1901–02 had established the poll tax as part of a package of voter-suppression provisions similar to those adopted by other former Confederate states between 1890 and 1910.

Poll taxes had come and gone over the previous decades in many states, even in the North, for various class- and race-discrimination purposes—or as a combination of both. But the year 1890, says voting rights historian Alexander Keyssar, "marked the beginning of systematic efforts by southern states to disenfranchise black voters legally" with "many of the disenfranchising laws ... designed expressly to be administered in a discriminatory fashion, permitting whites to vote while barring blacks."[2] Other disenfranchising devices during this period included literacy tests, secret ballot laws, lengthy residency requirements, complex voter registration systems, and White-only primaries.[3]

In addition, local voting officials—usually appointed by White-supremacist politicians—were empowered to judge the eligibility of voter-applicants as they saw fit. Such latitude often translated into denying countless Black applicants no matter how much they had prepared themselves.[4] Meanwhile, another set of laws stripped voting rights from men who were convicted of relatively minor crimes, such as vagrancy, bigamy and petty theft.[5]

Historians point out that many of the new provisions technically applied to Whites as well as to Blacks, a matter that at times generated debates among White politicians. However, the Southern states usually found ways to create loopholes for White voters, such as enacting "grandfather clauses" for sons and grandsons of earlier generations of voters. Many times, though, White politicians, especially from upper classes, did not seem too concerned if poor Whites also lost voting power, another indication of the fusion of class and race discrimination. As Keyssar observes, "Many of the landed, patrician whites ... were the prime movers of disenfranchisement," adding that suppressing African Americans and poor Whites helped reduce "the threat of a troublesome electoral alliance between blacks and poor whites."[6] On March 25, 1965, the Rev. Martin Luther King Jr. picked up on this theme in his speech at the end of the famous Selma-to-Montgomery voting rights march as he said, "The segregation of the races was really a political stratagem employed by the emerging Bourbon interests in the South to keep the southern masses divided and southern labor the cheapest in the land." The term "Bourbon," as King used it, referred to politically influential white Southerners who had sought to overthrow Reconstruction.[7]

The Virginia push for a poll tax and voter tests gained greater momentum after the U.S. Supreme Court ruled in 1898 in favor of Mississippi's disenfranchisement provisions.[8] White-supremacist Virginia politicians were unabashed in proclaiming their intentions at the 1901–02 constitutional convention. State Senator Carter Glass, among the leaders of the Black disenfranchisement initiative, boldly proclaimed:

Discrimination! Why that is exactly what we propose; that exactly, is why this was elected—to discriminate to the very extremity of permissible action under the limitations of the Federal Constitution with the view to the elimination of every Negro who can be gotten rid of, legally, without materially impairing the strength of the white electorate.[9]

When the Virginia convention wrapped up on March 28, 1902, the new constitution required a poll tax of $1.50 per year, payable six months before any election along with any delinquent payments from the previous three years, plus any late-payment fines. Frederic D. Ogden, one of the first political scientists to study the administration and impact of poll taxes, ranked Virginia's poll tax as the most burdensome "based upon poll tax rates, coverage, time of payment, and proof of payment" and its requirement for cumulative payments.[10] The basic payment of $1.50 per year in the early 1900s equates to $44.72 in 2020 U.S. dollars, and the cumulative $4.50 would now equal $134.16, according to an online inflation calculator.[11] The Virginia constitution also imposed an "understanding clause," meaning that voter-applicants had to successfully answer any questions related to government to the satisfaction of local voter registration officials. Yet another provision, taking effect in 1903, required would-be voters to submit written applications, completed without assistance. The constitution exempted Civil War veterans and their sons from all these mandates.[12]

The "understanding clause" amounted to a cruel game played time and again all throughout the South. White politicians appointed White voter-registration officials who would devise and administer these oral exams to voting applicants. The game was rigged because passing the test was left entirely to the discretion of the registrars, who had power to ask voter applicants any question they'd please. Here are a few examples as compiled by historian Brent Tarter:

Who discovered the Rocky Mountains and when?

What state passed the Port bill and when?

What state had its boundary changed three times by the U.S. Government and what was its number when admitted?

What state was originally named Albemarle?[13]

Carter Glass had vowed that the 1902 Virginia constitution "will eliminate the darky as a political factor in this state in less than five years."[14] He was correct. By 1904, Black voters in Norfolk, for example, decreased in number from 1,826 to 504, and by 1910, only 44 paid the poll tax in order to vote.[15] Statewide, there were about 147,000 African Americans eligible to vote in 1900, but only 21,000 remained on the voting rolls by October 15, 1902, according to Buni.[16]

Several years later, Carter Glass, by then a U.S. senator, continued to gloat about disenfranchising the South's Black populations. According to J. D. Smith,[17] Glass, in a national news interview, infamously declared that "people of the original thirteen Southern States [in the Confederacy] curse and deride and spit upon the 15th amendment—and have no intention of letting the Negro vote."[18] Reflecting upon the aims of the 1901–02 Virginia constitutional convention, Glass further boasted that:

> We obey the letter of the [14th and 15th] amendments and the Federal statutes, but we frankly evade the spirit thereof—and purport to continue doing so. White supremacy is too precious a thing to surrender for the sake of a theoretical justice that would let a brutish African deem himself the equal of white men and women in Dixie.[19]

Glass was not alone in expressing White-supremacist glee. As old voter-registration records across the state were purged on July 10, 1902, to make way for new registration, the *Richmond Times* newspaper proclaimed, "At the hour of noon today the dark cloud will be lifted, and peace and sunshine will come to regenerated Anglo-Saxon people."[20]

Scholars say it is impossible to tabulate exactly how many African Americans and poor or illiterate Whites lost or never gained voting privileges because of Southern disenfranchisement efforts.[21] But one indication of the devastation, says Keyssar, was the decline in overall voter turnout across the South, from a high range of 60 to 85 percent at the end of Reconstruction to only "50 percent for whites and single digits for blacks"[22] after 1900.

While African Americans bore the brunt of disenfranchisement, White elites celebrated the double victory over Blacks and many poor Whites. A 1904 *Richmond Times* editorial glowed: "We have eliminated the objectionable negro vote and many objectionable white voters have been retired. ... The Virginia electorate is now composed of the best white men in the State."

One other note regarding the class-driven clubbiness of White political insiders at the time: The delegates to Virginia's convention reneged on their promise to submit the new constitution to public referendum, fearing that most voters—especially the classes of poor Whites and Blacks—would not agree to disenfranchise themselves. Instead, the delegates proclaimed the constitution fait accompli.[23]

Many poor, illiterate whites may have been taken by surprise, according to Tarter, who illustrates this repercussion with a quote from William C. Pendleton, an early 20th century journalist, who wrote the following on what he observed in southwestern Virginia:

It was painful and pitiful ... to see the horror and dread visible on the faces of the illiterate poor white men who were waiting to take their turn before the inquisition. ... They had seen some of their neighbors and friends turned away because they were unable to answer satisfactorily the questions put to them by the registrars; and it required much earnest persuasion to induce them to pass through the hateful ordeal. This was horrible to behold, but it was still more horrible to see the marks of humiliation and despair that were stamped upon the faces of honest but poor white men who had been refused registration and who had been robbed of their citizenship without cause.[24]

Whether intended or not, a critical long-term result of the new Southern state constitutions, especially Virginia's, was the drastic shrinking of the list of qualified voters, Black and White, therefore making the remaining electorate "easily managed in the hands of skillful political manipulators."[25]

Virginia's most dexterous manipulator of political power was Harry Flood Byrd Jr., who had been just a teenager during the 1901–02 constitutional convention but quickly learned the ropes of politics when elected to Virginia's Senate in 1915. In 1922, he took over the chairmanship of the central committee of Virginia's Democratic Party and reigned near-supreme through his statewide machine, known as the Byrd Organization.

The poll tax remained as one of the Byrd Organization's "principal weapons of control," observes historian James R. Sweeney.[26] Until his death in 1966, Byrd continued to dominate his state's politics and governmental policies perhaps more completely than any other politician in America.[27]

While he was an avowed segregationist to the end, Byrd suppressed not only Black political advancement but effectively blocked most Whites who did not fall in step with him. As Tarter writes, the Byrd political organization had "racist origins and effects, and it also had elitist social and political origins and effects."[28]

Among those elitist effects was a long-running record of extremely low voter turnout even in a presidential election. In 1940, President Franklin D. Roosevelt won his third term in office with a 62.5% percent nationwide turnout among the voting-age population, according to the American Presidency Project.[29] Virginia, though, ranked 43rd of the 48 states with a 22% turnout.[30]

Virginia's turnout was even worse for gubernatorial elections—9.5% in 1937; 7.8%, 1941; and 9.4%, 1945, according to Heinemann.[31] Francis Pickens Miller, a fellow Democrat who unsuccessfully challenged a Byrd man in the party's 1949 gubernatorial primary, likened the Byrd-dominated Virginia to the Soviet Union.[32] In summarizing the legacy of the Byrd machine, Tarter provided this succinct but apt phrase: They "did worse than steal money. They stole democracy."[33]

Keyssar, too, presents a horrifying summary of the results of the class and race voter-suppression efforts. As he writes:

> Millions of people—most of them working class and poor—were deprived of the right to vote in municipal, state, and national elections. Their exclusion from the electorate meant that the outcomes of innumerable political contests were altered, different policies were put into place, different judges appointed, different taxes imposed. ... Many of the core institutions of the modern American state—institutions built between Reconstruction and World War I—were indeed shaped and accepted by a polity that was far from democratic.[34]

With limited means, African Americans tried to fight back against disenfranchisement and racist public policies where possible. The NAACP, created in 1909, began working on voting issues and eventually achieved several legal breakthroughs, including getting the Supreme Court to strike down the grandfather clause in 1915.[35]

Yet White supremacy would march hand-in-hand with Southern politics for decades to come. In Virginia, that frequently meant African Americans primarily served as scapegoats and cannon fodder in political demagoguery.[36] As Buni observed about the political campaigns in the 1920s and '30s: "The role of the Negro ... was not to be a voter but an issue. As of old, he was depicted as a threat to white supremacy."[37]

Blacks in Virginia continued to seek inroads, but the poll-tax hurdle remained high. Luther P. Jackson, the scholar-activist who chaired the history department at the Virginia State College for Negroes (now Virginia State University), hated the poll tax yet encouraged fellow African Americans to pay it and to follow through with registration and turnout. He co-founded the Virginia Voters League, whose motto was "Pay the poll tax in order to abolish the poll tax."[38]

Jackson also produced periodic reports on Black voting strength.[39] His 1941 compilation, for example, noted that Virginia had 329,000 African Americans of voting age but that only 25,000 had paid the poll tax for the requisite three consecutive years, merely 15,000 were registered voters, and no more than 12,000 actually voted.[40] Jackson sometimes scolded fellow Black Virginians, but more than apathy was to blame. As Edds writes, "hostile white registrars ... and a dearth of candidates with appeal to working-class blacks or whites curbed any incentive to participate."[41]

Along with intimidation, African Americans also encountered trickery when trying to pay poll taxes.[42] Ruses across the South allegedly included registrars failing to give or mail tax-paid receipts to Blacks, thereby frustrating them when they arrived to vote on Election Day and were asked to show proof they had paid their poll taxes.[43]

Voter-participation activists also often reported emotional barriers among would-be voter applicants. Some African Americans stayed so angry, Lewis reports, that even if they could afford the poll tax they refused to pay "$1.50 just for the privilege of voting for some white man."[44]

By the 1950s, Virginia's $1.50 per year poll tax had technically become a lighter financial burden for African Americans and low-income people because the $1.50 levy had not increased since enacted in 1902. However, Virginia required voter applicants to pay the $1.50 for three consecutive years and show proof, such as the receipts, before being approved.[45] In addition, the last

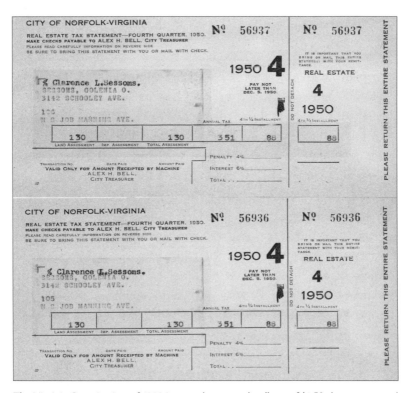

The Virginia Constitution of 1902 imposed an annual poll tax of $1.50 that suppressed voter registration among African Americans and many poor Whites until Evelyn Butts and her co-plaintiffs won a landmark victory at the U. S. Supreme Court in March 1966. This photo shows the 1950 poll tax receipt of Norfolk resident Clarence Sessoms. *Courtesy of Daun Hester.*

payment had to be made at least six months before the upcoming election, and Virginia also would impose a 5% penalty for late payment on delinquent accounts.[46]

By 1963, when Evelyn Butts filed her lawsuit, the $1.50 poll tax of 1902 was the equivalent of $5.34; and if one had to pay three years of poll taxes at once, that would equate to $16.01, according to the online inflation calculator.[47]

If the amount still sounds paltry, consider that Butts lived half of her life in an era when White society, especially in the South, consigned most African Americans to the lowest-paying, most menial jobs, such as those of maids, cooks, nannies, and other domestic service positions.[48] For example, Butts earned $20 per week as a domestic employee of two White women, the Lambert sisters, in the late 1940s. When she asked for a raise to $5 per day, the sisters agreed but then reduced her schedule to four days a week so Butts' take-home pay remained the same.[49]

By 1963, the year of Butts' lawsuit, domestic service workers with steady employment earned $800 per year before taxes on average across the United States, about a quarter of the annual average of $3,100 for all wage earners nationwide.[50] Also, simple math shows that the $800 annual pay for domestic service workers equated to $15.38 per week.

At the January 1966 Supreme Court hearing of Butts' lawsuit, then retitled as *Harper v. Virginia State Board of Elections*, Allison Brown Jr., a lawyer for Annie E. Harper, argued that requiring a poll tax for voting rights creates a financial hardship for the poor. "[P]aying a tax represents a choice between the necessities of life, food, clothing, shelter, medicine, and so forth," Brown said.[51]

He then noted that 28% of all Virginia families had annual incomes under $3,000, but by race, the figures broke down to 22% of White families and 54% of nonwhite.[52]

With evidence that the poll tax hurt greater percentages of Black citizens, Butts' lawyer Joseph A. Jordan Jr. told the Supreme Court in his oral arguments that "What Virginia accomplished by its action in 1902 was to create two body politics in Virginia, a white body politic and a Negro body politic."[53] The consequence, Jordan continued, was that "Negroes have been effectively eliminated from any political power in Virginia."

Front-page news story in the September 19, 1958, edition of *The Virginian-Pilot* reports that Governor J. Lindsay Almond Jr. shut down two public schools in Charlottesville to avoid court-ordered integration and that six all-White high schools and junior high schools in Norfolk could be next as part of Virginia's "massive resistance" policies. On September 27, the governor announced the Norfolk closings, effective September 29, a move that deprived nearly 10,000 students—most of them white—from several months of education. The six Norfolk schools remained shuttered until the federal courts reopened them on February 2, 1959. © *Virginian-Pilot. All rights reserved. Distributed by Tribune Content Agency, LLC*.

# CHAPTER 9

## Massive Resistance

On May 17, 1954, the U.S. Supreme Court handed down its famous school desegregation decision in *Oliver Brown et al. v. Board of Education of Topeka, Kansas*, a case that had combined five lawsuits, including *Davis v. County School Board of Prince Edward County, Virginia,* along with the Topeka matter and suits from South Carolina, Delaware, and Washington, D.C. The unanimous 9–0 ruling proclaimed "that in the field of public education the doctrine of 'separate but equal' has no place. Separate educational facilities are inherently unequal."[1]

The direct and indirect effects of this momentous ruling have continued into the 21st century, not only for school desegregation and better quality education for generations of African Americans but also for breaking down other racial barriers, refocusing the work of urban planners, and generating almost endless political debates about real-versus-imagined White flight to the suburbs as well as in the appointment of Supreme Court justices, to list just a few.

In the 1950s, political ramifications of *Brown v. Board* were among the most immediate effects. As law and history professor Michael J. Klarman notes in his prize-winning *From Jim Crow to Civil Rights: The Supreme Court and the Struggle for Racial Equality,* "politics in every southern state moved significantly to the right."[2] Political rhetoric got hotter and more extreme. "Georgia is going to resist mixing the races in the schools if it is the sole state of the nation to do so," promised Governor Herman Talmadge,[3] while racially moderate candidates throughout the South were condemned as cowards, traitors and "burglars ... (who) want to rob us of our priceless heritage."[4] There were also shifts in the common meaning of certain words, notes Woodward, who writes, "A 'moderate' became a man who dared open his mouth, an 'extremist' one who favored eventual compliance with the law, and 'compliance' took on the connotations of treason."[5]

Arguments about school integration shook even the sanctuaries of Norfolk's faith community as Jane Dailey shows in *Sex, Segregation, and the Sacred After Brown*. Anti-integrationist clergy, such as the Rev. James F. Burks of Bayview Baptist Church in Norfolk, preached that "This step of racial integration is but another stepping stone toward the gross immorality and lawlessness that will be characteristic of the last days, just preceding the Return of the Lord Jesus Christ."[6]

In contrast, clergy who applauded the *Brown v. Board* ruling issued remarks similar to those from the National Baptist Convention (a major group of Black Baptists), which said, "the Social Gospel of Jesus received its endorsement by the Highest Court of the nation."[7] Rejoicing African Americans felt that their claim on first-class citizenship was finally vindicated and that their long-held prayers for the end of Jim Crow would soon be realized. Yet, as Woodward observes, that "end was to be agonizingly slow in coming"[8] and often marred with violence.

As enforcement of school desegregation spread throughout the South, resistance stiffened among segregationists. Extreme White supremacists in Mississippi formed Citizens' Councils (also called White Citizens' Councils) to oppose all forms of integration and Black voter-registration efforts. The councils and similar groups started spreading across the South.[9] A favorite tactic of the councils was to discourage Black voter registration by threatening job loss for any African Americans who registered, voted, or were involved in voter-registration efforts. Civil rights historian Steven F. Lawson in *Black Ballots: Voting Rights in the South, 1944–1969*, quotes

Tom Brady, the White Mississippi judge credited for devising this intimidation initiative in 1954, as saying: "Over 95 percent of the negroes of the South are employed by white men or corporations controlled by white men. A great many negro employees will be discharged and a deplorable situation will arise for the negro."[10]

In some quarters, White anger over the *Brown v. Board* decision, conflated with other civil rights victories, spawned violence. The home of a Black family was bombed when they moved to Norfolk's then-all White Coronado neighborhood in 1954.[11]

Emmett Till, a 14-year-old African American who allegedly whistled at a White woman in Mississippi, was brutally murdered on August 28, 1955. J. W. Milam, one of the killers, was found not guilty in court, but he bragged about his motivations in a *Look* magazine interview. His reasons, he said, were to set an example of what will happen when a Black person steps out of line, including for attempts to integrate public schools or to register to vote. Milam told *Look*:

> I just decided it was time a few people got put on notice. As long as I live and can do anything about it, niggers are gonna stay in their place. Niggers ain't gonna vote where I live. If they did, they'd control the government. They ain't gonna go to school with my kids.[12]

In Norfolk, a local chapter of the segregationist Defenders of State Sovereignty and Individual Liberties came together and its president, James G. Martin IV, asserted that school integration was a communist plot to "mongrelize Americans."[13]

Virginia Senator Harry F. Byrd Sr., the state's political boss since the mid-1920s, organized a white-collar mob to try to stop school desegregation without violence. His "Southern Manifesto" of March 1956, signed by 101 members of both houses of Congress from the South, asked Southern states to disobey the *Brown v. Board* court order in a show of "massive resistance."[14] Byrd invoked the illegitimate legal theory of "interposition" through which states could supposedly claim the right to interpose themselves against Supreme Court rulings; in effect, nullify them. The interposition tactic was developed by Byrd's ally, James J. Kilpatrick, the White supremacist editorial page editor of *The Richmond News Leader*, who drew from former Vice President and former South Carolina Senator John C. Calhoun, a staunch defender of slavery and agitator for secession long before the Civil War.[15]

Kilpatrick continued to stir hate, defend separate-but-equal, and pine for the White supremacy of yesteryear into the 1960s. "The ingrained attitudes of a lifetime cannot be jerked out like a pair of infected molars, and new porcelain dentures put in their place," Kilpatrick wrote in his 1962 book, *The Southern Case for School Segregation*, before he launched a new career as a political commentator on nationwide TV and radio.[16] In throwback language reminiscent of Roger B. Taney's 1857 Dred Scott ruling, Kilpatrick added:

> On the contrary, the Southerner rebelliously clings to what seems to him the hard core of truth ... the Negro race, as a race, plainly is not equal to the white race, as a race; nor ... has the Negro race, as a race, *ever* been the cultural or intellectual equal of the white race, as a race. This we take to be a plain statement of fact.[17]

In summer 1956, Virginia took another major step in its attempts to block school integration. With spectators waving Confederate flags in the gallery, the General Assembly met in special session and approved several new laws as part of the now-formal Massive Resistance, as historian Andrew Buni describes in *The Negro in Virginia Politics, 1902–1965*.[18] These included the closing of any all-White public school that allowed Black students to enroll, pupil placement tests, rescinding public funding for integrated schools, and approval of public grants for students who wanted to attend segregated (all-White) private schools. Other Southern states followed Virginia's lead by adopting all or some of such policies.[19] New all-White private schools emerged throughout the South, a trend that continued for many years.

Meanwhile, Norfolk Public Schools Superintendent John J. Brewbaker had been trying to reassure White Norfolk residents that the *Brown v. Board* ruling would have little effect in their city because of "existing 'residential segregation.'" In a 1955 statement, Brewbaker added:

> We are all in favor of segregation. ... It is just a question of what is the best plan. ... I'm not in favor of integration, I'm in favor of carrying out the Supreme Court decree with the least harm to pupils ... and to the schools.[20]

As Virginia dug in for a protracted fight, the NAACP asked federal courts to enforce the *Brown v. Board* ruling. On June 7, 1958, U.S. District Court Judge Walter E. Hoffman ordered the Norfolk School Board to begin assigning Black students to all-White schools. Similar rulings affected other localities. But on July 17, the School Board listed 10 criteria that each student would have to satisfy before being allowed to transfer "to schools previously attended by the opposite race."[21]

That summer, Butts decided to have her daughter, Charlene, apply to integrate the nearby all-White Norview Elementary School for the fourth grade.[22] The process included academic and psychological examinations, and Black parents felt insulted because White children were not being tested.[23] The results: Norfolk's all-White School Board denied all 151 integration requests from the Black students.[24]

In August, when Butts was still hopeful that the School Board would approve Charlene's transfer, Superintendent Brewbaker appeared in front of the Butts' home in Oakwood to personally measure the distance between their house and the all-Black Oakwood Elementary and the all-White Norview Elementary. The School Board submitted Brewbaker's measurements to the federal court and claimed that Charlene needed to go to the all-Black Oakwood Elementary because it was closer. On August 29, 1958, Butts contradicted the superintendent in court by noting that Oakwood was 11 blocks away while Norview was only five blocks from their house. Despite the evidence, Charlene's application was rejected on grounds of traffic safety.[25]

Tensions continued to escalate.

On August 19, 1958, U.S. District Court Judge Walter E. Hoffman ordered the School Board to reconsider all the rejections. On August 29, the board announced its new results: It approved 17 black students for integrating six of Norfolk's all-White schools. Charlene was not among them.[26]

On September 27, 1958, Virginia Governor J. Lindsay Almond Jr. ordered the immediate closing of those six schools, a move that blocked nearly 10,000 students—most of them White—from several months of education. They became known as the "Lost Class of '59." The six schools remained closed until the federal courts reopened them on February 2, 1959.[27]

Pro-segregation Mayor W. Fred Duckworth and Vice Mayor George R. Abbott blamed the school closings on the 17 Black students seeking to integrate and suggested that racial tensions would resolve if the students withdrew their applications.[28] In a statement reminiscent of Virginia Way paternalism, Duckworth proclaimed that "The City of Norfolk has done more for its Negroes ... than any city in the South—barring none" and that the African Americans should have been better behaved and obedient in gratitude.[29]

Meanwhile, Norfolk was still intent on finding other avenues around integration, including using modular construction techniques to quickly produce two new elementary schools for African American students: Rosemont and Coronado. Charlene Butts was assigned to the temporary Rosemont modular school for her 1959–1960 fifth-grade year and found that the structure had 10 classrooms but only one girls' restroom and one boys' restroom, no cafeteria, no library, no gym—and no principal. Butts complained, "They built that school for Charlene because I applied to send her to Norview!"[30]

A year later, the new combined all-Black Rosemont Elementary and Junior High School opened, again undermining Butts' efforts to have Charlene integrate the nearby existing Norview Junior High School. [31]

On January 19, 1959, ironically, the birthday of Confederate General Robert E. Lee, federal and state courts decided two lawsuits that led to the reopening of Norfolk's schools in February. The first black students in previously all-White high and junior high schools in Norfolk were referred to as the "Norfolk 17," and they were greeted with racial taunts, bullying, threats of bodily harm, and other acts of humiliation and intimidation. At least two students had crosses burned in front of their homes.[32] Teachers were among the culprits in insulting African American students. Patricia Turner, one of the 17 black students, later recalled that her history teacher, Hal Bonney, a future U.S. Bankruptcy Court judge and bible class teacher, was among the worst. Bonney, said Turner, continually embarrassed Turner in front of other students by putting on rubber gloves every time he collected her test papers and homework.[33]

Virginia's Massive Resistance policy garnered volumes of negative news reports about Norfolk with in-depth stories appearing on CBS-TV and in *Life* and *Time* magazines, *The New York Times Magazine*, and *Boston Sunday Globe*. But as Parramore et al. point out, Norfolk was saved from more disastrous publicity because of a two-year battle over the integration of Little Rock High School in Arkansas at about the same time.[34] In Little Rock, President Dwight Eisenhower had to send the 101st Airborne Division and federalize the Arkansas National Guard to protect nine African American students from jeering mobs of anti-integrationist Whites. Even then, White students verbally and physically harassed their new classmates, and Governor Orval Faubus shut the school for a year in an attempt to undo desegregation.[35]

Attempts to maintain segregated schools in Norfolk continued on quite another track beyond the courts and schoolhouses. Duckworth devised a plan to circumvent the desegregation of neighborhood schools by using the powers of the Norfolk Redevelopment and Housing Authority to condemn and tear down integrated neighborhoods and nearby public schools in the name of slum clearance, public health and public safety.[36]

In February 1964, lawyer Joseph A. Jordan Jr. wrote to Robert C. Weaver, then head of the Federal Housing and Home Finance Agency, on behalf of Butt's neighborhood group, the Oakwood-Rosemont Civic League. Jordan complained that Norfolk planned to use federal urban renewal money to perpetuate residential and public school segregation, which prompted Weaver to invite Jordan, Butts and several other Norfolk residents to meet with him in Washington, D.C., on July 1.[37] Weaver then ordered an investigation into whether the Norfolk Redevelopment and Housing Authority and the School Board were collaborating to maintain segregation.[38]

Urban studies analyst Forrest R. White contends that Mayor Duckworth's dramatic bulldozer actions "do not appear to be unique" among cities that tried to stave off school integration.[39] He cited a report by Weaver, who charged that "urban renewal too often seemed to be an instrument for wiping out racially integrated living."[40]

Duckworth also figured in a controversy that ignited when the National Municipal League and *Look* magazine selected Norfolk in 1959 for an "All-American City Award," which cited Norfolk's new civic and medical centers as well as "the mighty citizen effort" to bulldoze "blight." On March 3, 1960, the mayor hosted the local award ceremony with more than 1,200 guests. However, 41 African Americans had signed a statement pointing out that no Blacks had been invited, so the city quickly added two Blacks to the luncheon. The damage was done, though, as members of the Congress of Racial Equality and other African Americans picketed outside against Duckworth's "malign neglect."

The peaceful assembly included lawyer Joseph A. Jordan Jr., who waved his protest sign from his wheelchair. It read, "Discrimination and Segregation are not All-American."[41]

# SECTION III

*Continuum of African American
Resistance and Resilience*

Under Evelyn T. Butts' stewardship, the Women of Virginia's Third Force not only helped register, inform and mobilize voters but also made annual visits to Virginia's General Assembly in Richmond to observe the state legislature, meet with politicians, and lobby for legislation. In this photo from March 1970, some Third Force members and elected officials pose in front of the Capitol. They are, left to right, Pearlene Jackson, Mozelle Mitchell, Melsie Giddens, treasurer Agnes Jordan, Del. William P. Robinson Sr., Pearl Robinson, president Evelyn T. Butts, Lieutenant Governor J. Sargeant Reynolds, Rebecca Williams, Everett Johnson, John Adams, Maria Jenkins, Josie Gazell, Del. Stanley Walker, Attorney General Andrew Miller, Annie M. Simons, and first vice president Alice Green. *Photo reprinted and used with permission courtesy of the New Journal and Guide.*

# CHAPTER 10
## Evelyn Butts Joins the Flow

On Evelyn Butts' 34th birthday, May 22, 1958, the Virginia State Board of Elections inadvertently gave her a gift that sharpened her leadership skills and focused her resolve in the fight for African American voting rights and self-determination.

Pursuant to General Assembly action that year, Virginia began to require that every voter-applicant use a totally blank piece of paper—"just a blank sheet of paper"—as a voter-registration "form." Each applicant had to correctly handwrite certain specific information in the presence of a voter-registration official but without being allowed to look at notes or other written material or ask anyone for help, including the registration staff.[1] The required information included name, age, birthdate, place of birth, current address and occupation, and any previous addresses and jobs for the past year, and the precinct location where the applicant last voted.[2] Civil rights advocates alleged that Virginia devised the rule to thwart the growing success of voter-registration campaigns among Virginia's African American citizens[3] during the state government's policy of Massive Resistance to public school desegregation.

Butts became involved through helping Norfolk civil rights attorney Joseph A. Jordan Jr. launch a "Third Force" initiative to fight the poll tax and "to register every Negro voter in every precinct" in Norfolk, an effort that included an affiliate called Women of Virginia's Third Force, with Butts as president.[4] The Third Force name (sometimes spelled "3rd Force" by various members and local newspapers) referred to the untapped political power represented by uncounted thousands of potential voters who were disenfranchised by the poll tax.[5]

One of the first projects of the Third Force women consisted of holding classes in Jordan's law office to teach voter-applicants how to correctly fill out Virginia's new blank application sheets from memory.[6] "We were teaching the people in the back room," Butts recalled when interviewed by Norfolk historian Tommy L. Bogger.[7]

The classes proved successful, along with similar efforts organized by other African American organizations across the state. Not only did Black voter registration continue to climb but the blank sheet voter-application forms confounded many White Virginians who did not have the benefit of training sessions, such as those offered by African American groups.[8]

Election officials from many localities complained to General Assembly members that the blank sheet law was not hurting Black voter-applicants as intended; instead, it was "creating confusion and ill will among whites, especially elderly people."[9] With the blank sheet tactic backfiring, Governor Albertis S. Harrison was forced to sign a law in 1962 that rescinded the provision.[10]

Meanwhile, the Women of Virginia's Third Force, under Butts' leadership, also tried to make sure that voter applicants could pay their poll taxes, taught them how to learn about political candidates, and organized precinct rides on Election Day. "We'd take up a collection in the [Oakwood-Rosemont] civic league, even if all anyone could give was a nickel or 10 cents or 25 cents," Marie G. Young recalled about one way the women's group raised money to help voter applicants pay their poll taxes.[11] Another source of poll tax payment money came from the Norfolk Branch of the NAACP, according to Butts.[12]

In stepping up to help fellow African Americans register to vote, Butts had joined the long continuum of African American resistance to White supremacy, a flow that had begun in Colonial times, and aimed to achieve full, unfettered citizenship as well as have a meaningful voice in determining the future of their communities.

Evelyn Butts would also assist Joe Jordan via her seamstress skills, making dress-like uniforms for the Jordanettes, a group of girls—her daughter Charlene and teenaged daughters of friends—who would pass out campaign material. One year Evelyn spent over 100 hours producing thirty-six uniforms. From left to right, top row—Margie Young, Martha Wills, Yvonne Wilson, Beulah Wilson, Minnie Green, Harriett Brownson. Bottom row—Joyce Knox, Charlene Butts, Joe Jordan, Patricia Gould, Karen Elizabeth James. *Courtesy of Charlene Butts Ligon.*

Butts' alliance with Jordan and her leadership of the Women of Virginia's Third Force continued to evolve, sometimes with surprising results.

In 1959, Jordan joined the growing list of African Americans in Virginia running for public office. His first parry came as a write-in candidate for the General Assembly's House of Delegates. Jordan's campaign, which he also seemed to use for overall consciousness-raising about the poll tax, included driving his "Vote Mobile," a 1948 Oldsmobile—equipped with a loudspeaker and decorated with "Pay Poll Tax" placards—through the streets of African American neighborhoods.

Butts sometimes accompanied Jordan and began developing her skills for political outreach and organizing. As part of Jordan's campaign, Butts and the Women of Virginia's Third Force assisted Jordan in setting up a rally that featured Rep. Adam Clayton Powell of New York, a well-known African American member of Congress. The event drew about 1,500 people.[13]

Jordan did not come close to winning the 1959 election, garnering less than 1,000 votes. But with Butts' leadership, Jordan and the Women of Virginia's Third Force gained insights and information that proved valuable in future elections.

One of Butts' greatest grassroots achievements derived from Jordan's failed request to Norfolk's voter-registration office to let him see the city's official list of voters as a public record. After the office denied Jordan, Butts assigned herself the tedious task of going to the registration office dozens of times over about two months and hand-copying the entire list.[14]

Not only did Butts get the voters' list, she also discovered that there were separate registration cards for White and Black citizens—white cards for White people and yellow cards for African Americans. Jordan later included that fact in preparing Butts' poll tax lawsuit in 1963. As Butts herself said of the different colored registration cards, "it was segregation in itself down at the registrar's office."[15]

Meanwhile, the registration list that Butts wrote out by hand became the basis of a massive store of voter information that Butts and the Third Force women built for future elections. With the list, they were able to cross-check the names of registered voters with addresses in a city directory and then look for names of neighbors who were not registered. "That way they could see who they needed to get to register to vote and what street they needed to work for more people to contact," Ligon explained.[16]

Over the next decade, Jordan, as well as several other Norfolk African Americans, would continue to run for City Council or General Assembly seats. Some strategy sessions were held in the living room of Walter and Alveta Green, where Butts would give "pep talk" speeches and assign tasks such as gathering signatures for petitions and distributing flyers.[17] Butts would also assist Jordan via her seamstress skills, making dress-like uniforms for the Jordanettes, a group of girls—her daughter Charlene and teenaged daughters of friends—who would pass out campaign material. One year, Butts spent "at least 108 hours" producing 36 uniforms.[18]

Butts and the Third Force women also were successful in persuading Norfolk to add more Monday-night voter-registration sessions in preparation for the 1968 City Council elections.[19]

The Women of Virginia's Third Force organization provided Butts with additional opportunities to educate voters—and politicians. The group not only helped register, inform, and turn out voters, but also worked to influence state legislators by making annual visits to Virginia's General Assembly under Butts' stewardship.[20]

Norfolk dentist Dr. Samuel F. Coppage, 1885–1977, linked several generations of African American professional, political, and civil rights leaders in Norfolk during his long and prolific life. The son of former slaves, Coppage was a charter member of the Norfolk Branch of the NAACP, a founder of the former Norfolk Community Hospital that served the city's Black residents, a director of a Black-owned bank, organizer of a free dental clinic for children during the Great Depression, crusader for Black voter registration during the poll-tax era, and a member of several political action efforts initiated by Joseph A. Jordan Jr., who was Evelyn Butts' friend and attorney. *Courtesy of Sargeant Memorial Collection, Norfolk Public Library.*

# CHAPTER 11
## Deeds of the Ancestors

African American resistance to the practices of White supremacy, even as far back as Colonial days, came in many forms:
physical and intellectual, street demonstrations and politics, and
business, arts and athletics. The wide range of individual and
collective activities dispelled popular notions over the years that
African Americans were not very engaged in seeking civil rights,
social equality, full political citizenship, and self-determination
before the Montgomery Bus Boycott of the mid-1950s—a misconception that continues in the 21st century.

"There's this idea that it's not a whole lot of black resistance
before the Montgomery Bus Boycott," observes former SNCC staff
member Judy Richardson.[1]

Many Black-resistance activities took place on a decentralized
and ad hoc basis through the work of local individuals, associa-
tions, and events overlooked by White-owned news media. Yet,
while resistance initiatives were often invisible to most of White
America, says historian J. Todd Moye, Black communities knew
about such efforts, so much so that local movements and social justice activists "drew inspiration, learned tactics from, and in many
cases included the same cast of characters of resistance movements
from previous eras."[2]

Gloria Richardson, a Cambridge, Maryland, 1960s civil rights
leader, for example, knew about the mid-1800s heroics of abolitionist Harriet Tubman from growing up in the same region of
Maryland's Eastern Shore. "I came from an area that's like fifteen

minutes from Harriet Tubman's home in Sharptown. And grandchildren of the Tubman family had gone to school with my children," Richardson explained.[3]

African Americans learned of efforts by earlier generations in many ways, including through churches, women's clubs, and community and fraternal organizations. Families also played a significant role as they pieced together genealogies, collected photographs, and held reunions.[4]

Annual Emancipation Day commemorations took place on January 1 in many communities for a number of decades. Events included parades, speeches, and ceremonies to reaffirm Black history and citizenship.[5]

African American historians also had important roles in motivating continued resistance to Jim Crow—and the efforts of these historians also constituted their own form of resistance by promoting African American history to dispel White-supremacist myths of Black inferiority as well as to encourage Blacks to learn more about their heritage. Carter G. Woodson (1875–1950) and Luther P. Jackson (1892–1950)—each of whom had significant ties to Virginia—were central leaders in advancing Black history and full citizenship.

Woodson, born in Virginia and known as the "Father of Black History," founded the Association for the Study of Negro Life and History to promote Black history among both scholars and grassroots organizations, as well as the *Journal of Negro History* and the annual Negro History Week, which was set in February to include the birthdays of Abraham Lincoln and Frederick Douglass. Negro History Week later evolved into Black History Month. Woodson also wrote histories of Black Americans to counter White denial of African American contributions and spoke to many Black organizations, including teachers. To supplement his work with teachers, Woodson produced and distributed "Negro History Kits" and other curriculum materials.[6]

Jackson, a history professor at Virginia State College (now Virginia State University) in Petersburg and a newspaper columnist, served as Virginia director of Woodson's Association for the Study of Negro Life and History, a position he used to promote Black political participation in the drive toward full citizenship. His pioneering books included *Free Negro Labor and Property Holding in Virginia, 1830–1860*; *Virginia Negro Soldiers and Seamen in the Revolutionary War*; and *Negro Office Holders in Virginia*.[7]

Black-owned newspapers were also key resources in transmitting knowledge about past and contemporaneous African American resistance, starting with *Freedom's Journal*, established in New York in 1827. Others followed, and enabled "African American leaders and masses to be in touch with each other ... express themselves, and opine about their burden, and ... reach out to each other beyond local and regional and state boundaries," writes Walton.[8] Walton adds that the existence of Black newspapers helped facilitate national conventions of Black people.

In the 20th century, many of the newspapers also shared news and features from across the country on topics important to African Americans via the Associated Negro Press, which had regular correspondents and other contributors in urban areas with large Black populations and provided member publications with a twice-weekly set of reports.[9] In Virginia, Black-oriented newspapers included the *Norfolk Journal and Guide*; the *Richmond Planet*; *St. Luke Herald*, also in Richmond; and the *Newport News Star*.[10]

Many publishers and editors were multi-talented as well as dedicated to the struggle against Jim Crow. Those men and women had their special roles in the history of resistance as did their newspapers. For example, Frederick Douglass published the abolitionist *North Star* and anti-lynching crusader Ida Bell Wells-Barnett co-owned *The Free Speech and Headlight* in Memphis, Tennessee, among their many other accomplishments.

Wells-Barnett's entry into journalism came as a result of her being dragged out of the White "ladies" car of a train in Tennessee and forced into the smoking car, where Black passengers were relegated. She had purchased a first-class ticket and had just made herself comfortable with a book, when a conductor demanded that she move. This was the post-Reconstruction South of 1883 and "no black woman was ever considered a lady."[11] She sued the railroad and, surprisingly, won a $200 award from the company. A similar incident in 1884 won her $500 from the railroad, and a Memphis newspaper carried the headline, "A Darky Damsel Obtains a Verdict for Damages Against the Chesapeake & Ohio Railroad."

Other Black women were excited, and she was asked by a Black church magazine to write about what had happened. Soon other Black magazines, along with newspapers, sought her out as well. In 1889, she invested in the Memphis paper and in 1892, she conducted a three-month investigation into over 700 lynchings after a friend, a Black grocer named Tom Moss, had been lynched. In 1896, Wells-Barnett co-founded the National Association for Colored Women, the first nationwide network of its kind, which later became the National Association of Colored Women's Clubs. Ending lynching and elevating the image of Black women were among its goals.[12]

In Virginia, leading Black newspapers, publishers, and editors during the post-Reconstruction and Jim Crow eras included *The True Southerner* with Joseph T. Wilson; *Richmond Planet* with John Mitchell Jr.: and the *Norfolk Journal and Guide* with P. B. Young Sr.

Wilson also developed a literary reputation by authoring *The Black Phalanx; A History of the Negro Soldiers of the United States in the Wars of 1775–1812, 1861–66*, in 1887, a book that was hailed in 1891 as exceeding the sales of "any other work written by an Afro-American."[13]

Black-owned newspapers also helped launch the anti-segregation "Double V" campaign of the World War II era, which linked the goals of fighting fascism overseas with battling against Jim Crow in the United States. As early as 1938, the *Pittsburgh Courier* worked with several African American military officers who had endured racism in World War I to create the Committee for Participation of Negroes in the National Defense Program. The group aimed to foster "a more dignified place in our armed forces during the next war."[14]

Inspiration for resistance also came from the writings and speeches of intellectual activists, such as sociologist-civil rights leader W.E.B. Du Bois; Frances Ellen Watkins Harper, a poet and abolitionist, and women's suffragist; author-educator Anna Julia Cooper; Mary McLeod Bethune, an educator and humanitarian; and Maggie L. Walker, a business entrepreneur and civic leader based in Richmond, Virginia, who also promoted voting rights for Black women. Many African Americans followed the work of civil rights organizations, such as the NAACP, and its legal representatives, especially lawyer Thurgood Marshall.

Resistance began in the earliest days of Colonial Virginia of the 1600s. Blacks fled enslavement and sometimes joined with White indentured servants in conspiracies to rebel.[15] Also, there were many instances of slaves filing lawsuits in attempts to win their freedom, although with mixed results, and trials of female slaves who killed their masters for forcing them into sexual relations, according to the Law Library of Congress.[16]

Ona "Oney" Judge escaped from President George and First Lady Martha Washington on May 21, 1796, while the Washingtons and their presidential mansion were based in Philadelphia, then the nation's temporary capital. Smuggled aboard a schooner, Judge successfully made her way to New Hampshire, where she lived in freedom for the rest of her life.[17]

Slave-initiated efforts to rebel include a planned insurrection in 1800 that became known as "Gabriel's Conspiracy," named for an enslaved blacksmith who was a key leader. The scheme would involve abducting Virginia Governor James Monroe and burning Richmond, the state's capital. Scholars consider this plot among the most important of such activities even though it was discovered and stopped before the rebellion could begin.[18]

Virginia was the scene of another famous slave insurrection, Nat Turner's Revolt, which began overnight on August 21–22,

1831, in Southampton County. In this slave rebellion, considered the most deadly in American history, Turner and his co-conspirators killed 55 White men, women, and children. The uprising was put down within several days. White mobs killed more than 30 Blacks before they could be tried; another 19, though, were executed after convictions. As for Turner, he was finally captured on October 30 and executed on November 11.[19]

Slave Dred Scott and his wife, Harriet Robinson Scott, sued for freedom in separate legal petitions on April 6, 1846, in what became the most infamous of such court cases. The suit entailed 11 years of hearings and appeals before the U.S. Supreme Court ruled against the Scotts with a 7–2 vote on March 6, 1857. At the time, other slaves also were suing for freedom if they had lived in free states, but the Supreme Court, in an opinion written by Chief Justice Roger B. Taney, ruled that Dred Scott was not a citizen of the United States and, therefore, was not eligible to file suit in a federal court.[20]

Perhaps the greatest mass participation in resistance came in the form of the Underground Railroad, a far-flung network of Blacks and Whites, in slave states and free states, who smuggled tens of thousands of slaves to freedom largely via secret routes and safe houses. Escaped slave Harriet Tubman, from Maryland's Eastern Shore, was the Underground Railroad's most famous "conductor" because of fearlessness, resourcefulness, and daring in returning at least 13 times to slave territory to free about 70 people.[21]

The Underground Railroad was very active in Virginia, which had the largest slave population in the South and was geographically close to several free states, such as Pennsylvania and Ohio. Virginia also had a number of port cities that frequently hosted commercial visits from Northern ships with sympathetic captains and crew members. The ports gave Virginia's fugitive slaves another option for escape in addition to land routes, as historian Cassandra describes in *Virginia Waterways and the Underground Railroad.*[22]

One of the oddest escapes came in 1849, when Henry Brown had friends ship him in a box from Richmond to Philadelphia, where he then worked as a magician, writer, and abolitionist.[23]

Underground Railroad activities in Norfolk included the stealth assistance of two slaves, Annetta M. Lane and Harriet Taylor, who were said to have used tents to shelter refugees from slavery until they could be taken north to free states or Canada.[24] After the Civil War, Lane and Taylor evolved and formalized their organization and network into the United Order of Tents in 1867 with a new mission: "to uplift the African-American community through mutual-aid and personal betterment."[25] The "tents" part of the name then came to refer to how the founding members viewed their organization as a "tent of salvation."[26] The order continues to have chapters in several states.

African Americans had been forming mutual aid societies at least since 1787 with the founding of the Philadelphia Free African Society, followed by similar organizations in Newport, Rhode Island, Boston, Massachusetts, and New York, New York. A fraternal group, the Negro Masonic Order, was chartered the same year.[27]

Free Blacks also asserted claims for a fuller citizenship, even in the midst of the American Revolution. In 1780, brothers Paul and John Cuffe (sometimes spelled "Cuffee") forged their own brand of "no taxation without representation" by refusing to pay their real estate taxes in Massachusetts unless they were permitted to vote. Their case led to the Massachusetts legislature approving voting rights for all free Blacks in 1783.[28]

The need for voting power continued to be a major advocacy theme among African Americans throughout United States history, especially during the worst days of Jim Crow oppression. "The ballot was expected to bring both material and psychological rewards," explains historian Steven F. Lawson,[29] who continues:

Once Negroes exercised their vote, they could help elect sheriffs who would be less likely to brutalize them; they would select officials who would see to it that ghetto streets were paved and cleaned; and ultimately they would use their ballots to dismantle the entire Jim Crow caste system.[30]

------- • -------

Stories about African Americans and Black organizations involved in resistance are rich, varied and extensive enough to fill a massive library. This book presents only a sampling to show the diversity as well as creativity, resourcefulness, and determination of African American resistance and resilience.

**Boycotts, sit-ins, lawsuits.** When federal Reconstruction efforts ended in the 1870s, Southern Blacks were left to find ways to resist the resurgence in White supremacism even "as the noose of Jim Crow segregation tightened," both figuratively and sadly literally, as noted in the words of Parramore et al.[31] This subsection includes examples.

In 1896, the U.S. Supreme Court ruled that racially segregated public accommodations on railroads were constitutional as long as there were equal facilities for Blacks and Whites. In 1904, the Virginia General Assembly codified permission to streetcar companies to follow suit, thereby enabling the Virginia Passenger and Power Company to devise and enforce segregated seating on streetcars in Richmond. Thousands of Blacks responded with a boycott that lasted more than a year. The General Assembly tightened the law in 1906, and the boycott foundered.[32] Meanwhile, similar boycotts arose in Lynchburg, Newport News, Portsmouth, and Norfolk, although they did not last as long as in Richmond.[33]

In Norfolk, however, African Americans not only boycotted segregated streetcars for a while, they also created the alternative Metropolitan Transfer Company. The enterprise, though, could not draw enough regular riders and collapsed, along with the boycott.[34]

On the national level, the NAACP was formed on February 12, 1909, the 100th anniversary of Abraham Lincoln's birth. Its goals were to protect the rights guaranteed in the 13th, 14th, and 15th amendments to the Constitution,[35] which ended slavery, promised equal protection under the law, and enabled universal adult male voting rights.

In its early years, NAACP activities included protesting President Woodrow Wilson's concurrence in segregating employees, toilets, and lunchrooms at the Treasury and Post Office departments of the U.S. government and the removal of more than 100 Black federal employees in favor of Whites.[36] The NAACP also helped to organize demonstrations in several cities against Wilson hosting a White House showing of *The Birth of a Nation*, the infamous pro-Ku Klux Klan, pro-White supremacy movie on February 18, 1915.[37]

No Hall of Fame of resisters would be complete without Charles Hamilton Houston, the World War I veteran who vowed to dedicate his life to civil rights after enduring bitter Jim Crow experiences in the military. In 1929, at age 33, Houston began his work as the legendary vice-dean of the Howard University School of Law and built the program into a civil rights incubator that would produce transformative lawyers such as Thurgood Marshall, Oliver Hill, and Spottswood Robinson Jr. Throughout his tenure, Houston would tell his students time and again that "a lawyer's either a social engineer or a parasite on society" and focus them on the mission of using the 14th Amendment's equal protection clause to bring down Jim Crow through "innovative and ambitious intervention."[38]

Some Howard-trained civil rights attorneys handled important cases for the NAACP, some in Norfolk. The work of the lawyers also helped revive the dormant branch in that city, along with the initiative of Daisy E. Lampkin, an NAACP regional field secretary, whose focus on Norfolk included the recruitment of 800 local residents in 1934 and 600 more in 1935.[39]

In the late 1930s and early '40s, a pair of pay-discrimination lawsuits by two Norfolk teachers in Norfolk became the main focus of the local African American resistance to White supremacy.[40]

First, Aline Elizabeth Black, a chemistry teacher at Norfolk's black Booker T. Washington High School, agreed in 1938 to be the plaintiff in an equal-pay, equal-protection test case to challenge the city's two-track salary scale for teachers; e.g., $970 per year for White high school teachers, $699 for Blacks with similar training.[41] The Norfolk School Board admitted that its pay scale discriminated against Blacks,[42] but in May 1939, a state judge sided with the city attorney in ruling that Black had waived her 14th Amendment rights when she signed a work contract to teach under the existing scale. A few weeks later, the Norfolk School Board denied her a new contract for the upcoming school year, and Black was jobless.[43] In addition, the School Board charged Black $4.01 for the workday she missed while being in court.[44]

The story then took some twists and produced some new resisters. On June 25, 1939, dozens of Black students carrying signs, such as "Dictators: Hitler, Mussolini, Norfolk School Board," led about 1,200 Black Norfolkians in a demonstration against the dismissal of Aline Black.[45]

Lead attorney Thurgood Marshall then decided to try again, but this time with another teacher, Melvin O. Alston, president of the Norfolk Teachers Association. Like Aline Black, Melvin Alston lost in court on the first round, but he decided to appeal in late 1940. A three-judge federal appeals panel then ruled that Norfolk's two-track salary schedule was a discriminatory violation of the 14th Amendment as well as the separate-but-equal precedent of *Plessy vs. Ferguson*.[46] Soon, Black teachers, with the help of NAACP-affiliated lawyers, were filing similar lawsuits throughout Virginia and the South.[47]

The public library in Alexandria, Virginia, became the scene of another grassroots act of resistance in 1939 with an unusual sit-in—or "sit-down" strike, as it was called then. Samuel W. Tucker, a 26-year-old lawyer, walked into the public library two blocks from his home and filled out an application for a library card for a friend, George Wilson, who had accompanied him. An assistant librarian then told the two men that the public library "does not issue cards to colored persons." Two weeks later, Tucker returned and the city's librarian told him that the city was discussing plans to open a library for "colored people."[48]

As Alexandria officials continued their discussions, Tucker filed a lawsuit on behalf of Wilson, and at a hearing in July 1939, Tucker asserted that because Alexandria's public library "was maintained by the taxes of all the citizens," that African American residents "had a right to the use of its facilities." The judge gave time for the city to resolve the issue, but on August 21, 1939, Tucker moved ahead with other plans to force the issue. He arranged for five Black residents of Alexandria to enter the library, one at a time, and for each to request a library card.[49]

Upon refusal by the librarian, each young man selected a book from the library shelves and sat down to quietly read. The librarian called the police, and they told the men they would be arrested if they didn't leave. The men politely refused, and the police escorted them out under arrest about an hour later.[50]

Meanwhile, Tucker, who had planned this very civil protest, had tipped off the press. When the police and the five Black men exited the library, they found several reporters and photographers and a crowd of 200 to 300 onlookers. By then, the police had become confused about what crime to charge the five men with because there was no law prohibiting Blacks from entering the library, only a library policy that they could not get library cards for the "White" library. The city manager then directed that they be charged with disorderly conduct. The next day in court, however, the police admitted that they had witnessed no disorder, and Tucker asked if "they were disorderly because they were black,"[51] presaging by more than 70 years the phrase "driving while Black" used by Black Lives Matter activists and similar groups.

The two cases—Tucker's original discrimination lawsuit on behalf of Wilson and the arrest of the five young Black men—dragged on for months. Then, on January 10, 1940, Judge William Wools rejected the Wilson lawsuit on a technicality but declared that the city must allow Blacks to use the "White" library and not be denied library cards that were properly applied for. However, two days later, the Alexandria City Council found money to build a "Black" library, and the judge's decision became moot. Black newspapers and some leaders proclaimed victory when the Black library opened in April 1940. But Tucker said he was disgusted because White paternalists had controlled the process, resolving the protest with yet another so-called separate-but-equal public accommodation and again relegating Blacks to second-class citizenship.[52]

**Resistance through sports, arts, and business.** Denied meaningful political expression, African Americans still sought to resist the culture of White supremacy in other ways, even if momentarily. Sports sometimes became that arena, even though most professional leagues and events prohibited interracial participation.

On July 4, 1910, in Reno, Nevada, Jack Johnson, a Black heavyweight boxing champion, defended his crown from former champion Jim Jeffries, who was known as "the Great White Hope" because he challenged Johnson with the intent of restoring the championship to a White man. In the lead-up to the fight, Jeffries said, "I am going into this fight for the sole purpose of proving that a white man is better than a negro." Billed as "the fight of the century," the event "became a metaphor for an age," says historian Earl Lewis.[53]

Whites, shocked by Johnson's victory over Jeffries, responded with racial violence in several cities across the country, including in Norfolk, where Whites pulled Blacks off streetcars and beat them. On July 5, 1910, the local White-owned *Virginian-Pilot* newspaper blamed the rioting on the "insolence of jubilant negroes" who had dared to celebrate Johnson's victory in public.[54]

Black sports fans in the Norfolk area also showed their resilience by finding ways to support baseball player Jackie Robinson—usually from afar but sometimes close up. In 1947, Robinson became the first African American to break Major League Baseball's modern-era color line when he joined the Brooklyn Dodgers. Local fans, though, already had received a glimpse of what was coming thanks to the *Journal and Guide* newspaper. The Black-owned newspaper had chronicled many of Robinson's activities even when he played for the Kansas City Monarchs minor league team in 1945 and it was clear that the Dodgers were considering him for the majors.

When he finally came to the Dodgers, the *Journal and Guide* frequently highlighted Robinson's batting average and other achievements throughout his rookie season. Norfolk fans also got into the act as many traveled to New York to attend Brooklyn Dodgers games.[55] Norfolk-area African Americans also turned out by the thousands when Robinson visited the region, including when he and his wife, Rachel, attended a Hampton Institute (now Hampton University) basketball game in 1948 and with a barnstorming team with other pioneering Black baseball players in the late 1940s and early 1950s.[56]

Robinson's baseball breakthrough helped inspire local African American sports fans to boycott the Norfolk Tars minor league team until management agreed to integrate both the team and stadium seating arrangements in 1954.[57] Such actions were not just about satisfying the sporting interests and comfort accommodations of Black fans. Desegregated teams and stadiums represented another step toward full citizenship as shown in the words of Cal Jacox, sports columnist for the *Journal and Guide* newspaper: "Democracy in action was the keynote at Norfolk's Myers Field for the first time in history when ... [a]n overflowing throng of an estimated 8,000 fans experienced the simple act of colored and white fans entering the same gate and ... sitting together in the same sections."[58]

Public beaches, too, became arenas for African American aspirations.

Blacks living in southeastern Virginia used several strategies to gain access to the region's bountiful beaches after area localities, including Norfolk, closed such waterfront recreational areas to African Americans in the early 1900s. Black businessman Lem Bright opened three acres of his land in Norfolk's Willoughby Bay area around 1905 and built several shelters. A few other private property owners made similar arrangements. A fire of suspicious origins destroyed Bright's site in 1927. African Americans didn't give up. They called on the City Council to designate a beach area for Black residents, even though many Whites voiced opposition. A court battle ensued before the council finally allowed Blacks to use a small, sandy tract in a then-rural section of neighboring Princess Anne County. That beach opened in 1934.[59]

African Americans also resisted White supremacy by giving homage to historical figures and through business aspirations. In Norfolk, the two came together in the 1919 construction of the Attucks Theatre on Church Street, then the "Main Street" of the city's Black population. The facility asserts African American culture in two ways: It celebrates its namesake, Crispus Attucks, who was considered to be the first Colonial American killed by the British in the Boston massacre, an important prelude to the American Revolution; and it was conceived, designed, financed, and developed entirely by African Americans.[60]

For decades before and after the development of the Norfolk theater, the Attucks name, because of its power in Black communities, was also attached to a range of African American entities across the United States, including political and social clubs, schools, apartment buildings, service and relief organizations, women's auxiliary groups, and fraternal orders.[61]

As Kachun observes, the invocation of the Attucks name has been more than a salute to one brave African American. The power of the Attucks name has been a symbolic reminder of the resilience of African Americans to persevere for freedom, equality, and full rights as citizens of the United States.[62]

Sadly, the African American out-of-town entertainers—greats such as Louis Armstrong, Nat King Cole, Count Basie, Billy Eckstine,

Cab Calloway, and Ella Fitzgerald—were prohibited from staying at Norfolk's White-owned hotels while performing at Norfolk's Attucks Theatre and even at local White venues. Bonnie McEachin, the African American owner of the Plaza Hotel on Church Street, used the opportunity to enhance her business and became nationally known for her hospitality and contributions to charity.[63]

Many concerned and inventive African Americans used their ingenuity to assist their immediate and widespread communities. In so doing, they found their niche in resisting Jim Crow.

Victor Hugo Green, a mailman in New York City, created such a role for himself. From 1936 to 1966, Green compiled and published *The Negro Motorist Green Book,* an annually updated travel guide to advise African Americans about safe places to stay, eat, and buy gasoline while driving through the South and other regions. For the depth of care poured into every edition, Calvin Ramsey, who wrote a play about the Green Book, likens Green's work to "a love letter" to fellow African Americans.[64]

**Politics.** In Norfolk, Black freedom and pride after the Civil War translated into demands for full citizenship and self-determination. As Lewis points out, in the decades between the Civil War and the modern Civil Rights Movement, Norfolk African Americans not only "struggled to improve their material conditions, they also fought for equal treatment, sometimes quietly and sometimes visibly. They never abided racism, 'polite' or otherwise, well; instead, they boycotted, rioted, petitioned, cajoled, demonstrated, and sought legal redress."[65]

One of the first post-Civil War indications that Norfolk's Black leaders were serious about asserting full citizenship for African Americans arose in 1865 with the creation of the Colored Monitor Union Club[66] to advance Black unity and to seek Congressional action on voting rights.[67] On June 5, 1865, Union Club members and other Black men convened a mass meeting that produced the *Equal Suffrage Address from the Colored Citizens of Norfolk, Va., to the People of the United States.*[68] Some 5,000 copies were disseminated across the United States, making "Norfolk's black community ... the first in the nation to argue for equal rights on a national level."[69]

The *Equal Suffrage* manifesto asks fellow citizens to recognize African American rights to "the full enjoyment of those privileges of full citizenship," including for unfettered political participation. The document makes clear that voting rights were fundamental to everything else, declaring: "give us the suffrage, and you may rely upon us to secure justice for ourselves."[70]

The phrase "give us the suffrage" would reverberate through the decades. In a May 17, 1957, speech, the Rev. Martin Luther King Jr. proclaimed the same demand in his famous "Give Us the Ballot" speech, which, in part, read, "Give us the ballot, and we will no longer have to worry the federal government about our basic rights."

The demands from Norfolk's Black community reflected a broader movement for full citizenship that included the National Convention of Colored Men in October 1864 in Syracuse, New York.[71] African Americans in other Virginia communities organized political entities similar to Norfolk's Colored Monitor Union Club, and together they held a statewide convention August 2–5, 1865, in Alexandria.

Presaging the equal protection clause of the 14th Amendment, which was to come in 1868, and the voting rights 15th Amendment of 1870, Virginia's Black convention of 1865 called for equal protection and "the elective franchise," as noted in historian Brent Tarter's 2015 article, "African Americans and Politics in Virginia (1865–1902)," in the online *Encyclopedia Virginia*. In doing so, the convention invoked the concept of inalienable rights from the Declaration of Independence, again well before Martin Luther King Jr. and his ringing reminder in his 1963 "I Have a Dream" speech that America had long ago "defaulted on this promissory note" to African Americans.

In addition to the Colored Monitor Union Club and other Black political organizations, the early years of emancipation and the Reconstruction era produced Black political luminaries such as John Mercer Langston, who in 1888 became the first African American from Virginia elected to the U.S. House of Representatives, although Congress did not seat him until 1890.[72] Langston was the only Black Virginian to serve in House until 1993, when Bobby Scott won election in Virginia's 3rd District.

After Langston, political victory became impossible for Virginia's African Americans as they were largely disenfranchised by the Virginia Constitutional Convention of 1901–02. Also, both major political parties, Democrats and Republicans, made it clear by words and actions that Blacks were not welcome as active participants in the political process and that Blacks were to serve only as negative campaign fodder when one candidate or party attacked its rival. White politicians seemed bent on outdoing each other in labeling competitors as "Negro lovers" or "the party of Negroes.[73] To that, Buni adds, "The role of the Negro, however, was not to be a voter but an issue."[74]

Blacks, however, sometimes turned to the ballot box to make symbolic protests, such as when the "lily-black Republican" slate ran in 1921 after the Republican State Convention, held in Norfolk, proclaimed that "the Negro was of little or no value,"[75] adding further insult to decades of similar treatment from Democrats. The lily-Black slate included *Richmond Planet* publisher John Mitchell Jr. for governor and entrepreneur Maggie L. Walker for superintendent of public instruction,[76] and the Black candidates knew they had no chance of winning.[77]

An observation that historian Earl Lewis makes about the early 20th century Black community in Norfolk seems to have applied throughout Virginia for several decades: "They understood ... that a loss of power never meant absolute powerlessness."[78] However, with the end of World War II, many African American veterans returned home to places like Norfolk with ideas and the courage to help transform that sentiment into a robust political citizenship, as we will see in Chapter 12.

On August 26, 1961, Rowena Stancil (left) and 12-year-old Charlene Butts, participated in a protest against segregation that Charlene's mother, Evelyn T. Butts, had helped to organize. The demonstrators were picketing a preseason NFL game between the Washington Redskins and the Baltimore Colts because the Redskins did not have any Black players and seating at Foreman Field in Norfolk was racially segregated. Charlene's sign read: "In War We Fight Together. Why Not Sit Together In Peace?" *Copyright Virginian Pilot. All Rights Reserved. Distributed by Tribune Content Agency, LLC.*

# CHAPTER 12
## Double V on the Home Front

On August 26, 1961, Charlene Butts joined a pro-integration demonstration that her mother, Evelyn Butts, had helped to organize. There, one of the other adults gave the 12-year-old girl a picket sign that read: "In War We Fight Together. Why Not Sit Together In Peace?"[1]

The target of the protest had nothing to do with military integration. Evelyn Butts and her allies were picketing a preseason exhibition professional football game between the Washington Redskins and the Baltimore Colts, and they had three demands: that the Washington Redskins must hire Black players; that seating at state-supported Foreman Field in Norfolk must become permanently integrated; and that the local Kiwanis Club, the game's sponsor, must open its membership to African Americans.

Many memories of World War II and the Korean War had receded, yet military-oriented slogans adapted for civil rights issues—such as the one lettered onto Charlene's placard—now resonated among African Americans, especially in Norfolk with its huge naval base and the region's extensive collection of defense-related industries.

Thousands of Black men and women living in the Norfolk area belonged to the great generation of Americans who had endured the devastating 1930s economic depression and then served in the wartime military or had worked at defense installations. Such African Americans, with all due respect to journalist Tom Brokaw, should be known as the "doubly greatest generation." They not only fought for democracy and self-determination overseas as soldiers and sailors or manufactured crucial munitions and supplies as civilians, they had little choice but to continue fighting after the war—for freedom in their home communities.

The Black press had even popularized a term for this extraordinary calling—the Double V campaign, for victory on both fronts.[2]

The families of these Double V African American warriors should be considered members of the era's heroic cadre, especially the wives of the Black servicemen. Like the wives of White soldiers, the Black spouses remained home to raise children on their own and find work to help make ends meet, but many African American wives did so while continuing to endure the Jim Crow humiliations of the era.

Evelyn Butts, who worked throughout World War II while also rearing two of her three children, had her own special affinity toward military veterans. Her husband, Charlie Butts, returned from World War II severely wounded and eventually became 100% disabled and dependent on Evelyn's caregiving. Butts' close friend and civil rights collaborator, attorney Joseph A. Jordan Jr., an Army sergeant in the war, was paralyzed from the waist down from a landmine explosion suffered at age 19 and relied upon a wheelchair for the rest of his life. Proud of his service, Butts would quickly correct people who thought Jordan was suffering from a birth defect.[3]

Norfolk, which hosts Naval Station Norfolk, headquarters of the Atlantic Fleet, has a military history dating to the American Revolution. The Black community's long collective memories about African American civilian and military experiences with U.S. armed forces includes Civil War liberation from enslavement, segregated units during World Wars I and II, and the integrated forces that came with the Korean War in the early 1950s.

While African American experience with World War II and the Korean War had far-reaching effects on the Civil Rights Movement, these were not the first times that Blacks returned from wartime service intent on overthrowing racial oppression in the United States. The story began during earlier conflagrations, especially with the Civil War and World War I (although African Americans also participated in the American Revolution, War of 1812, and Spanish American War).

Famed abolitionist, orator, writer, and statesman Frederick Douglass, who had escaped enslavement in 1838, lobbied President Abraham Lincoln to allow free African American men to join the Union military and fight against the pro slavery Confederacy. Douglass then encouraged African Americans to enlist and offered a variety of reasons in compelling speeches and articles, asserting that joining Union forces would help prove that Blacks are entitled to full citizenship and that military service in the fight against slavery would be an ennobling effort that bolsters self-respect.[4]

Even after African Americans began enlisting, Douglass continued to remind them of the importance of their service. For example, in a January 29, 1864, speech to the 29th and 30th Connecticut Volunteer Infantry, made up of African American troops, Douglass implored:

> You are the pioneers of the liberty of your race. With the United States cap on your head, the United States eagle on your belt, the United States musket on your shoulder, not all the powers of darkness can prevent you from becoming American citizens. And not for yourselves alone are you marshaled—you are pioneers—on you depends the destiny of four millions of the colored race in this country. ... If you rise and flourish, we shall rise and flourish. If you win freedom and citizenship, we shall share your freedom and citizenship.[5]

Those inspired by Douglass included William H. Carney, who was born in Norfolk but had migrated to Massachusetts with his parents before the start of the Civil War. Intending for a career in the ministry, Carney changed course and enlisted in the all-Black 54th Massachusetts Volunteer Regiment, where he was quickly promoted to sergeant and became famous during the Union's attack on Fort Wagner, South Carolina, on July 18, 1863. While severely wounded, Carney saved the United States flag from Confederate capture.[6] He later recalled his actions with pride and how his battlefield comrades were equally proud of his heroics. "When they saw me bringing the colors," Carney said, "they cheered me, and I was able to tell them that the old flag never touched the ground."[7] He was among the first African Americans awarded the nation's Medal of Honor for bravery under fire but had to wait until 1900 to be so honored.[8]

Free men were not the only Blacks who heeded the call to join Union forces. The Civil War increased opportunities for African Americans to escape from slavery, and many joined the Union Army and Navy. Michael Hucles notes that the Norfolk area, occupied by federal forces since 1862, "proved to be fertile ground for ... eager black recruits"[9] from throughout southeastern Virginia. About 1,200 Black men from the Norfolk area alone joined the federal forces,[10] including Evelyn Butts' great-grandfather, Smallwood Ackiss.[11] Smallwood Ackiss had fled a nearby plantation and enlisted in a division of the United States Colored Troops in Norfolk in 1863, while the plantation owner, John Ackiss II, went off to fight for the Confederacy.[12]

Actions taken by African Americans during the Civil War had an even deeper meaning, according to Foner,[13] Southern Blacks, like Ackiss, hastened the dismantling of slavery by fleeing the plantations and enlisting with the Union. These initiatives, Foner writes, "were crucial to placing the issue of black citizenship on the national agenda."[14]

One proof of Foner's assertion can be seen in a founding document of the National Equal Rights League (NERL), which 145 African American leaders from Northern and Southern states created at the National Convention of Colored Men in Syracuse, New

York, October 4–7, 1864. The NERL's *Address to the American People* posed the following questions:

> Are we good enough to use bullets, and not good enough to use ballots? May we defend rights in time of war, and yet be denied the exercise of those rights in time of peace? Are we citizens when the nation is in peril, and aliens when the nation is in safety? May we shed our blood under the Star-Spangled Banner on the battlefield, and yet be debarred from marching under it to the ballot-box? ... Shall we toil with you to win the prize of free government, while you alone shall monopolize all its valued privileges?[15]

Blacks, whether born free or formerly enslaved, were proud of their participation in the Civil War and their role in liberating other African Americans. In all, about 200,000 African Americans fought for the Union and nearly 40,000 died in the cause.[16]

In Norfolk, such pride manifested itself in a movement to create a cemetery for African American veterans of the Civil War, a project headed by James E. Fuller, one of the first two Blacks elected to the Norfolk City Council. Fuller, a war veteran, finally succeeded in 1885 when the council designated a section of a former pauper's cemetery for Black veterans and renamed it West Point because it was on the westerly margin of the then-all-White Elmwood Cemetery.[17] However, the city separated West Point from Elmwood with a 10-foot-high brick wall, a physical symbol that the Civil War did not win first-class citizenship for African Americans. The wall, a reminder that Blacks were to be segregated even in death, remains as a historic artifact in Norfolk[18] even though Elmwood Cemetery is now an integrated burial ground.

Led by Fuller, Norfolk's African American residents also strove to honor native son Sgt. William H. Carney by planning a monument to him as the main feature of West Point Cemetery. Over a course of about 20 years, the mostly low-income Black community raised money through chicken dinners, pie sales, raffles, and concerts to build the base of the monument and then, for almost 15 more years, to top the structure with a statue of Carney, which was dedicated in 1920. As extra historical significance, the monument is the only known memorial in the South that salutes Black veterans of the Civil War and Spanish-American War.

After the Civil War, a pattern emerged: Blacks continued to serve in the U.S. military, albeit in segregated units and usually with low-level assignments—yet with the quest for full citizenship and self-determination high in their minds. President Woodrow Wilson's rhetoric about America's World War I goal of saving democracy in Europe reinforced these dreams, but, again, the targets proved elusive. African American soldiers and sailors endured harsh treatment, racial indignities, and segregated facilities, including the latrines and showers.[19] Their contributions were downplayed by high-ranking officers and politicians, and their efforts to succeed were often ridiculed or undermined by Whites.

Such racist sentiments are expressed, for example, in World War I-era correspondence from members of the White Fife family from Charlottesville. In a letter to his sister, James D. Fife, a doctor, writes about seeing "a couple of American coons today" but none "of our good Virginia niggers."[20] Fife's sister, Ella, also in Europe as a nurse, writes to another sister in America that she sometimes had to sit "at the next table to the blackest shines you ever saw." While noting that the African Americans were "excellent soldiers," Ella added, "I'm afraid there are going to be some spoiled darkies coming back home."[21]

Yet Black soldiers and sailors persisted both during their active-duty years and when they returned to civilian life, even when knowing that displaying public pride in their military service could bring deadly consequences.[22] At least 10 Black veterans were lynched while wearing their military uniforms in riots instigated by White mobs in 1918 and the bloody "Red Summer" of 1919.[23] Atop the violence, U.S. Senator James K. Vardaman of Mississippi added insult: He warned fellow senators not to commend African Americans for serving patriotically in World War I because Blacks would then conclude that their "political rights must be respected."[24]

More than 370,000 African Americans served in the U.S. military during World War I, which meant 9% of American troops.[25] Among them was Charles Hamilton Houston, a young officer who became so angry about Jim Crow conditions in the Army that he dedicated himself to a lifelong fight against discrimination as a civil rights lawyer, Howard University law professor, and a leading mastermind of the NAACP's strategy to dismantle White supremacy.[26] Houston would later explain:

> The hate and scorn showered on us Negro officers by our fellow Americans convinced me that there was no sense in my dying for a world ruled by them. I made up my mind that if I got through this war I would study law and use my time fighting for who could not strike back.[27]

Houston's World War I military experience and subsequent engagement in civil rights foreshadowed what was to emerge from the Black experience in World War II more than two decades later.

As World War II approached, many African Americans likely knew the racial-horror stories of grandparents and parents who served in the Civil War, Spanish-American War, and World War I, or held their own memories of Jim Crow experiences in the military and of the poor treatment Black veterans endured from White politicians. Recalling the mistreatment, a group of Black opinion-makers and African American former officers from World War I formed the Committee for Participation of Negroes in the National Defense Program in 1938.[28] The committee, historian, C. S. Parker says, "sought to avoid the disappointment of the First World War and the immediate postwar period by ensuring African Americans' access to full, unencumbered military participation."[29]

Parker also cites the words of Roy Wilkins, editor of the NAACP's *Crisis* magazine, who wrote that equality in the military and defense sector was a top priority, along with antilynching efforts, "among all classes (of Blacks) in all sections of the country."[30]

So, with World War II approaching, many African Americans stepped forward once more as patriots willing to serve their country and its ideals. As in earlier wars, they also saw opportunity along with the risks: opportunity for work, for learning new skills, for self-respect, for proving again to America that they were deserving of first-class citizenship. The long-running battle with Jim Crow was also central as evidenced in the following statement by African American civil rights and labor leader A. Philip Randolph:

> Though I have found no Negroes who want to see the United Nations lose this war, I have found many who, before the war ends, want to see the stuffing knocked out of white supremacy and of empire over subject peoples. American Negroes, involved as we are in the general issues of the conflict, are confronted not with a choice but with the challenge both to win democracy for ourselves at home and to help win the war for democracy the world over.[31]

Randolph concluded:

> A community is democratic only when the humblest and weakest person can enjoy the highest civil, economic, and social rights that the biggest and most powerful possess. ... By fighting for their rights now, American Negroes are helping to make America a moral and spiritual arsenal of democracy. Their fight against the poll tax, against lynch law, segregation, and Jim Crow, their fight for economic, political, and social equality, thus becomes part of the global war for freedom.[32]

In all, about 1.2 million African Americans served in the U.S. military during World War II—and many who survived came back with a keener sense that the United States was not living up to its creeds about democracy, equality, liberty, and justice.[33] They had endured indignities from White officers and comrades as they fought overseas and from White civilians as they waited for deployment in places like Norfolk. Tempers flared, especially on crowded streetcars and buses where Black soldiers and sailors had to join with civilian African Americans pushing their way past White passengers in order to sit in the back seats, historian Marvin W. Schlegel reports in *Conscripted City: Norfolk in World War II*.[34] Many Black military men from more "liberal" parts of America were not accustomed to the requirements of Jim Crow segregation in mass transit.

Norfolk's African American civilians—men and women—also continued to face discrimination on the home front. The Great Depression of the 1930s had taken a greater toll on Norfolk-area Blacks than on Whites, as Blacks were often the first to lose their jobs or were laid off and replaced by Whites.[35] When World War II began and jobs started opening in defense-related industries, blacks rushed forward for the opportunities, and many times went away bitterly disappointed. For example, dozens of Black carpenters who responded to an emergency hiring announcement for several regional military installations were sent home by the contractor who told them "we cannot mix the races."[36]

Women—Black and White—also answered the call for defense workers, given that many men had joined the military. But, as noted in Chapter 6, African American women often discovered that their skin color disqualified them.[37] Black women and men who did manage to find defense employment were confronted with many other forms of discrimination, including exclusion from proper training, placement in segregated working facilities, assignment to the lowest-paying jobs, and being overlooked for promotions.[38]

Even though African Americans in Norfolk, as elsewhere throughout the country, wanted to participate in America's war effort, they saw daily instances of racism that tested their good faith. Norfolk's Civilian Defense Office, for example, issued identification cards to Blacks that contained descriptions such as "woolly hair and maroon eyes."[39] African American residents of Norfolk had to also endure—and deny—rumors that they were arming themselves with ice picks for a plot to rise up and murder thousands of Whites in nighttime attacks.[40]

African Americans stationed or training in Norfolk were excluded from many venues for wholesome recreation. They were denied entry to the Navy YMCA and at most USOs. Finally, the Black Smith Street USO was opened, but it was located in one of Norfolk's worst slums, which had streets that were almost impassable during rainstorms.[41]

Blacks also served in Jim Crow conditions within the military's segregated units during World War II, although they sometimes fought alongside Whites in certain warfront battles.[42] The *Norfolk Journal and Guide* and several other Black-owned newspapers helped keep up morale, especially in their home communities, by sending their own correspondents and running feature stories about the heroics of African American soldiers and sailors who were usually overlooked by White-owned periodicals.[43]

Many African Americans serving in World War II knew how African American veterans of World War I had felt betrayed by America after fighting for democracy in Europe; still, they felt pride in wearing a United States military uniform and being part of the Allied effort to defeat fascism in Europe and Japan's aggression in the Pacific.[44]

"Fighting for democracy ... symbolized the equality to which African Americans aspired," writes Christopher S. Parker,[45] who interviewed a number of Black veterans for his book, *Fighting for Democracy: Black Veterans and the Struggle Against White Supremacy in the Postwar South*. "Bearing arms to preserve

America's democratic ideals ... meant full membership in the political community, which included enjoyment of civil as well a political equality."

One such veteran, a "Mr. Carter" (first name not provided in C. S. Parker's book), who enlisted in 1940 and spent his career in the Army, told Parker that wearing his uniform "made me feel as though I was a true American—that I merited everything that I received."[46] Parker concludes that the military uniform, especially for Southern Blacks, "symbolized their equality, their membership in the political community" and a "sense of accomplishment" and a "commitment to American ideals."[47]

Wearing the uniform added also to both the resolve and the embitterment many Black veterans felt as they experienced the disparity between the democratic ideals for which they fought and the racial realities they encountered in service and when they returned to their communities. "They returned with a new set of expectations, confident of their ability to achieve them," C. S. Parker writes. "Black veterans returned home determined to secure the rights to which they, and the community they represented, were entitled,"[48] echoing the sentiments that Charles Hamilton Houston expressed after the First World War.

Poet Langston Hughes tapped into similar moods, albeit more cynically, with his bitter World War II-era poem, "Beaumont to Detroit: 1943."[49]

Although they were battle-worn, many Black World War II veterans followed through on the second leg of their Double V mission by joining or forming grassroots organizations to pursue civil rights, voting rights, or community improvement—all in the quest of first-class citizenship for African Americans.[50] Some became well-known nationally during the civil rights struggles of the 1950s and '60s, including brothers Medgar and Charles Evers, Hosea Williams, Aaron Henry, and Whitney M. Young Jr.[51] "It was my Army experience that decided me on getting into the race relations field after the war," said Young, who became executive director of the National Urban League. "Not just because I saw the problems, but because I saw the potentials, too."[52]

C. S. Parker, though, goes to the heart of experience as he writes:

> By virtue of their sacrifice, black veterans believed themselves—and the black community—to be entitled to first-class citizenship. Since this wasn't forthcoming, military experience gave them the confidence to take it. Compared to what they were forced to endure in the military—that is, fighting the enemy in addition to racism in the ranks—black veterans were eager to fight Jim Crow upon their return, something at which it's clear many of them excelled.[53]

Despite their determination and confidence, Black veterans found that Southern White supremacists remained intent on denying full citizenship to African Americans, including those who had fought overseas for democracy. Here are just three of countless examples:

In February 1946, Army veteran Isaac Woodard Jr., a 27-year-old decorated sergeant who served 15 months in a Pacific combat zone, was arrested and beaten in Batesburg, South Carolina, on the same day he had been discharged from the military. He was still wearing his uniform. An Atlantic Greyhound bus driver cursed Woodard and accused him of taking too long in the colored restroom, and an argument between the two men escalated. The driver called local law enforcement, reporting that Woodard was drunk—even though the sergeant did not drink—and officers arrested Woodard at the next bus stop. The officers then beat Woodard with nightsticks, which resulted in Woodard becoming totally blind.[54]

President Harry Truman, a veteran of World War I, took notice of the Woodard beating and other incidents of White violence against Black World War II veterans and spoke out, according to C. S. Parker, who quotes Truman declaring:

> When a mayor and a City Marshal can take a negro Sergeant off a bus in South Carolina, beat him up and put out one of his eyes, and nothing is done about it ... something is radically wrong with the system. ... I am going to try to remedy it.[55]

Partly with such incidents in mind, Truman appointed a 15-member Commission on Civil Rights in December 1946 and directed it to devise a strategy to protect the rights of African Americans. The report, *To Secure These Rights*, issued the following October, called for the desegregation of the military, creation of a permanent Fair Employment Practices Committee, passage of federal anti-lynching laws, the banning of poll taxes, and "elimination of segregation ... from American life."[56] Contemporary analysts and historians have noted that Truman was also motivated by wanting to preserve America's international reputation against the Cold War propaganda of the Soviet Union, which seemed to celebrate "every blunder committed by white supremacists" in order to undermine "America's fitness to lead the 'free world.'"[57]

Nevertheless, Southern White-supremacist politicians blustered about leaving the Democratic Party of which Truman was a member. Some did, led by South Carolina Governor J. Strom Thurman, who unsuccessfully ran for president against Truman in 1948 under the new States Rights Democratic Party, nicknamed the "Dixiecrats."[58] Mississippi Senator James Eastland condemned the civil rights report and recommendations as confirming "that organized mongrel minorities control the government" and were now aiming "to Harlemize the country," while a Georgia congressman likened the recommendations to "the platform of the Communist Party."[59]

African Americans, though, stepped up their call for voting rights. On July 2, 1946, Medgar and Charles Evers tried to register to vote in their hometown of Decatur, Mississippi. A group of Whites blocked their way to the courthouse. The Evers brothers continued to advocate for voting rights for many years, with Medgar falling to an assassin's gunfire in 1963.[60]

Another veteran, Maceo Snipes, actually voted in a Georgia primary in July 1946, but one day later he was confronted by a gang of White men in a pickup truck and gunned down by one of them.[61]

Air Force veteran James Howard Meredith fared better in his struggle with Jim Crow. After leaving the military in 1960, he said, "I returned to my home state [Mississippi] to fight a war. ... My objective was total victory: victory over discrimination, oppression, the unequal application of the law, and, most of all, over 'White Supremacy' in all of its manifestations." [62]

Inspired by the inaugural speech of President John F. Kennedy, Meredith decided to break the color line at the University of Mississippi. He eventually needed court orders, the intervention of President Kennedy and Attorney General Robert F. Kennedy, and the protection of hundreds of U.S. Marshals, federal troops, and federalized National Guard members to enroll on October 1, 1962.

Black veterans persisted, and many helped to give courage, confidence, and wise counsel to their home communities for decades to come. Such veterans in Norfolk were no different—and Evelyn Butts' life was influenced by her association with them, especially a trio of attorneys, Victor J. Ashe, J. Hugo Madison, and Joseph A. Jordan Jr., each of whom became political activists as well as civil rights crusaders.[63]

Among their many activities: Ashe and Madison challenged Whites-only use of Seashore State Park in nearby Princess Anne County, now known as First Landing State Park in the city of Virginia Beach;[64] Madison and Jordan represented the concerns of Butts and other Oakwood residents in the community's fight against Norfolk's proposed urban redevelopment project in the

1950s;[65] and Ashe, Madison, and Jordan took on lawsuits related to trying to integrate Norfolk's public schools after the U.S. Supreme Courts' 1954 *Brown v. Board of Education* decision.[66]

Jordan and Butts, of course, worked closely on many civil rights and political issues, including Butts' 1963 lawsuit to overthrow state and local poll taxes.

Evelyn T. Butts carrying a placard that reads, "School Board Unfair," picketed in front of the Norfolk School Administration Building in September 1963 to protest poor conditions at Booker T. Washington High School and the slow pace of integration in Norfolk. *Copyright Virginian Pilot. All Rights Reserved. Distributed by Tribune Content Agency, LLC.*

# CHAPTER 13
## Schooling the School Board

When Evelyn Butts discovered in 1960 that her daughter, Charlene, and other children at their all-Black school were given hand-me-down books from a nearby all-White school, she voiced outrage at the next meeting of the Norfolk School Board. Then, within days, new books replaced the old, Charlene Butts Ligon recalls about this example of how her mother confronted racism.[1] "She didn't wait for others to do something for her. She just did it, and she always took a leadership role," Ligon said.[2]

Evelyn Butts was not always as successful challenging White supremacy as she was when obtaining new textbooks for her daughter and other students at the all-Black combined Rosemont Elementary and Junior High School in 1960. Butts had been defeated in efforts to integrate Charlene into an all-White school before the city opened the combined Rosemont school; Butts had also unsuccessfully battled against the very creation of the Rosemont school as well as the nearby Coronado Elementary School.[3] Norfolk developed both of these hastily constructed all-Black schools to circumvent local enforcement of court-ordered school desegregation, as discussed in Chapter 9.[4]

Years later, in a newspaper comment she made for Martin Luther King Jr. Day 1986, Butts said she had long believed that "if you have two schools, one for black students and one for white students, there would be no quality education" and that "segregated schools means inferior education."[5]

Education had long been a central issue in Butts' life even though she had dropped out of high school in the 10th grade after becoming pregnant with her first child.[6] In addition, Butts made sure her siblings stayed in school and that her own children valued education.[7]

It is not known when Butts moved from being an education advocate for her family to an advocate for equal opportunity in education for all African Americans. But pivotal times in her advocacy seemed to have occurred in the early 1950s after she joined the Norfolk Branch of the NAACP and again when the Supreme Court abolished segregated public schools in the 1954 *Brown v. Board of Education* decision, according to Butts' daughter, Charlene.[8]

Virginia's policy of Massive Resistance to public school integration certainly sharpened Butts' activism on educational issues. Like many African American parents, Evelyn and Charlie Butts hoped that the Supreme Court's decree would mean that their children would soon be able to attend better and integrated public schools closer to their homes.

The stakes were extra-personal for the Butts' household. The "woefully inadequate"[9] and overcrowded Oakwood combined elementary and high school that Evelyn Butts had attended as a youngster had closed in the early 1950s. That meant that her eldest daughter, Patricia Ann, had to ride by bus to the next closest Black high school some 15 miles away in an area outside the city of Norfolk then known as Norfolk County. (Virginia has separate cities and counties.) The county's school buses were not always reliable, so students were sometimes stranded.[10] At some point, Evelyn and Charlie Butts decided to devote part of their meager budget to enrolling Patricia into the all-Black St. Joseph's Catholic Church and School in downtown Norfolk, which was only seven miles away.[11]

The *Brown v. Board of Education* ruling, however, did not take immediate effect, and integration of public schools was delayed by several years of legal and political wrangling. In Virginia, key entities in the litigations and community activism included the Norfolk Branch of the NAACP.[12]

During this time, Butts tried to have daughter Charlene trans-ferred from the all-Black Oakwood Elementary School and be among those seeking to integrate the nearby all-White Norview Elementary School for the fourth grade.[13]

Butts' advocacy on school issues did not end with her efforts on behalf of Charlene. By the early 1960s, she had become an important mobilizer on many aspects of African American political citizenship and self-determination in Norfolk. She continued to speak out in fa-vor of integrated schools for all students at various city government meetings.[14] She also pursued avenues to give the Black community a voice on the city's then all-White School Board, and she helped students and parents organize a protest against rundown and inade-quate conditions at the all-Black Booker T. Washington High School as well as Norfolk's foot-dragging on school integration.[15]

In July 1963, the terms of four School Board members had just expired, so Butts saw her chance to speak out on the need for African American representation on this powerful policy-making panel. Citing her stature as president of the Oakwood-Rosemont Civic League, Butts addressed Norfolk's Citizens Advisory Com-mittee (CAC), a 25-member biracial board that the City Council had created to study Norfolk's racial problems and issue recom-mendations. In her remarks, Butts said that Norfolk should appoint an African American to the School Board for the first time.[16] Butts came prepared on the issue and informed the CAC that "most of the larger cities in Virginia,"[17] such as Hampton, Newport News, Portsmouth, and Richmond, had already appointed Black citizens to important public commissions, and that Richmond had a Black vice chairman on its school board.[18] The CAC agreed with Butts, adopted her recommendation, and sent it to the City Council. On July 30, 1963, the City Council unanimously approved attorney Hilary H. Jones Jr. as Norfolk's first African American member of the School Board.[19]

Then, in September 1963, Butts and a woman named Mary Humphrey helped organize a two-part protest of poor conditions

169

at Booker T. Washington High School and the slow pace of school integration in Norfolk. Over 2,200 students left classes for a protest march, while parents and other adults picketed the school administration building in downtown Norfolk.[20]

Students walked out of the school on September 20, 1963, and paraded about two miles to the administration building, where they presented nine grievances about "unbearable and over-crowded conditions, and the lack of facilities."[21] The list noted that Booker T. Washington High School had been built in 1924 with a capacity of 1,400 students but that 2,450 were enrolled in 1963; that it was so cold in the winter that teachers had to wear coats and gloves; that plaster was falling from the ceilings; and that the cafeteria, bathrooms, and gymnasium were grossly inadequate and outdated.[22]

Students returned to school the next day, but adults, including Butts, continued their picketing on the integration issue for several more days.[23]

The picketing drew a public rebuke from Robert Ripley, chairman of Norfolk's biracial Citizens Advisory Committee, who said: "I personally feel that picketing is an insult to the committee. ... I think it's wrong, but it's up to the Negroes if that's what they want." Butts shot back:

> I regret very much that the CAC has chosen to use its valuable time to criticize our conduct in the picketing of the Norfolk School Administration. In the first instance, it shows a serious lack of understanding of the Norfolk Negro citizens, and in the second instance it is a waste of time if this is intended to discourage us.[24]

The year 1963 already had proved to be an especially active one for Butts in her advocacy for civil rights and equal opportunity. Then, on August 28, she joined the March on Washington for Jobs and Freedom and heard her hero, the Rev. Martin Luther King Jr., deliver his iconic "I Have a Dream" speech.[25]

Butts returned from the march further determined that she would no longer wait for Norfolk's White power structure to parcel out small favors to obedient Black citizens under the etiquette of the Virginia Way. For Butts and her allies, African Americans deserved to have a meaningful voice in decisions that affected their lives and the right to determine their own future.

In November 1963, Evelyn T. Butts helped launch a Norfolk chapter of Martin Luther King, Jr.'s Southern Christian Leadership Conference. SCLC chapter leaders included, left to right, Elmer Harris, board member; Joseph A. Jordan, Jr., treasurer; J.D. Speller, Sr., second vice president; Evelyn T. Butts, secretary; and the Rev. Donald W. Johnson, president. *Courtesy of Harrison B. Wilson Archives, Norfolk State University.*

# CHAPTER 14

## A New Generation, A New Frontier

During the 1940s and '50s, several events and trends in Butts' personal and civic spheres likely helped to ignite her civil rights activism and emergent leadership skills. During World War II, Butts joined the Oakwood Civic League, a neighborhood group that advocated on community issues, and was mentored by the organization's president, Annie Nickens, a woman several years her senior. Then, in the early 1950s, Nickens invited Butts to a meeting of the Norfolk Branch of the NAACP.[1] Butts already had a long-established interest in keeping up with current events on the news, but her appetite probably was heightened when the U.S. Supreme Court declared segregated schools unconstitutional in 1954, a case closely watched by the national NAACP and branches all across the country.

At about the same time, the city of Norfolk was moving to expand its boundaries by annexing an adjacent part of old Norfolk County then known as the Tanner's Creek district, which included Butts' Oakwood neighborhood and the nearby Rosemont and Lincoln Park communities—a total of 370 acres with more than 1,000 dwelling units. Oakwood, Rosemont, and Lincoln Park were populated by low-income African Americans, many of whom lived on dirt roads in substandard housing without indoor plumbing. Other parts of this county were later merged into what became today's city of Virginia Beach.[2]

The Tanner's Creek annexation went into effect on January 1, 1955.[3] By mid-1956, the city's Norfolk Redevelopment and Housing Authority had proposed a massive urban redevelopment project for Tanner's Creek, including tearing down many of the 1,000-plus homes and rebuilding the area with an assortment of 2,500 single-family and semi-detached houses and garden apartments, playgrounds, an elementary school, and a small shopping center.[4]

Residents of Oakwood, where Butts lived, strongly opposed the redevelopment proposal, with many contending that they would not be able to afford the new homes or they would not be treated fairly in the real estate condemnation and compensation process. "There would have been many elderly that would have been out of a home," Butts recalled in an interview decades later.[5] The scared Oakwood residents also cited stories about African Americans who had lost their homes in the city's downtown-area redevelopment project that began in 1951. Local civil rights attorneys J. Hugo Madison and Joseph A. Jordan Jr. added another objection: that the proposed redevelopment project would perpetuate segregation instead of promote residential integration.[6]

In light of neighborhood resistance and faced with increasing controversy over court orders to desegregate public schools, the city indefinitely postponed action on the Oakwood-Rosemont-Lincoln Park urban renewal project and turned its redevelopment efforts elsewhere.[7] Norfolk's redevelopment and public school policies, however, would soon tie together in new ways, drawing Butts deeper into battles against the city's system of institutionalized racism. However, the link between the city's urban renewal program and public school policies also heightened Butts' awareness on two concerns: the importance of voter turnout in local elections, and how the poll tax impeded that participation for many African Americans, according to one of Butts' closest friends, the late Marie G. Young.[8]

Butts was still in her early 30s and economically struggling as a mother of three daughters, wife of a disabled World War II veteran, and sometimes a substantial provider of her family's income. Yet she found motivation, time, and energy to step up her activism, while becoming more confident in her skills.

"I believe this is when my mother became president of the Oakwood and Rosemont Civic League," adds Butts' daughter, Charlene Butts Ligon. "The threat of redevelopment made her intensely political."[9]

Although Butts' experiences under Jim Crow varied in specific details from other emerging and resilient African American activists of the 1940s and '50s, they shared an overwhelming desire to protect their families and their own well-being. From diverse tributaries, members of this new generation of civil rights risk-takers were immersing themselves in the continuum of Black resistance. These new protagonists seemed to step forward from almost anywhere. The hallowed list of names includes two Virginia African American women who refused Jim Crow seating arrangements on bus transportation in 1944, preceding the famous Rosa Parks incident that sparked the Montgomery, Alabama, bus boycott by 11 years.

In one 1944 incident, Sara Morris Davis, a teacher, sat between two Whites on a Norfolk bus—the only seat she could find—and was arrested when she did not comply with the driver's order to move. She appealed, and the Virginia Supreme Court overturned her conviction on grounds that the driver did not give a similar order to a White passenger sitting in the Black section of the bus. It was a narrowly focused ruling as the court did not overturn the law on segregated seating, ruling only that the driver had discriminated in how he enforced the law.[10]

In the other incident, Irene Morgan, a 27-year-old mother recovering from surgery, had spent some time convalescing at her mother's home in Gloucester County, Virginia. Returning to Baltimore, Morgan boarded an interstate Greyhound bus but had to sit on an uncomfortable bench-like seat in the back of the crowded bus. At a stop in Saluda, Virginia, Morgan and another Black woman, Estelle Fields, took the seats vacated by a White woman and her child. Several minutes later, two White people climbed aboard, and the driver ordered Morgan and Fields to "get up so that the white couple might sit down." Morgan refused and was charged with violating Jim Crow seating and resisting arrest. The case eventually went to the U.S. Supreme Court, which ruled in 1946 that interstate transit required "a single uniform rule to promote and protect national travel," meaning that Blacks and Whites must be treated alike when journeying on interstate vehicles, thereby trumping Virginia state law, as noted in Margaret Edds'[11] *We Face the Dawn: Oliver Hill, Spottswood Robinson, and the Legal Team That Dismantled Jim Crow*, and in Woodward.[12]

Courtroom victories and prominent news media coverage of civil rights activities emboldened increasing numbers of African Americans seeking equality as first-class citizens. Younger Blacks, along with White student allies, found creative ways to contribute as the movement surged into the 1960s.

The often-told stories of the decade include the Freedom Rides of 1961, in which mixed groups of Blacks and Whites rode interstate buses in the South to thwart Jim Crow segregated seating and the three Selma-to-Montgomery voting-rights marches of March 1965, especially the March 7 "Bloody Sunday," when state and local law enforcement officers beat demonstrators with billy clubs and dowsed them with tear gas.[13]

Many protests and peaceful gatherings were met by brutality, either from police, the Ku Klux Klan, White-supremacist mobs, or combinations of the three. Acts of deadly violence included the White terrorist bombing of the 16th Street Baptist Church in Birmingham, Alabama, in which four Black girls were killed on September 15, 1963; the June 1964 murders of civil rights workers James Chaney, Andrew Goodman, and Michael Schwerner; and the assassination of Martin Luther King Jr. on April 4, 1968.[14]

Sit-ins became popular among students. On Monday, February 1, 1960, four African American freshmen at the North Carolina Agricultural and Technical College—Joseph McNeil, Franklin McCain, David Richmond, and Ezell Blair Jr.—who were tired of Whites-only service at restaurants, sat down at the F.W.

Woolworth Company five-and-dime store in Greensboro, North Carolina. They refused to leave when a waitress told them, "We don't serve colored here."

The four remained until 5:30 p.m., when the store closed,[15] but they returned Tuesday with more students and on Wednesday with even more, now filling 63 of the lunch counter's 66 seats— but never being served. White customers jeered at and threatened them, but the sit-in spread to the nearby S.H. Kress store. Then thousands of Black students, joined by some Whites, picked up on the idea and organized similar sit-ins at dozens of lunch counters across the South, including in the Virginia cities of Norfolk, Portsmouth, Richmond, and Petersburg.[16] Some protests drew violence and arrests. But, one by one, the managers relented and dropped their Jim Crow policies.[17]

In Norfolk, Evelyn Butts helped back up the sit-in participants at the segregated lunch counters of the downtown W. F. Woolworth and W. T. Grant five-and-dime stores. James F. Gay, interviewed by a *New Journal and Guide* reporter in 2003, recalled being arrested with two other young men but that Butts and attorney Joseph A. Jordan Jr. "came and got us" before they could be taken to a police lockup.[18]

The tumult of the Civil Rights Movement in the 1960s invigorated Evelyn Butts. She and other members of the Women of Virginia's Third Force seemed to show up everywhere, making their voices heard on a plethora of issues, demonstrating against injustices, intent on breaking barriers every day. "When anything came up," Alveta V. Green recalled, "she had somebody, some man with a car, one of her drivers, and she could say, 'Go take this petition to this one and that one,' and she knew we would get it done. We were like her army."[19]

Borrowing a term from a famous speech by President John F. Kennedy, Butts aimed high in her quests. She called for "a New Frontier in Race Relations" in Norfolk,[20] but it looked easier for the country to launch an astronaut into the frontiers of outer space than it was for local White politicians to include Black citizens in decision-making about their own communities.

In the early 1960s, a semi-dormant urban renewal proposal threatened to fall out of its sleepy orbit and crash-land on Evelyn Butts' Oakwood neighborhood, demolishing nearby Rosemont and Lincoln Park as well. Now well-skilled at resistance, Butts counter-proposed a protective shield, at least for Oakwood.

Butts organized her Oakwood neighbors to show that they would take responsibility for renovating their own homes if the city paved the streets, installed sidewalks, and make other infrastructure improvements. In February 1961, she told the City Council that Black citizens wanted a voice in determining the future of their neighborhoods.[21] The city's new plan then split the project area, with many Oakwood community residents allowed to keep their homes but Rosemont and Lincoln Park being largely demolished and rebuilt.

"She saved this neighborhood out here," longtime neighbor Herbert Smith said of Butts.[22] "The city had put us on the demolition list" but "[s]he went around and got people to upgrade their bathrooms to get hooked into the city's water system. Then she went down to City Hall and stayed in their faces until they agreed."

Another longtime neighbor, Claude Stevens, remembered how Oakwood had been "nothing more than a set of houses sitting along muddy unpaved streets with septic tanks and outhouses. But because of the work and persistence of Mrs. Butts, it was brought to a respectable level by the city."[23] Other neighbors also credited Butts with prodding City Hall to build the nearby Norview Recreation Center in the mid-1960s, a facility which was then replaced by an even larger center in 2009.[24]

However, Butts wasn't done with making sure that the city lived up to its word. In November 1963, she helped start a Norfolk chapter of the Rev. Martin Luther King Jr.'s SCLC, and this local unit hosted a visit by King in June 1964, and gave him a tour of the Oakwood-Rosemont area.[25]

On July 1, 1964, Butts, attorney Joseph A. Jordan Jr., and several of their allies traveled to Washington, D.C., to meet with Robert C. Weaver, administrator of the Federal Housing and Home Finance Agency about school and redevelopment issues. Weaver then ordered an investigation into whether the Norfolk Redevelopment and Housing Authority and the School Board were collaborating to maintain segregation.[26]

In 1968, Butts' deep admiration of King and his style of nonviolence, as well as her semi-public expression of grief after his April 4 assassination, may have gotten her fired from a seasonal seamstress job. Stein's men's clothing store in downtown Norfolk had already hired Butts to do alterations on Easter clothing, a popular sale item at the time. Although she was upset about King's murder, Butts followed through on her tailoring commitment to Stein's, but she reported to work decked out with "all the buttons she could find from the March on Washington and anything to do with King."[27] She also talked nonstop about her sadness and anger. However, she made the store owners uncomfortable with her style of grieving and was not asked to return for the Christmas buying season later in the year.[28]

King's assassination weighed heavily on Evelyn Butts. As daughter Charlene Butts Ligon later recalled, "That day marked the first time I saw my mother cry in front of her children."[29]

Evelyn T. Butts was called "a wizard of grassroots organization" for her dynamic leadership and organizational skills and style, door-to-door canvassing, and civic participation efforts. She also carefully maintained rosters of registered voters and leaders. ©*Virginian Pilot All rights reserved. Distributed by Tribune Content Agency, LLC.*

# CHAPTER 15
## Demanding Democracy

Evelyn Butts' opportunity to strike at the poll tax came on November 29, 1963, when she agreed to be the plaintiff in a lawsuit being prepared by Joseph A. Jordan Jr. The civil rights attorney had considered another possible plaintiff, an elderly man remembered in history as only "Mr. Timberlake," who worked making deliveries by horse and wagon. Timberlake fell ill, though, so Butts stepped in.[1]

*Evelyn Butts v. Albertis Harrison, Governor, et al.* was destined to be a tough lawsuit to win. The U.S. Supreme Court had unanimously ruled in support of poll taxes in a 1937 Georgia lawsuit, *Breedlove v. Suttles*, which had been brought by a White man who refused to pay the tax. Judge Pierce Butler wrote: "Privilege of voting is not derived from the United States, but is conferred by the State and, save as restrained by the Fifteenth and Nineteenth Amendments and other provisions in the Federal Constitution, the State may condition suffrage as it deems appropriate."[2]

Several lawsuits also arose in Virginia, including a 1950 challenge by Jessie Butler, a Black resident of Arlington. All failed, usually with the courts citing the precedent of the 1937 *Breedlove* decision.[3]

Undaunted, Butts and Jordan persevered, even when lower courts ruled against their case, citing the *Breedlove* precedent among other reasons for denial. Along the way to the Supreme Court, the Butts lawsuit was combined with one from several low-income plaintiffs in northern Virginia to become *Annie E. Harper v. Virginia State Board of Elections.*

The courts, though, had not been the only avenues for challenging poll taxes. White allies were growing in number since the early 1940s because, as historian Peter Wallenstein writes, they "had a profound interest in curtailing the inordinate power of a few senior members of Congress—elected by unrepresentative electorates in the poll-tax states—to thwart progressive federal legislation on a wide range of issues."[4]

Labor unions, the ACLU, and the National Committee to Abolish the Poll Tax all tried repeated appeals to politicians, including early on to President Franklin Roosevelt and First Lady Eleanor Roosevelt. Nothing worked. They could not overcome the institutional unwillingness of both the Democrats and the Republicans to make poll taxes a high-priority issue,[5] especially against the wishes of White-supremacist Southern politicians, such as Virginia's Harry F. Byrd Sr.[6]

Byrd and other Southerners in Congress even fought against World War II legislation to exempt all men and women serving in the military from paying poll taxes. Any federal bill to eliminate poll taxes, Byrd argued, would "destroy the last vestige of States Rights and would give the New Deal, with its 3,000,000 civilian employees, the Negroes, and the labor unions control of the country."[7]

African Americans and voting-rights activists and organizations employed other tactics as well, especially at the grassroots level in local communities.[8] Tactics included paying poll taxes for Black citizens who could not afford these levies and conducting educational sessions on how to register, including how to prepare for literacy tests and similar roadblocks—initiatives similar to those organized by Evelyn Butts and the Women of Virginia's Third Force.

They made some inroads. As evidence, Buni notes that Black voter registration in Virginia climbed from 32,889 in 1944 to

38,020 in 1945,[9] although it still represented little more than 10% of the 365,717 voting-age Blacks in the state.

Energy for the voting-rights push, as well as other civil-rights causes, then began to pulse from new generations of African Americans, especially from Black veterans returning from service in World War II as discussed in Chapter 12.

American rhetoric about saving democracy overseas even spurred Black veterans to run for office.[10] As Buni writes, African Americans after World War II felt that "since Negroes had served the nation in its time of need, they should be allowed to do so in time of peace."[11]

Black voter registration continued to increase in Virginia. Numbers climbed to 43,945 in 1946; 45,737 in 1947; 53,035 in 1948; and 65,286 in 1949.[12] As a result, or perhaps in tandem, the late 1940s saw more Black Virginians willing to run for political office. The two trends fed on each other: rising Black voter registration encouraged new candidates, and the appearance of more African American candidates motivated more Black Virginians to pay their poll taxes and register.[13]

Among the Black candidates, World War II veteran Victor J. Ashe made one of the strongest runs for office in his 1946 campaign for Norfolk City Council. He lost, although the 3,101 votes he had garnered represented about two-thirds of Norfolk's 4,235 Black voter registrants that year. In Richmond, attorney Oliver W. Hill, also an Army veteran and well-known for his civil rights work with the NAACP, produced an even stronger showing in 1947, losing by only 101 votes for the Virginia House of Delegates.[14] Hill, though, continued to capture the political imagination of Richmond's Black community by running for the Richmond City Council in 1948. African American voter registration in that city soared from 6,374 in 1945 to 11,127 in 1948—and Hill won.[15]

During this time, national momentum for abolishing poll taxes also finally took hold. On August 27, 1962, Congress authorized sending the 24th Amendment to the states for ratification. That amendment, however, pertained only to poll taxes for federal elections, leaving the matter of poll taxes for state and local elections up to individual states to decide. Section 1 of the amendment read:

> The right of citizens of the United States to vote in any primary or other election for President or Vice President, for electors for President or Vice President, or for Senator or Representative in Congress, shall not be denied or abridged by the United States or any State by reason of failure to pay any poll tax or other tax.[16]

Ratification came swiftly, with the necessary 38 states giving their approval by January 23, 1964.[17] President Lyndon B. Johnson signed the amendment on February 4, 1964. Although the amendment went into effect, Virginia, North Carolina, Alabama, and Texas did not join in until years later, with Virginia ratifying the 24th Amendment in 1977. Five other Southern states never approved it.[18]

The 24th Amendment that banned poll taxes for federal elections had immediate and dramatic results in the 1964 election campaign between President Lyndon B. Johnson and Barry Goldwater. Voter registration among African Americans in the South climbed by more than 40% that year,[19] with up to 200,000 new Black voters in Virginia.[20]

Still, White political prognosticators predicted that African Americans would continue to be mostly powerless in state and local governments because Virginia maintained its poll tax system for such internal elections. A 1964 *New York Times* news report even noted that:

> The quickened Negro interest in national politics bears little immediate chance of Negro influence in state elections. Registrars in Portsmouth and Norfolk estimate that 10 per-cent or less of the new Negro voters are also paying

the $1.50-a year poll tax still demanded as a state and local voting requirement.[21]

On route to a national landslide in 1964, Johnson carried the Old Dominion with 558,038 votes to Goldwater's 481,334, a difference of 76,704. White journalists and political observers at the time apparently did not look far enough below the surface for signs of greater significance.

Historians, such as James R. Sweeney, came to ascribe Johnson's victory in Virginia largely to the rise in Black registration there.[22] But Sweeney also argues that the 24th Amendment likely produced another "important long-term result" in Virginia, a "surge in political activity among the state's African-American population."[23]

"It revealed that black Virginians had for the first time in the twentieth century become a major voting bloc," says Sweeney.[24]

The Byrd Organization apparently understood early on that a surge of African American voting strength hovered in the horizon. In 1963, the machine sought to protect its power—and to continue to thwart Black participation—by enhancing Virginia's poll tax before complete ratification of the 24th Amendment in January 1964. A special session of the General Assembly convened in November 1963 to maintain the poll tax for state and local elections and add another requirement, an annual residency certification form that a voter would submit six months before an election.[25] The new certificate, described by political scientist Ronnie Bernard Tucker as "an obstacle to voting more onerous than the poll tax"[26] allowed a citizen the option of voting only in federal elections without paying a poll tax but not in state and local elections unless the tax was paid.[27] The U.S. Supreme Court unanimously struck down Virginia's residency certificate in *Harman v. Forssenius* on April 27, 1964.[28]

By the time that the 24th Amendment was ratified in 1964, most Southern states had already abolished poll taxes for state and local elections. Alabama, Mississippi, and Texas joined Virginia in holding out—and a frustrated Butts and Jordan persisted with the poll-tax lawsuit that had been filed on November 29, 1963.

Friend Alveta V. Green lauded Butts as "courageous" for taking up the poll-tax fight against the powerful machine of political boss Senator Harry F. Byrd Sr. "Evelyn wasn't scared of the governor [a Byrd man, Albertis Harrison] or anyone. I can't think of anybody else who would have taken that up because we were afraid of losing our jobs or something like that," says Green, who had worked as a public school teacher at the time.[29] Friend Herbert Smith agrees, saying "She had more nerves than a red fox."[30]

In March 1964, four residents of Fairfax County, Virginia, joined the battle with a lawsuit similar to the one filed by Butts. They were Annie E. Harper, 79, a retired domestic worker; World War II veteran Curtis Burr, 41, a brick mason; Burr's wife Myrtle, 37; and Gladys A. Berry, 42, a divorced unemployed domestic worker; who were represented by attorney Allison W. Brown Jr. of the American Civil Liberties Union.[31]

Butts and Jordan encountered several legal setbacks in their suit and had to refile twice. Jordan and his partners, Edward Dawley and Leonard Holt, also had to fend off the Committee on Offenses Against the Administration of Justice,[32] which the Virginia General Assembly created to obstruct and intimidate supporters of integration, especially the NAACP and lawyers doing civil rights work.[33] The committee had tried to raid the law firm's offices in 1961 to seize all files dealing with the SCLC, Congress of Racial Equality, and Student Nonviolent Coordinating Committee. A lawsuit followed but dragged on, diverting the firm's resources for four years and causing the law partners to split apart.[34]

By late 1965, the Butts case was bundled with the suit from Fairfax County, and the combined lawsuit became known as *Harper et al. v. Virginia State Board of Elections et al.* Nationally

The U.S. Supreme Court's 6-3 decision to outlaw poll taxes for state and local elections was the lead story in *The Virginian-Pilot* newspaper on March 25, 1966. The front page included a photo of plaintiff Evelyn T. Butts celebrating with her attorney, Joseph A. Jordan Jr. *©Virginian Pilot. All rights reserved. Distributed by Tribune Content Agency LLC.*

famous civil rights attorney Thurgood Marshall, then serving as U.S. solicitor general under President Johnson, joined in as a friend of the court on the side of the plaintiffs.[35]

The U.S. Supreme Court heard oral arguments for *Harper v. Virginia* on January 24–25, 1966, with Butts as the only one of the five plaintiffs to attend. On March 24, 1966, the Court announced its 6–3 decision in favor of the plaintiffs. The majority opinion, written by Justice William O. Douglas, agreed that Virginia had violated the 14th Amendment by denying equal protection of the laws when the state had imposed the poll tax. Yet the court went even further by emphasizing and re-emphasizing that "Fee payments or wealth, like race, creed, or color, are unrelated to the citizen's ability to participate intelligently in the electoral process." The ruling continued:

> Voter qualifications have no relation to wealth nor to paying or not paying this or any other tax. ... To introduce wealth or payment of a fee as a measure of a voter's qualifications is to introduce a capricious or irrelevant factor. The requirement of fee paying causes an 'invidious' discrimination that runs afoul the Equal Protection Clause. ... For to repeat, wealth or fee paying has, in our view, no relation to voting qualifications; the right to vote is too precious, too fundamental to be so burdened or conditioned.[36]

Accounts vary about Butts' reaction. *The Virginian-Pilot* newspaper displayed a photo of a jubilant Butts and Jordan on page A1, but the news story reported a low-key response from Butts in contrast to the picture. The article quoted her saying that "the impact will just be that we will have more registered voters" and that there will be "better treatment" of Blacks trying to register or vote.[37] The report continued with a few more brief quotes from Butts:

"I was sewing this morning when a friend called me about the decision. I was very glad it was over," she said. "It will help the state of Virginia to progress."

"No, I don't feel much different today," she said in response to a question. "All the decisions on civil rights make me feel better."[38]

A forthcoming book on Norfolk's African American history reports that Butts "was unflappable as always."[39] Daughter Charlene remembers her mother being "pragmatic" and already focusing on "registering voters—thousands of them" through her efforts with the Women of Virginia's Third Force.[40]

Neighbor Herbert Smith, though, paints a more vivid and active image of Butts' reaction as he recalls, "Oh yeah, she was happy! My goodness, she's running around telling everybody, 'We won! We won!'"[41]

Either way, Butts poured herself into even more voter-registration efforts, and was reported to have guided the registration of 2,882 (although some news reports say "about 3,000") new African American voters during one six-month period.[42] It was through such work that the milestone victory at the U.S. Supreme Court in 1966 translated into political victory for Norfolk African Americans in 1968 with the election of Butts' friend, civil rights lawyer Joseph A. Jordan Jr., to the Norfolk City Council.

Jordan drew 13,551 votes out of a record 28,000-plus that June.[43] That put him second among eight candidates vying for three seats on the City Council—and it made him the first African American elected to Norfolk's council since Reconstruction. A year later, William P. Robinson Sr., a political science professor at Norfolk State College (now Norfolk State University), became the first African American from Norfolk elected to Virginia's House of Delegates.

The victories were sweet for Butts and Jordan and vindicated one of the essential points of their 1963 poll tax lawsuit: that during the post-Civil War Reconstruction Era, African Americans often won political seats in Virginia's General Assembly and on local city councils, but such victories had become impossible after Virginia's 1901–02 state Constitutional Convention imposed the poll tax and other voter-suppression devices. In his 1966 oral arguments, Jordan had told the Supreme Court, "Negroes have been effectively eliminated from any political power in Virginia—eliminated and separated from the political power which is now exercised by the whites exclusively, to the exclusion of Negroes."[44] Such exclusion was no longer the case.

The Jordan and Robinson victories were not the only local political dividends from the 1966 poll-tax ruling. African Americans made similar breakthroughs in nearby Portsmouth, electing Dr. James W. Holley III and Raymond Turner to that city's seven-member City Council in 1968. Black candidates also won that year in several other Virginia cities, including Fairfax, Buena Vista, Martinsville, Danville, and Staunton.[45] "The elimination of the poll tax opened the door of opportunity," said state Del. William P. Robinson Jr.,[46] who succeeded his father in Virginia's House of Delegates.

In addition, Butts' political power continued to rise. The Concerned Citizens for Political Education, which she now chaired, became a sought-after endorsement by candidates until the mid-1980s. Butts and other leaders of the group would interview candidates and then print its endorsements on yellow-colored paper under the title "Goldenrod Ballot." Political scientists Elsie M. Barnes and Ronald E. Proctor observe that, "In its heyday, in the 1970s, it was considered to be the most influential endorsement a candidate in Norfolk could receive. Such an endorsement would reap several thousand black votes."[47] The Concerned Citizens organization had evolved from the Committee of Forty and the Citizens United for Representative Government (CURG), the latter founded in the 1960s by Thomas W. Young who had succeeded his father, P. B. Young Sr., as publisher of the *Journal and Guide*, but then died in 1967.[48]

The Supreme Court's *Harper v. Virginia* decision has also had profound impact beyond its effects on Black voter registration and electoral victories, according to voting rights experts and legal scholars. Political historian Alexander Keyssar says the poll tax ruling was innovative in its use of the 14th Amendment and historic in that it drove "the final nail" into a "vestigial class limitation" on voting. "Almost two centuries after the nation's founding, economic restrictions on voting had been abolished in all general elections," Keyssar writes. "What once had been believed to be the most essential qualification for the franchise—the possession of property—officially had been judged irrelevant."[49]

Other commentators have asserted that the *Harper* ruling had even more beneficial effects on American democracy.

Voting rights attorney John Bonifaz, founder of the nonprofit, nonpartisan National Voting Rights Institute and the Free Speech for People organization, calls Butts a hero. He notes that her victory over the poll tax became a legal precedent for the 1972 *Bullock v. Carter* Supreme Court ruling that struck down high filing fees for candidates in Texas primaries.[50]

Ronnie L. Podolefsky, in her 1998 law review analysis, *Illusion of Suffrage: Female Voting Rights and the Women's Poll Tax Repeal Movement after the Nineteenth Amendment*, writes that the poll-tax decision should be regarded as an important intersectional achievement for poor African American women. The ruling, she says, "was not decided as an issue of race or of gender, but rather upon one manifestation of the intersection of the two: the inability to participate in the political process by reason of poverty."[51]

Historian Brent Tarter includes Butts in a book chapter about Virginia's modern transforming revolutionaries and revolutionary actions in his *The Grandees of Government: The Origins and*

*Persistence of Undemocratic Politics in Virginia.* Tarter notes that the *Harper* case (1966)—in combination with the 24th Amendment ban on poll taxes for federal elections and the 1965 Voting Rights Act—"finally removed the most important of the barriers that for more than a century had prevented most black Virginians and many poor white Virginians from registering and voting."[52] The *Harper* case, Tarter continues, was also among "the most import- ant of the civil rights cases that arose in Virginia" because it helped to fundamentally change "the course of American law and race relations" and begin "a slow transformation of the ways in which black people lived in their home state."[53]

Furthermore, Tarter suggests that the *Harper* (1966) case in combination with other Virginia civil rights cases helped to forge the Civil Rights Movement in Virginia as "both a democratic and a democratizing event."[54] By that, Tarter means that the movement in Virginia was democratic in that it sprung from the grassroots and from community activists—like Butts—who "pushed further and faster against racial segregation than the state's principal civil rights organization, the NAACP, wished to move," and "democ- ratizing in that it brought into the political process many people who had been disenfranchised or excluded from participation in public life."[55]

Such democratic and democratizing aspects of the Supreme Court's poll-tax ruling also amount to a victory for the political citizenship of all Americans. Bruce Ackerman and Jennifer Nou, in *Canonizing the Civil Rights Revolution: The People and the Poll Tax,* suggest that our society should celebrate the *Harper* victory because it codifies "a larger effort by the American peo- ple, during the 1960s, to create a more egalitarian democracy. *Harper* is not the product of an activist Court, but of an activist People."[56]

For Evelyn Butts, her victory over the poll tax went hand- in-hand with her overarching quest for African American self-determination. "Mrs. Butts realized the power of the vote. She realized how much of a voice Black people could have if only we had access to the vote," close friend Marie G. Young recalled for a news reporter a few years after Butts died.[57] Young conveyed similar information in a 2001 newspaper interview as well, emphasizing that Butts "was talking about the poll tax long before the lawyers carried it to the courts."[58]

# SECTION IV

*A New Beginning*

Evelyn T. Butts at age 51, as depicted in her official portrait as then-new member of the Board of Commissioners of the powerful Norfolk Redevelopment and Housing Authority. The City Council appointed her in 1975, making her the first African-American woman named to the board. *Courtesy of Norfolk Redevelopment and Housing Authority.*

# CHAPTER 16
## The Evelyn Butts Way

Getting people involved in our American democracy was the essence of the Evelyn Butts Way of leadership. Her approach made for a sharp contrast to the predominant Virginia Way elitist culture of top-down decision-making that offered mostly vague and paternalistic promises to African Americans and poor Whites of the sort: "Trust us. We'll take care of you down the road, but you must stay out of politics."

Many times, the Evelyn Butts Way of encouraging democratic participation equated to voting—and encompassed voter registration, education, and turnout activities. But not always, and not in the majority of instances. The Evelyn Butts Way included many forms of political citizenship, including organizing petition drives, picketing, speaking out at public forums, educating fellow citizens about the workings of government, and devising creative methods of giving courage and confidence to others.

In terms of leadership practices, Evelyn Butts exemplified citizen leadership and bridge leadership styles, especially those used by the crucial, adaptive grassroots leaders in the civil rights movement, as described by scholars Richard A. Couto and Belinda Robnett (as discussed in this book's introductory chapter).

At their core, Couto's citizen leaders are often "transforming leaders who engage others in efforts to reach higher levels of human awareness and relationships."[1] Their truest "distinguishing characteristic of leadership," Couto writes, is the "gift of trust" that has been bestowed upon them by the people with whom they work or work for.[2]

As for Robnett's bridge leaders, they generally operated "through one-on-one, community-based interaction" to help fellow citizens "cross the boundaries between the public life of a movement organization and the private spheres of adherents and potential constituents." In such work, Robnett says, bridge leaders were "critical mobilizers of civil rights activities." As longtime friend Alveta V. Green said of Butts, "She had a personality for winning people over because she could explain something so they would know what she was talking about."[3]

The Evelyn Butts Way of leading also entailed many "community mothering"[4] activities that came naturally to her, such as dual-purposing her kitchen get-togethers. Butts' kitchen served not only as a place for neighborhood women to share culinary tips but also an important civic space for nourishing grassroots activism. Butts practiced this form of political creativity in the 1950s and '60s, long before it was described by scholars such as Zenzele Isoke (1995) in *Urban Black Women and the Politics of Resistance* and Philomena Essed (1996) in *Diversity: Gender, Color, and Culture.*

Although Butts was not mentioned in such books, her entrepreneurship in combining homemaking talents with civic activism was noticed where it mattered most—that is, by Oakwood neighborhood women, especially those whom Butts connected to community issues or the Civil Rights Movement. For example, longtime neighbor Annette Bryant observed that Butts was always available to help with a question about cooking or sewing and then used such opportunities to pass on information about civil rights or politics. "And we always got a good laugh out of her. She was an all-around person. She loved her family, loved her neighborhood and, oh yeah, she could cook!" Bryant said.[5]

We can learn many such commonsense lessons from the Evelyn Butts Way of leadership. They include:

- Personal communication is effective for building momentum or support for a cause or a political candidate.

Butts' daughter, Charlene Butts Ligon, and surviving friends described Butts as tireless in going door to door and in telephoning neighbors about community, civil rights, and political issues.

- Even if you do not possess many tangible or financial resources, be creative and entrepreneurial with what you do have. When Norfolk's voter-registration office refused to give Joseph A. Jordan Jr. a copy of registered voters, Butts assigned herself to go to City Hall and copy the list of thousands of names by hand, a task that took about two months. She also acquired a voting machine to take to community meetings, where she demonstrated how to vote. And she tried to encourage voter registration through a PTA project until stopped by a school principal.

- Be persistent. Friends remembered how Butts would return to speak out at City Council meetings week after week after being initially turned down on requests. She applied similar persistence to making sure her neighbors paid their poll taxes, registered to vote, and showed up on Election Day. She and her lawyer, Joseph A. Jordan Jr., had to refile her poll tax lawsuit three times before it was combined with another lawsuit and considered by the U.S. Supreme Court.

- Don't be afraid to speak up when trying to right a wrong. Butts did not hesitate to challenge local and state government officials, newspaper editors, ministers, NAACP leaders, and anyone else she thought was blocking the way to social justice for marginalized people.

- Be a good organizer or have someone on your team who has such skills. And be prepared. Butts realized the importance of having lists of registered voters and used them well to recruit new voters and also for voter turnout on Election Day. She also prearranged for volunteer drivers to make sure that voters would show up at the polls. "This way," Butts explained to a newspaper reporter, "I can check who voted against the master list. Then I can go send somebody out to get those people."[6]

- Follow through on promises. If someone had a community- or government-related question that Butts could not immediately answer, she would find out the information and report back. As neighbor Rachel Smith said, "If we had a question about something and she didn't know, she said she'd look into it. And she did. ... Ms. Evelyn was the go-to person to get stuff done in Oakwood, and you saw every day she was doing something."[7]

- Stay connected with your base but also reach out to forge additional alliances. The Oakwood neighborhood remained as Butts' anchor throughout her many activities, but she built bridges across Norfolk through Women of Virginia's Third Force and the Concerned Citizens for Political Education, as well as to national civil rights organizations, such as the SCLC.

- Teach others. As a young mother, Butts learned about politics, community organizing, and cooking from the likes of her Aunt Roz, civic league mentor Annie Nickens, and other Oakwood neighborhood women. Over the years, she gave similar lessons to younger generations, even inspiring some of her mentees to eventually run for political office.

- Walk the talk. Butts had a reputation for never asking others to do things she had never done. Neighbors witnessed her working in the trenches alongside them every day. Sometimes this lesson was forgotten by younger politicians and activists. For example, by 1992, a year before Butts' death, several up-and-coming Norfolk leaders admitted to a news reporter that they did not include voter registration as part of their strategies because they thought other people and organizations would do it for them.[8]

• Build bridges—and not only to help people connect their lives with larger causes and movements. Butts also served as a bridge between her struggling low-income neighborhood and the Norfolk city government. She attended and spoke out at City Council and School Board meeting and returned home with information; she learned the rules of voter registration and gave confidence to thousands of first-time voters; she brought political candidates, Black and White, to her home for meals, showing neighbors that politicians needed them as much as they needed the ear of City Hall.

In addition, Butts encouraged neighbors and mentored others to join with her when she crossed bridges—and, like the heroic abolitionist Harriet Tubman, she returned time and time again to pull more people over the bridges with her.

As Butts built bridges to City Hall and to other neighborhoods, she also helped Oakwood neighborhood children build bridges to their future by encouraging them to do well in school, behave in the community, and use her name as a reference when looking for jobs. Friends knew that Butts was helping to build a different type of future for Norfolk's African Americans than they knew under Jim Crow domination.

Describing a few of her youthful encounters with Evelyn Butts, neighbor Rachel Smith recalled some incisive words from Butts that proved apropos to the overall African American quest for full citizenship and self-determination. As Butts often said:

"Your moment is going to come, but you got to be ready for it."

Evelyn Butts and other jubilant supporters of Joseph A. Jordan Jr. celebrate Jordan's 1968 swearing-in as the first African-American member of the Norfolk City Council since the Reconstruction Era some 80 years earlier. The "V" for victory hand symbols were for themselves and other Black voters as well as for Jordan because his election signified an important breakthrough in the long quest of Norfolk's African-American community for meaningful votes, full citizenship, self-determination, and a seat at the table of the city's highest governing body. Evelyn Butts, a friend and civil rights ally of Jordan, helped make Jordan's victory possible. With Jordan as her attorney, Butts successfully sued to end Virginia's poll tax on state and local elections, thereby knocking down a formidable barrier to Black voter participation. Butts also spearheaded many grassroots initiatives for voter registration, voter education, and voter turnout. In this photo, Butts stands in the third row back, slightly left of center, with her fingers in a "V" symbol pointing upward to the "C" in "COURTS." *Courtesy of Charlene Butts Ligon.*

# EPILOGUE
## Valorizing Leadership

I write this Epilogue in the year 2020, a momentous time in our nation's history—and our planet's.

As Americans, we endured an often bitter and deeply divisive presidential campaign season that tested our faith in democracy; as humans, we faced a worldwide existential crisis in the form of a lethal coronavirus known as COVID-19. These experiences were frustrating and sorrowful, yet they also contained some positive common denominators, especially in the crucial role of grassroots organizing and our ability to learn from such activism.

My book focuses on the grassroots leadership of Evelyn Butts but also discusses the continuum of grassroots African American resistance, resilience, and creative social justice advocacy. So, whenever I hear the words "grassroots organizing" these days, I can't help but reflect on the history I had explored and continue my learning. Attuned this way, I noticed many instances of grassroots organizing and civic engagement both in the presidential election and in community responses to the pandemic. I also saw that many of the activities recalled the spirit and resolve of Evelyn Butts and other grassroots leaders of the 1950s and '60s and of earlier eras. Later in this Epilogue, I will note examples of grassroots organizing and civic engagement from our 2020 election season and from diverse community responses to the COVID-19 pandemic.

From a historical perspective, 2020 was also a year for commemoration of progress in voting rights. This year, Americans observed the 150th anniversary of the 15th Amendment, which prohibited federal and state governments from denying voting rights based on race, and the 19th Amendment, which extended suffrage to women. Grassroots movements were heavily involved in promoting support for both amendments, including in Norfolk. For example, as discussed in Chapter 11 of this book, Norfolk's Colored Monitor Union Club issued a widely distributed *Equal Suffrage Address* making the local Black community "the first in the nation to argue for equal rights on a national level."[1] As mayor of Norfolk, I am proud of that heritage.

In this Epilogue I continue to reflect on the contributions of Evelyn Butts and how the lessons from her activism and leadership style continue to apply to my public life and our own times. The discussion that follows is divided into four sections:

- Valorizing Leadership
- The Grassroots Factor in 2020 Politics
- Grassroots Responses to COVID-19
- The Grassroots Heritage in my Public Life

**Valorizing Leadership**

My observations and thoughts from the past year, combined with my study of Evelyn Butts' grassroots activism, have helped me discern the outlines of a new leadership dynamic for public officials, which I now call "civic valorization." I chose this term to describe the process of validating and strengthening the political or civic contributions of people who are often marginalized with the aim of helping them to fully participate in the political or civic life of a community.

A unique characteristic of a valorizing leader is that they are or have been a public official, either elected, politically appointed, or administratively hired. I suggest this dimension because public officials usually possess the advantages of access to governmental decision-making and resources, publicity, and the community-wide stature often necessary to build helping coalitions. Marginalized people have historically lacked serious attention from public officials and have lacked meaningful access to the assets that public officials can harness.

"Valorization" is not a new term. In economics and the physical sciences, it refers to assigning or increasing value or converting some material into a more useful product. In human services, the phrase "social role valorization" entails "a dynamic set of ideas useful for making positive change in the lives of people disadvantaged because of their status in society," especially those with physical or cognitive impairments or who are elderly, according to the International Social Role Valorization Association, or ISRVA.[2]

The ISRVA continues:

A basic tenet of role-valorizing efforts is the notion that the good things any society has to offer are more easily accessible to people who have valued social roles. Conversely, people who have devalued social roles, or very few or marginally valued ones, have a much harder time obtaining the good things of life available to those with valued social status. Therefore valued social roles and the positive status that typically attends them are a key to obtaining the benefits inherent in any given culture.[3]

In the political or civic sphere, there are communities that are often disadvantaged or marginalized because of racial, gender, ethnic, economic, educational, environmental, geographic, religious, or historical factors and, therefore, are devalued by the mainstream. This can result in being excluded from or being given only watered-down access to meaningful opportunities for public decision-making or to "the good things any society has to offer." Sometimes, the people within disadvantaged groups buy into this devaluation of themselves or their community and their potential abilities. This dispiritedness can cause groups to further separate themselves from the mainstream, such as by not taking part in opportunities afforded to their fellow citizens or by not voting.

A valorizing leader seeks to turn around the devaluation of a group of people and help to validate them as full-fledged, valued citizens whose concerns are important to the overall civic life of a community. In the valorizing process, a public official meets the marginalized or devalued group on their own ground; listens and observes well; keeps an open mind while learning their concerns, values, and aspirations; and acts in good faith.

It can be difficult to observe valorizing leadership in action. However, I have collected a few news reports of activities by public officials that seem to represent the spirit of valorization. One of my favorites concerns Mayor Aja Brown of Compton, California.

When Brown became mayor in 2013, Compton was infamous for a host of severe urban problems, including a $43 million deficit, an unemployment rate double the state average for California and triple the national average, and an ongoing plague of gang violence.[4]

As Brown tells it, she asked certain influential community residents to help invite gang members to the table for a frank discussion about crime and violence.

Think about this. When we talk about marginalized people, gang members are so marginalized that we rarely even think about reaching out to include them in discussions on how to improve our communities.

In Compton, more than 75 male and female gang members came to the first meeting on a Sunday afternoon in June 2014. Brown said she was "amazed and humbled" and she introduced herself "to every single one of them and thanked them for coming.[5]

Brown described what happened next:

> I asked (them) to pull up a chair in a circle, because we are all equal and we're all connected. Many of [them] were shocked, yet touched. They couldn't believe that I actually

wanted to speak with them and that I treated them with such respect.

I was open and honest, and told them I was tired of seeing them kill one another. I asked them what I could do to help them stop the violence and if we could work toward peace for the benefit of our children. Their ask was simple: They needed jobs, opportunity, access and understanding. And in return, they would work with their individual neighborhoods to bring peace and create a community where our youth could thrive.

From that meeting, Compton Empowered was created—a community-based gang reduction and intervention initiative focused on empowering ex-gang members to take back their neighborhoods through peace treaties, unity activities and employment opportunities. We committed to work together on a cease-fire and started meeting every other Sunday.[6]

According to a news report from August 25, 2020, Brown and the gang members began meeting every other Sunday and worked on reducing violence by arranging cease-fire treaties among the gangs. As the effort evolved into a formal program, the city hired 13 ex-gang members to manage these "peace treaties" and to create opportunities for employment and for healthy activities for at-risk youth. As a result, Compton reports a 64% reduction in homicides without diverting additional funding to law enforcement or policing.[7]

My take on the work of Mayor Brown: She valorized many of the gang members and at-risk youth by showing that she would genuinely listen to them, treat them as fellow citizens, and make sincere efforts to address their concerns. She earned their trust.

Earning trust is part of the valorizing dynamic.

Evelyn Butts earned the trust of her neighbors and many more African Americans in Norfolk. However, in the valorizing leadership dynamic that I propose, Evelyn Butts—despite all of her leadership talents and energies—would not be defined as a valorizing leader during her heyday as a grassroots civil rights leader because she did not serve at that time as a public official in any capacity. (She was not appointed to the Norfolk Redevelopment and Housing Authority's Board of Commissioners until 1975 and to the Virginia Board of Housing and Community Development until 1982.)

Butts, though, knew the value of attaining validation from public officials and often sought valorization for her activities as well as for the concerns and untapped problem-solving potential of neighbors and other low-income African Americans. In July 1963, Butts called upon Norfolk's Citizens Advisory Committee, a 25-member biracial problem-solving commission, to recommend that the City Council appoint an African American to the School Board for the first time. As my book discusses in Chapter 13, the CAC agreed, and on July 30, 1963, the Council followed through with such an appointment.

Many times, though, Butts was denied validation, especially early in her activism and sometimes for simple good-citizenship activities. As I noted in Chapter 2, Butts, as president of a PTA chapter, set up a cardboard display to salute parents who were registered to vote in hopes that such recognition would motivate more parents to register. However, the school's principal removed the chart either on orders from the superintendent of Norfolk public schools or in fear of losing his job.

A public official, such as a mayor or school principal or superintendent, could be considered a valorizing leader—and a wise one, at that—if he or she recognized the civic contributions and concerns of Evelyn Butts and her neighbors and stepped forward in partnership to validate and strengthen the marginalized citizens and their communities.

Valorizing experiences can benefit public officials as well as marginalized people. By rejecting Butts' PTA display, the school principal lost an opportunity to gain the confidence and trust of parents, a dynamic that he could have tapped when striving to enhance the school's learning environment.

Good leadership matters at all levels of government, especially in an era when we cannot expect government or afford for it to solve many of our public concerns without authentic community engagement. Public officials would serve more effectively if they have the interest and ability to valorize our nation's grassroots civic leaders and work with them in strengthening our communities.

As a society, we do not seem to take our civic sector as seriously as we should. Scholars and political analysts probe the depths of government at the national, state, and local levels but often overlook or downplay the importance of the mostly volunteer formal and informal organizations, networks, and social systems that work at the grassroots level to stabilize and improve our communities. Evelyn Butts, as this book presents, excelled as a leader in the civic sector especially through three community groups that were her domain for many years: the Oakwood-Rosemont Civic League, made up of her neighbors; Women of Virginia's Third Force, which channeled the voter-participation energies of women citywide; and Concerned Citizens for Political Education, with citywide male and female membership.

I may be biased about the great value of grassroots engagement because of my own civic roots. You see, despite my multiple election victories as a Virginia state delegate, state senator, and Norfolk mayor, my greatest honor came at age 29 when my neighbors elected me president of the Beacon Light Civic League, the longest continuously operating neighborhood organization in Norfolk. As part of my Beacon Light leadership, we promoted nonprofit housing development and a community credit union as well as our decades-long tradition of encouraging neighbors to vote in every election.

Most importantly, it was through the Beacon Light Civic League that I learned the value of taking time to listen to the concerns and ideas of neighbors and that I practiced the democratic art of engaging fellow community members in finding solutions. I was becoming not only a steward for community improvement but also a servant-leader for advancing the tangible—but also often-intangible—hopes and aspirations of my neighbors.

## The Grassroots Factor in 2020 Politics

As I briefly mentioned in Chapter 2, several community leaders, including my grandmother, Ruby Rose Cooper, got me involved in voter-turnout efforts in our neighborhood, such as distributing flyers door-to-door as a youngster and driving people to the polls on Election Day as a young man. Voter-turnout activity is a major grassroots theme throughout my book as that was among Evelyn Butts' greatest passions and skills. So, I was excited to see the news media devote so many stories to the voter-turnout topic in the 2020 news coverage of the election—and I was delighted to learn that the 66.5% turnout rate[8] was the highest since 73.7% in 1900.[9]

The news stories that probably fascinated me the most were those reporting on the grassroots tactics deployed to get the vote out, especially in the swing states that saw narrow margins of victory, such as Georgia and Arizona.

According to many news reports, the resurgence of old-fashioned, door-to-door canvassing proved to be important to both Republican and Democratic voter-turnout initiatives, although each party took a different approach because of the COVID-19 pandemic. The GOP seemed to have the early advantage by not hesitating to send swarms of door-knocking volunteers into the neighborhoods; Democratic organizations and their liberal and progressive allies mostly held back because of virus concerns—opting for personal phone calls, text messages, online Zoom meetings, and postcard writing—before unleashing its street teams in October.[10]

"There's nothing that replaces the basic blocking and tackling of campaigns, and that's the pounding of the pavement, walking door to door," said Joe Gruters, chairman of the Florida Republican Party.[11]

As political scientists Alan S. Gerber and Donald P. Green observed in *Get Out the Vote: How to Increase Voter Turnout*, "Face-to-face interaction makes politics come to life and helps voters establish a personal connection with the electoral process."[12]

Meanwhile, Democrats like Danielle Friel Otten, a state representative in Pennsylvania, expressed frustration at not being able to fully utilize door-knocking, which she described as "our superpower" in past campaigns. She explained that door-to-door canvassing not only could risk the health of volunteers but also send the wrong public message about safety during the pandemic.[13]

Interestingly, the door-knocking tactic—which had been a staple of Evelyn Butts' crusades—had fallen out of favor among political operatives for many years in the 20th century.[14] "[S]hoe leather politics gradually faded away," Gerber and Green have noted. "The shift from door-to-door canvassing occurred not because this type of mobilization was discovered to be ineffective, but rather because the economic and political incentives facing parties, candidates, and campaign professionals changed over time."[15]

But as both parties revived door-knocking in 2020, Democratic grassroots organizers augmented their voter-outreach with dimensions that Evelyn Butts might well have appreciated. The enhancements entailed deeper conversations with voters, even electronically via telephone and Zoom before returning to face-to-face visits, and through "relational organizing,"[16] which involves peer-to-peer outreach by canvassers to people they already know.[17]

"Just knocking on the door doesn't turn out a voter. It's having a conversation with a voter that turns out a voter," contended David Broockman of the University of California Berkeley.[18]

For example, many political analysts and pundits cite the grassroots voter-registration and turnout work of a widespread coalition of grassroots groups led by Democrat Stacey Abrams, former minority leader of the Georgia House of Representatives. Abrams had lost her 2018 bid to become Georgia's first African American governor by 55,000 votes, or 1.4%,[19] the closest margin that state had seen since 1966. In 2020, Abrams and a coalition of progressive and young-adult voter outreach organizations, built upon the momentum she had achieved in 2018 to help deliver Georgia for presidential candidate Joe Biden by a 12,000-vote margin. That marked the first time Georgia went Democratic in a presidential election since Bill Clinton in 1992.

"This is not magic," said the Rev. Raphael Warnock. Instead, the Democratic gains in Georgia were the result of building grassroots coalitions and "hard work over time" as well as "a deep commitment to the noble idea that your vote is your voice and your voice is your human dignity," Warnock added.[20]

The grassroots voter-outreach activities in Georgia included two initiatives that Abrams founded to combat voter-suppression and to encourage voter-registration, especially among minorities and young adults—the New Georgia Project, which included young progressives, African Americans, Asian Americans, LGBTQ voters, and Latinx citizens, and the newer Fair Fight Action.

"You cannot expect national entities, DC-based organizations, to do real, authentic work in states," observed LaTosha Brown, co-founder of Black Voters Matter.[21]

Or as Marcus Ferrell, former deputy campaign manager for Abrams, explained, "Stacey understands that you have to talk to Georgians ... in a language that they understand and an authentic manner that they understand.[22]

In addition, Abrams aimed to persuade new voters "that voting can actually yield change."[23]

Indeed, Abrams and her allies invested in the hard, one-on-one work of building relationships at the grassroots level, just as Evelyn Butts had done in Norfolk along with many other pioneering Black community-based civil rights leaders in the 1950s and 1960s. As historian Martha S. Jones observes, "Abrams knows the political tradition out of which she comes, and she stands on the shoulders of generations of Black women.[24]

### Grassroots Responses to COVID-19

Grassroots activism in 2020 was not limited to politics. All across our country, citizens organized community-based responses to the impact that the deadly COVID-19 virus has had on local economies and the wellness needs of vulnerable populations. As reported by Noa Gafni, executive director of the Rutgers Institute for Corporate Social Innovation, "Grassroots organizations are key to addressing the coronavirus crisis.[25]

Here is just a small sampling of the diverse array of volunteer grassroots efforts from across our country:[26]

> The Ohio Service Workers Mutual Aid Fund came together to raise money for service workers who became unemployed when restaurants and small businesses shut down in Ohio.
>
> In New York City, the Nail Salon Worker Resilience Fund helped those who lost work when salons closed.
>
> Medics made and distributed hand sanitizer in Portland, Oregon.
>
> Knox Makes Masks coordinated the sewing of masks for health care workers in Knoxville, Tennessee.
>
> An outreach program in South Los Angeles set up a safe parking lot with security and portable toilets for people living in their motor vehicles.
>
> Uncertain about the federal COVID-19 relief package, residents of the Beloit, Wisconsin, area set up a Facebook group, Save Our Local Businesses … Now! to promote local merchants.
>
> Volunteers stepped forward in many locations, including the Rio Grande Valley of Texas, Chicago, Brooklyn,

Philadelphia, and San Diego to buy and deliver groceries to shut-ins who could not shop during the pandemic.

In my own city of Norfolk, grassroots efforts to make sure elderly shut-ins and other needy citizens had meals and groceries included the We Care Project affiliated with the Burning Bush Worship Center. The initiative began in March with outreach to 50 households. By September, volunteers assisted by the Norfolk Police Department served 900 meals to people in their homes and delivered 150 bags of groceries.

The willingness and generosity of many citizens and organizations at the grassroots level rises not only during crises but year-round. What I have observed reinforces my belief that public officials need to step away from the halls of government as often as they can, talk with citizens in their neighborhoods, and learn how best to valorize their civic concerns and aspirations.

### The Grassroots Heritage in my Public Life

In the preface of this book, I noted that I had never met Evelyn Butts but was mentored by some of the people she influenced, as well as by my grandmother, Ruby Rose Cooper. They, too, were dedicated to working toward a better future for new generations and believed it crucial to involve young people in community efforts. From them I learned persistence, how to speak up, organizational skills, and the importance of getting to know my neighbors and staying connected with them—and with many other fellow citizens all across Norfolk—as I rose in leadership. It all paid off not only in my electoral successes but, more importantly, in feeling that I have been able to represent a broad base of our citizenry as mayor.

My grandmother and mentors Horace Downing, George Banks, Minnie Madrey, Yvonne Miller, and so many others, never said, "this is how Evelyn Butts did it and you should do it that way too." Instead, they encouraged me to "hope someone"—as my grandmother used to say—by showing up where help was needed, by helping to give hope to other people, by knowing my neighborhood and making myself known, by remembering my roots but also having the self-confidence to believe "I belong here," by being persistent and focused in striving for social justice and a better world. In those ways, I feel connected to the Evelyn Butts Way.

It wasn't until after I was elected mayor of Norfolk in 2016—50 years after Butts achieved her great voting rights victory at the Supreme Court—did I start intentionally learning so deeply about Evelyn Butts. Yet, it is now clear that the quests for inclusiveness, self-determination, and full citizenship that Butts and her generation set forth also motivated and invigorated those who taught me. I became amazed at both what Butts had to overcome and how she transformed Norfolk. I also better understood the lessons from my elders and often think about them, as well as Evelyn Butts and her allies as I work on issues facing Norfolk today.

One of Butts' achievements—one that came even before her successful lawsuit against Virginia's poll tax—was her insistence upon community involvement in the city's redevelopment of her Oakwood neighborhood. Instead of massive demolition and displacement, Butts got the city government to agree to work in partnership with the neighborhood; the government rebuilt the streets and infrastructure, while residents renovated their homes.

Redevelopment of low-income communities continues as a concern in Norfolk. Details are greatly different from the 1950s and '60s, but Evelyn Butts' principle of community partnership remains the same. I will explain.

As mayor, I inherited the city government's momentum to redevelop three public housing neighborhoods that flank our burgeoning central business district. Redevelopment needs to happen because we cannot maintain the aging complexes indefinitely and the rising sea level is undermining some buildings and streets built upon a flood plain.

However, since becoming mayor, I learned that previous administrations had done little to include the public housing residents in the planning activities for this area, which had the bureaucratic name, "St. Paul's Quadrant." While the residents were being left out, it seemed that communication was occurring with everyone else, especially owners of downtown commercial property and leaders of our business community. The mantra was "we'll include the public housing residents when the time is right."

Having grown up in a low-income marginalized community (although not a public housing neighborhood), I knew that public housing residents resented the failure of the city to reach out to them. This exclusion also generated suspicion, anger, fear, and despair for their future. It made for a bad mix.

With such concerns in mind, I halted the planning process until we could devise better ways to include the voices of the public housing residents and work with them on improving their lives even before they have to move. I also said that we cannot proceed with any plans until we have made sure that everyone who could be impacted had a seat at the table. We must always ask: Who is at the table? Who is not here?

My efforts included arranging a series of discussions within the affected communities and mailing personal mayoral invitations to every household, marking the first time public housing residents received invitations from a Norfolk mayor for any event. After holding these meetings, our redevelopment plans became more comprehensive. They now encompass education, job training, wellness and health care, transportation, and recreational programs in addition to relocation assistance.

Through this holistic approach, called the Mayor's People First Initiative, we aim to enable residents to achieve their own aspirations and become partners in ending intergenerational poverty within their families. We also launched People First well before requiring anyone to move out of the three public housing communities and, of course, before any demolition began.

June 12, 2020, Norfolk removed the "Johnny Reb" statue from the top of the 80-foot Confederate monument in the central business district. The pedestal part of the monument soon came down as well. *Courtesy of City of Norfolk.*

In the inaugural year, our People First worked with 984 individuals in the Tidewater Gardens community to create Individual Development Plans that address the strengths, desires, and challenges that each person would like to address. As a result, we saw the average annual income in the Tidewater Gardens rise from $11,900 to $18,005. That's not all. The proportion of children involved in early childhood education programs rose from 38% to 68%, and the percentage of individuals with health insurance increased from 22% to 89%.

We pay for the Mayor's People First Initiative with proceeds from a 10-cent increase in the city's real estate tax. The tax hike, enacted in 2018, generates an additional $23 million a year for a variety of city operations, including $3.5 million annually for People First. Incidentally, I was reelected mayor in spring 2020 without any opposition, and the tax raise was not an issue.

Evelyn Butts was a strong advocate of social justice and human dignity in many ways. I think about her not only as we strive to improve the lives of public housing residents but also as we address so many other city issues. For example, her spirit, along with that of other civil rights activists, resonates through Norfolk's efforts to help remove the Jim Crow-era Confederate monuments that glorify men who committed treason against the United States in order to preserve slavery. Working with other Virginia cities as well as civic leaders, Norfolk encouraged the Virginia General Assembly to rewrite state laws that, until recently, made it difficult to remove these statues from public sites.

The new law took effect on July 1, 2020. However, in the weeks leading up to that date, the Black Lives Matter movement inspired angry public demonstrations against the monuments. Some of the protests damaged statues in a few Virginia communities—and even contributed to serious injury to protestors. Mindful of the risk for more injury, I directed our city manager to accelerate the safe removal of the 80-foot-high "Johnny Reb" monument that had stood prominently on downtown Main Street. I was able to accomplish this before the advent of the new law because I attained the concurrence of the Virginia Chapter of the Sons of Confederate Veterans by reaching out to them in advance. This avoided potential on-the-street conflicts between opposing protest groups as the nation has seen in some other cities. I cannot presume, of course, what Evelyn Butts would have done on the Confederate monument issue, but I do know that building bridges with unlikely allies was an essential component of her activism.

In 2016, I ran for mayor of Norfolk on a theme of unifying the diverse sections of our city and being mayor for all our residents. Since becoming mayor, I have continued my efforts and have become known throughout the city for my willingness to meet on the home turf of any community group in any part of the city, even in precincts that cast more votes for my two opponents than for me in the mayoral election. I try to help neighborhood leaders solve problems just as I would any other section of Norfolk, and I've received comments of appreciation for making them feel that their neighborhoods are important part of the city.

Leaders can do much to set the tone and expectations for public problem-solving—and to valorize them. I hope I am doing my part to make sure that all Norfolk citizens are treated with dignity, respect, and civility even when we debate the hot-button issues of our time. Here is an example of how such an approach succeeds—an example that also derives from the Black Lives Matter demonstrations against Norfolk's Confederate monument.

Our police chief, Larry D. Boone, decided to march beside Black Lives Matter supporters and reach out to many demonstrators for one-on-one conversations. The chief and I also involved ourselves in meaningful discussions with the community about what some call "defunding the police." In Norfolk, people and government agree that we need to reshape police training, priorities, and partnerships with other agencies, such as those that deliver mental health services.

My thoughts about building and maintaining good relations between our police department and our communities continue to evolve as I learn about best practices—and also about needless tragedies—from other cities across the country as well as from our nation's history in race relations and civil rights. As Chief Boone says, "the Norfolk Police Department views authentic community outreach as an opportunity to be transparent and a way to show the community it cares."[27] During my administration, the Police Department has expanded programs for nontraditional interactions between officers and young people, such as in sports, literacy, haircuts, and after-school meals. Our chief also believes that such visibility, coupled with authenticity, helps build citizen trust in the police, which, in turn, can help resolve tensions and reduce crime.

As mayor, I have launched other new initiatives to strengthen police-community relations. When a police officer shoots someone, we no longer assign our police department to conduct an internal investigation. Instead, we turn the investigation over to the Virginia State Police, which adds an element of outside review. We are also planning to establish a police-community relations commission, and we are awaiting legal guidance from the state on how to best create and empower such a panel under Virginia law.

My administration is continually seeking additional proactive opportunities as we aim to tackle some of the most deep-rooted and long-lasting social problems in our neighborhoods. My research into the life of Evelyn Butts and the context of her struggles has deepened my resolve to help our society, especially the most marginalized, move forward and upward over the minefields of systemic and structural racism that warp all of our major institutions, including education, health care, housing, finance, criminal justice, and the media.

In June 2020, I led our City Council in establishing our Mayor's Commission on Social Equity and Economic Opportunity because I knew we needed to do much more to remedy our community divisions than removing Confederate statues from prominent public perches. I said at the time—and still believe—that many of our citizens continue to experience "some of the same economic and social inequalities of 50-plus years ago" and that "the bigger conversation for all of us is addressing poverty and social and economic inequalities in housing and wages and homeownership and access to health care for black and brown people."[28]

Studying the life and contributions of Evelyn Butts has made me better appreciate the importance of leaders in setting standards for ethics and achievement, modeling the values of human rights, and setting the tone for community discourse and problem-solving.

Although I never met Evelyn Butts, I have learned so much from her. That is why I want to do all I can to make sure that Evelyn Butts and her crusades will never be forgotten in Norfolk as we move forward in making Norfolk a more dynamic and inclusive city. Specific issues may differ from her era to ours, but the underlying principles and values remain the same: dignity, respect, self-determination, equality, equal justice, and dedication to uplifting the lives of fellow citizens.

Butts' life and contributions help us to better understand what we have inherited and how to continue transforming the legacies of earlier generations into lessons for future generations.

How Butts organized and activated her quests also remains relevant. Her actions not only provide lessons about how the Civil Rights Movement thrived at the local level. Her accomplishments can also teach and inspire us if we expand our notions about leadership and explore ways to adapt her methods to today's lifestyles and concerns. Evelyn Butts changed the course of history by knocking out the suppressive poll tax, plus knocking on doors to motivate thousands of people to vote, thereby helping African Americans get elected in Norfolk for the first time since the Reconstruction Era. As a result of her accomplishments, the style and substance of Norfolk's government changed for decades to come.

Hand-in-hand with Butts' social justice advocacy was her tireless work to register, educate, and motivate voters to turn out. The results from such voter-participation work made the Norfolk government more inclusive, and we continue to build upon that inclusiveness for the common good of all. Butts holds an uncommon place in history because she was among a handful of plaintiffs who beat back the poll tax in a landmark U.S. Supreme Court case. Therefore, her name has been permanently and rightly inscribed into history books and law journals. It is the other work that Butts did as a civil rights bridge leader before and after the court's 1966 poll-tax decision that makes her life so interesting and enriching to study. In that regard, Butts was not so rare—and that thrills me because I maintain faith in the potential of fellow citizens to refresh our democracy.

As I've studied her life, I have gained not only a better appreciation for Butts' social justice activism and transformational grassroots civil rights leadership. I also see how her efforts were undergirded with persistence, great organizational abilities, and an independence of spirit. She was a presence to behold. She generously shared the force of her agency with neighbors and others trying to change the politics and policies of her time. Butts always encouraged them to believe that their voices, actions, and lives mattered, and to live in ways that made a difference. That was the essence of the Evelyn Butts Way.

Yet, as I finish writing this portion of my book, I am also saddened. Had Evelyn Butts lived into old age, she would have celebrated her 96th birthday on May 22, 2020. She died, though, at age 68 in 1993. More members of her great generation of civil rights activists are leaving us every day as well.

We owe it to history and to future generations to discover many more grassroots leaders and activists from the era of the Civil Rights Movement and document their stories before it is too late. For continued progress, we need to understand what they can teach us about citizen leadership, community self-determination, and changing the course of history.

—Kenneth Cooper Alexander
Norfolk, Virginia
December 8, 2020

# ACKNOWLEDGMENTS

When I embarked on my doctoral work at Antioch University's Graduate School of Leadership and Change in 2015, I knew I would eventually share the fruits of my studies with my hometown of Norfolk, Virginia, which has given so much to me. I did not know at the time, though, how much the history of Norfolk would help me choose my dissertation topic, sharpen my insights about what my forebears endured, and strengthen my resolve to pass these lessons forward to future generations.

Delving into the life and activism of voting-rights champion Evelyn T. Butts and her persistent fight for rights of poor and marginalized people was challenging, stimulating, and rewarding; yet my journey was never a lonely one. Throughout my quest, I was blessed with the support, patience, and enduring love of my wife, Donna, and our two sons, Kenneth II and David, young men who will soon begin their own pursuits in higher education. Their embrace of my studies constantly reminded me of how important family and community have been throughout my life. This remarkable achievement is also theirs.

My deepest thanks also go to my late parents, David Alexander and Ruby Rebecca Cooper, and my late grandmother, Ruby Rose Cooper, and to many community mentors. A complete list of people who gave me positive guidance from childhood through my formative years in the public and political arenas might resemble a village telephone book, but I must single out a few. They include Elwood "Coach" Williams, the former director of the Southside Boys & Girls Club; the late George Banks; Izaak David Glasser,

223

longtime family friend; the late Horace C. Downing; the late Minnie Madrey; the late Yvonne B. Miller, Ph.D., the first African American woman elected to the Virginia House of Delegates, the first African American woman elected to the Senate of Virginia, and the first to chair a Virginia General Assembly standing committee; and my Antioch Missionary Baptist Church family.

I also owe a great debt of gratitude to so many other people who were generous with their time and insights, including Dr. Stephen Shaw, faculty research librarian at Antioch's Graduate School of Leadership and Change; and Norfolk City Hall clerk's staff, especially Mary Lou Stone, special assistant to the Mayor, and Norfolk Public Library, especially Troy Valos, special collections librarian, Sargeant Memorial Collection.

The resources at Old Dominion University's Patricia W. and J. Douglas Perry Library and Norfolk State University's Harrison B. Wilson Archives, and especially the efforts of NSU's Annette Montgomery, proved invaluable.

There are so many friends to thank, but I want to give special recognition to Michael Knepler and his wife, Barbara Taychert, both retired journalists, and Dr. Battinto Batts, Journalism Fund director, Scripps Howard Foundation, all of whom rendered much constructive advice about writing, and to Rodney Jordan for sharing archival material from his late uncle, Joseph A. Jordan Jr., who was Mrs. Butts' close friend and attorney. Thanks, too, to political scientist Dr. Leslie A. Caughell of Virginia Wesleyan University as well as to the university's Center for the Study of Religious Freedom, to historian Dr. Charles Ford of Norfolk State University, and to my great team of employees at Metropolitan Funeral Service for easing my professional burdens to allow me more time for my studies.

I found enthusiasm and encouragement for my study of Evelyn Butts from so many people but especially from Dr. Laurien Alexandre, provost, professor, and director of Antioch's Graduate School of Leadership and Change, my leadership studies adviser, Dr. Jon Wergin, professor of Education Studies in Antioch's Graduate

School of Leadership and Change, and my dissertation committee members, Dr. Philomena Essed, professor of Critical Race, Gender and Leadership Studies in Antioch's Graduate School of Leadership and Change; Dr. Elizabeth L. Holloway, professor of psychology in Antioch's Graduate School of Leadership and Change; and Dr. Tommy L. Bogger, professor of history and university archivist at Norfolk State University. Each of you presented me with thoughtful challenges and pushed me to clarify where needed, sharpen my focus in various sections, and made sure I produced a dissertation that I could build upon for future publication. Hence, *Persistence: Evelyn Butts and the African American Quest for Full Citizenship and Self-Determination*.

Of course, I never would have gotten very far in this project if not for the people who knew Evelyn Butts and agreed to be interviewed. Thank you not only for sharing your experiences but also for providing priceless personal and historical context for what happened in Norfolk during the years of Evelyn Butts' heyday as a grassroots activist.

The names of my interviewees are scattered throughout this book, but I honor them here with the following rollcall:

*Alveta V. Green*, a retired educator and longtime friend of Evelyn Butts. She hosted many meetings in her home that Butts led or in which Butts was involved. Green's late husband, Walter H. Green Sr., was also a stalwart ally of Butts in many of her activities.

*Herbert Smith*, a retired brick mason and longtime neighbor of Evelyn Butts. He frequently volunteered to drive Butts to many of her public appearances (e.g., City Council meetings) and other events.

*Rachel Smith*, daughter of Herbert Smith and a longtime neighbor of Evelyn Butts. She provided memories of how neighborhood children looked up to Butts and appreciated her efforts.

*Ellis W. James*, a longtime civil rights activist in Norfolk. His late daughter, Karen James, was one of the "Jordanettes," a group of teenaged and pre-teen girls who campaigned for Butts' ally,

Joseph A. Jordan Jr., and wore outfits made by Evelyn Butts. Ellis W. James also knew Jordan's father, Joseph A. Jordan Sr.

*Walter Dickerson*, a World War II veteran, longtime neighborhood activist, and husband of Lola Dickerson. He observed Evelyn Butts' activities over the years.

*Lola Dickerson*, longtime secretarial employee of Tidewater Legal Aid, precinct poll worker, neighborhood activist, and wife of Walter Dickerson. She observed Evelyn Butts' activities over the years. She had been in declining health when I interviewed her and died on January 17, 2019.

*G. Conoly Phillips*, retired businessman and former Norfolk City Council member. He knew the grassroots power of Evelyn Butts' voter-participation activities. He died on April 22, 2020.

*Charlene Butts Ligon*, the youngest and only surviving daughter of Evelyn Butts. She wrote a self-published memoir, *FEARLESS: How a Poor Virginia Seamstress Took On Jim Crow, Beat the Poll Tax and Changed Her City Forever*, about her mother and for which I had the honor to write the foreword. Ligon's 2017 book was valuable in several ways, including providing biographical information about Butts' childhood and years as a struggling young mother and emerging activist, information that could not be collected from any other source. Ligon's book also offered behind-the-scenes looks at some of Butts' activities, eyewitness accounts that were mostly not reported in contemporaneous newspaper stories. My personal interview with Ligon added further details and clarifications.

Because each of you so generously shared your stories, you have helped our Norfolk community and students of the Civil Rights Movement in general understand how much we have benefited by the social justice activism, leadership, and legacy of Evelyn T. Butts and her persistent fight for the rights of poor and marginalized people in America.

# ENDNOTES

## PREFACE

[1] Ligon (2017) p. 73
[2] "The Referendum" (1958); "Referendum Post Mortem" (1958); Littlejohn & Ford (2012) p. 100
[3] Altman (2017)
[4] Colvin (1996)
[5] Roberts (2006) B-3
[6] Barnes & Proctor (1994)
[7] McCartney (2018)
[8] Virginia Museum of History & Culture (n.d.)
[9] Moye (2013) p. 9
[10] Garrow (2005) p. 196
[11] Alston & McClellan (2011) p. 54
[12] James (1997) p. 97
[13] Robnett (1997) p. 191
[14] Collier-Thomas & Franklin (2001) pp. 3–4
[15] "What the Life of Martin Luther King, Jr. Has Meant to Me" (1986)

## CHAPTER 1 Evelyn Butts and Her Quests

[1] Knepler (2001a)
[2] A. V. Green, personal communication (June 1, 2018)
[3] Chadwick (1969)
[4] "Legendary Local Activist" (1993)
[5] Bennett (1967) p. 83
[6] Robnett (1997) pp. 19 & 143

## CHAPTER 2 Life and Leadership

[1] Ligon (2017) pp. 11–12
[2] Ligon (2017) p. 14
[3] Ibid., p. 15
[4] Ibid., pp. 15–17
[5] Ibid., pp. 15–18
[6] Ibid., pp. 17–18
[7] Ibid., pp. 18–19

227

[8] Bogger, et al. (2018) p. 231

[9] Ligon (2017) pp. 17–20

[10] C. B. Ligon, personal communication (January 11, 2018)

[11] Ibid. (April 1, 2019)

[12] Ibid. (January 11, 2018)

[13] Ligon (2017) p. 20

[14] C. B. Ligon, personal communication (January 11, 2018); H. Smith, personal communication (February 20, 2018)

[15] Knepler (2001)

[16] Isoke (2013) p. 35

[17] Essed (1997) p. 97

[18] Ligon (2017) pp. 187–193

[19] Ibid., p. 20; Swift (1993); E. W. James, personal communication (February 7, 2018)

[20] Ligon (2017) p. 20

[21] Ligon (2017)

[22] Knepler (2001)

[23] "A Worthy Celebration" (2006)

[24] Ligon (2017) pp. 100–101

[25] Bogger et al. (2018) pp. 262–266

[26] Barnes & Proctor (1994) p. 91

[27] G. C. Phillips, personal communication (November 28, 2018)

[28] Colvin (1993) p. 1

[29] Swift (1993) p. D-1

[30] A. V. Green, personal communication (June 1, 2019)

[31] as quoted in Knepler (2001a)

[32] H. Smith, personal communication (February 20, 2018)

[33] Ibid. (February 19, 2018)

[34] Ibid.

[35] Bogger, et al. (2018) p. 289

[36] H. Smith, personal communication (February 20, 2018)

[37] A. V. Green, personal communication (March 1, 2018)

[38] H. Smith, personal communication (February 20, 2018)

[39] Colvin (1996)

[40] A. V. Green, personal communication (March 1, 2018, & June 1, 2018)

[41] C. B. Ligon, personal communication (January 11, 2018)

[42] as quoted in Ligon (2017) p. 94

[43] as quoted in Knepler (2001a)

[44] Isoke (2013) p. 81

[45] T. L. Bogger, personal communication with E. T. Butts (1989); Ligon (2017) p. 76

[46] A. V. Green, personal communication (March 1, 2018)

[47] C. B. Ligon, personal communication (January 11, 2018)

[48] Coit (1979)

[49] Spratley, personal communication via Ligon (February 15, 2019)

[50] Ligon (2017) p. 188

[51] C. B. Ligon, personal communication (January 11, 2018)

[52] H. Smith, personal communication (February 20, 2018)

[53] C. B. Ligon, personal communication (January 11, 2018)

[54] A. V. Green, personal communication (June 1, 2018)

[55] Ibid.

[56] Ligon (2017) pp. 185–186
[57] R. Smith, personal communication (February 20, 2018)
[58] Ibid.
[59] Ibid.
[60] Ibid.
[61] Ibid.
[62] Couto (1995) p. 12
[63] Ibid.
[64] Ibid., p. 13
[65] Ibid.
[66] Couto (1995) pp. 13–14
[67] Robnett (1997) p. 20
[68] Ibid., p. 19
[69] Ibid., p. 21
[70] Ibid., p. 143
[71] Ibid., p. 19
[72] Ibid., pp. 20–21
[73] Robnett (1997)
[74] A. V. Green, personal communication (June 1, 2018)
[75] S. M. Whitley, personal communication (June 2, 2018)
[76] B. Thompson, personal communication (June 2, 2018)

## CHAPTER 3 Political Citizenship and Self-Determination

[1] Charlene Butts Ligon, personal communication (January 11, 2018)
[2] as quoted in Ligon (2017) p. 91
[3] T. H. Marshall (1964) p. ix
[4] Ibid., pp. 71–72
[5] Eric Foner (1998) p. xvii
[6] "You've got it" (n.d.)
[7] Bloom (2019) p. 177
[8] Brooks & Houck (2011) p. 62
[9] Moye (2011) p. 159
[10] Ibid., p. 166
[11] Dennis (2005) p. 197
[12] Ibid.
[13] Ibid., p. 196
[14] Ibid.
[15] Bogger et al. (2018) p. 257
[16] Ligon (2017) p. 117
[17] Moye (2011) p. 148
[18] Ibid., pp. 151–152
[19] Ibid.

## CHAPTER 4 The Virginia Way

[1] J. D. Smith (2002) p. 4
[2] J. D. Smith (2002) p. 4); Titus (2011) p. 11; Hayter (2017)

[3] Taylor (2002); Hall (2001) pp. 81–82

[4] Hall (2001) p. 83

[5] Titus (2011) p. 11–12

[6] Ogline (2007) p. 37

[7] Thomas (2019) p 160

[8] J. D. Smith (2002) p. 10

[9] Epps-Robertson (2013) p. 138

[10] J. D. Smith (2002) p. 4

[11] as quoted in Tarter (2013) p. 314

[12] J. D. Smith (2002) p. 128

[13] Ibid., p. 133

[14] Ibid.

[15] Ibid., p. 273

[16] Wynes (1961) p. 89

[17] Tarter (2013) p. 329

[18] Heinemann (1996) p. 62

[19] J. D. Smith (2002) pp. 108–109

[20] Ibid.

[21] as quoted in J. D. Smith (2002) p. 167

[22] Bogger et al. (2018) p. 182

[23] Ibid., p. 266

[24] Heinemann (1996) p. 80

[25] Ibid., p. 256

[26] Rose (2008) p. 465, fn. 10

[27] as quoted in Heinemann (1996) p. 329

[28] Ibid., p. 256

[29] Ibid., p. 27

[30] Ibid., p. 63

[31] Ibid., p. 476–477, fn. 9

[32] Berman (2015) p. 122

[33] Equal Justice Initiative (2017) *Lynching in the South, Table 1*

[34] L. M. Smith (2001) pp. 270–271; Heinemann (1996) p. 329

[35] J. D. Smith (2002) p. 297

[36] Thomas (2019) pp. 23, 160

[37] Martin & Shear (2014)

[38] J. D. Smith (2002) p. 258

[39] Ibid., p. 275

[40] as quoted in Suggs (1988) p. 126

[41] as quoted in J. D. Smith (2002) p. 275

[42] Ibid., p. 276

[43] Parramore et al. (1994) p. 349

[44] Ibid., p. 347

[45] D. M. Watson (2017)

[46] "Support grows for 'our man Joe'" (1968)

[47] Colvin (2003b)

[48] "People Express Desire For Change" (1968)

## CHAPTER 5 Born in Virginia

[1] Lichtman (2018) pp. 164–165
[2] Meacham (2018) p. 36
[3] Tarter (2013) p. 6
[4] Senate Clerk's Office (n.d.) para. 1
[5] Tarter (2013) Chapter 1
[6] Ibid., p. 31
[7] Gottlieb (2018); Virginia Historical Society (n.d.)
[8] Tarter (2013) p. 24
[9] Ibid., p. 13
[10] McCartney (2018)
[11] Tarter (2013) p. 31
[12] Ibid.
[13] Welch (2004) p. 16
[14] Ibid., p. 8
[15] Virginia Museum of History & Culture (n.d.)
[16] Tarter (2013) p. 31
[17] Ibid., p. 332
[18] Foner (1998) p. 74; Woodward (2002) p. 70; Wynes (1961) pp. 109, 125, 145
[19] as quoted in Kluger (2004) p. 502
[20] Bogger (1982) p. 10; J. D. Smith (2002) p. 36
[21] Bly (2019) para. 1
[22] Bly (2019)
[23] Ibid.
[24] Ibid.
[25] Foner (1998) p. 75; Glass (2018); M. S. Jones (2018) pp. 131–132; State Historical Society of Missouri (n.d.)
[26] Africans in America: Judgment Day (n.d.)
[27] Foner (1992), p. 55; M. S. Jones (2018) pp. 5, 152
[28] Meacham (2018) pp. 98–100
[29] as quoted in Lepore (2018) p. 319
[30] Tarter (2013) p. 244
[31] Parramore, Stewart, & Bogger (1994) p. 245
[32] as quoted in Woodward (2002) p. 96
[33] Meacham (2018) p. 94
[34] Ibid., pp. 95–96
[35] Ibid., pp. 96–97
[36] Guelzo (2018) Race and Reconstruction section, para. 2
[37] Foner (1992) p. 55; Meacham (2018) pp. 109–110
[38] Foner (1992) p. 63
[39] Lichtman (2018) pp. 94, 137; Ogden (1958)
[40] as quoted in Tarter (2019) p. 46
[41] Breitzer (2015); Lichtman (2018) p. 94; Woodward (2002) p. 84
[42] as quoted in J. D. Smith (2002) p. 151
[43] Ibid.
[44] Tarter (2013) pp. 258, 260, 346–350
[45] Wynes (1961) p. 102
[46] Ibid.
[47] as quoted by J. D. Smith (2002) p. 33

48 J. D. Smith (2002) p. 33
49 Ransby (2003) p. 39
50 Tarter (2013) p. 318
51 Lewis (1991) p. 156; J. D. Smith (2002) p. 259; Wynes (1961) pp. 88–89, 116–119
52 Wynes (1961) p. 88
53 Ibid., pp. 88–89, 116–119
54 Lewis (1991) p. 156
55 Wynes (1961) (pp. 116, 119
56 Bogger et al. (2018) p. 139
57 Ibid., pp. 183–184
58 Kneebone (2016)
59 Kluger (2004) p. 88
60 Jones (1982) p. 58
61 Ibid.
62 as quoted in Wynes (1961) p. 95
63 Dabney as quoted in Wynes (1961) p. 122
64 as quoted by Wynes (1961) p. 102
65 Martinot (n.d.)
66 Buzard-Boyett (2011) p. xvi
67 Tarter (2013) p. 313
68 Kluger (2004) p. 86
69 Klarman (2004) pp. 16–23; Wynes (1961) p. 76
70 Lewis (1991) p. 22
71 Woodward, (2002) p. 140
72 Kluger (2004) p. 88
73 Parramore et al. (1994) p. 276; J. D. Smith (2002) p. 140; Bogger et al. (2018) pp. 177–178
74 Kluger (2004) p. 88
75 Ibid.
76 Ibid., p. 213
77 Lewis (1991) p. 156
78 L. M. Smith (2001) p. 8
79 Tarter (2013) p. 258
80 J. D. Smith (2002, p. 234
81 Lindgren (1993) p. 9
82 Maxwell (2010) p. 2
83 Bayless (2011); Tarter (2013) p. 349
84 Tarter (2013) p. 349
85 Bayless (2011) p. 20
86 Ibid., p. 101
87 Smith (2001) p. 27
88 Eichelman (1976) pp. 456–458; Tarter (2013) pp. 345–349; Springston (2018); Huffman (2019); Minton 2020)
89 Huffman (2019)
90 Minton (2020)
91 Huffman (2019)
92 Wynes (1961) p. 143
93 as quoted in J. D. Smith (2002) p. 289
94 Ibid.
95 Ibid.

[96] Ibid.
[97] Ibid.


## CHAPTER 6 Let the Men Lead

[1] Modern History Sourcebook (n.d.) para. 2
[2] Ligon (2017) p. 86; "Many Witnesses Are Heard" (1960)
[3] Alston & McClellan (2011) pp. 52–55; Gilkes (1994) p. 232; Isoke (2013) pp. 14–26, 33–35; Zinn & Dill (1994) pp. 4–5
[4] as quoted in Walker (2012) p. 1023
[5] as quoted in Edds (2018) p. 298
[6] Olson (2001) p. 35
[7] Davis (1983) p. 175
[8] Ibid., p. 70
[9] Davis (1983) p. 7
[10] Ibid., p. 175
[11] Ibid.
[12] McGuire (2011) p. xviii
[13] Hale (1998) p. 32
[14] Olson (2001) p. 35
[15] Ibid., p. 35
[16] Hale (1998) p. 32
[17] Wallace-Sanders (2008) p. 2
[18] J. D. Smith (2002) p. 110
[19] Lewis (1991) pp. 56–57
[20] as quoted in Lewis (1991) pp. 56–57
[21] J. D. Smith (2002) p. 49
[22] Ibid.
[23] Lewis (1991) p. 191; Odum (1943) pp. 67–95; Parramore et al. (1994) p. 339; Schlegel (1991) p. 194
[24] Zeitz (2017)
[25] Armstrong (2012); Lin (2013); Winter (2010)
[26] Winter (2010)
[27] McGuire (2011) p. 59
[28] T. L. Jones (1982) p. 60; Lewis (1991) p. 190; McGuire (2011) pp. 40–43, 58–61
[29] McGuire (2011) p. 59
[30] Ibid., pp. 60–61
[31] Ransby (2003) p. 127
[32] Olson (2011) pp. 117–118
[33] Lewis (1991) p. 157
[34] Ibid., p. 158
[35] Ibid., p. 178
[36] Ibid.
[37] Ibid.
[38] Ibid.
[39] Keyssar (2009) p. 5
[40] Lichtman (2018) p. 16
[41] Ibid., p. 100

[42] Collier (1992) p. 22

[43] Lichtman (2018) p. 111

[44] Keyssar (2009); Lichtman (2018)

[45] McDaid (2018) The Suffrage Argument section, para. 4

[46] as quoted in Lichtman (2018) p. 117

[47] Keyssar (2009) p. 169

[48] Buni (1967) p. 73

[49] McDaid (2018) Suffrage and Race, para. 1

[50] Lichtman (2018) p. 104

[51] Ibid., p. 117

[52] Terborg-Penn (1998) pp. 108–109, 120

[53] Hale (1998) p. 108

[54] Olson (2001) p. 46

[55] McDaid (2018) Suffrage and Race, para. 2; Terborg-Penn (1998) p. 125

[56] L. M. Smith (2001) p. 44

[57] Buni (1967) p. 75

[58] Jones (2019)

[59] Tarter (2013) p. 270

[60] Buni (1967) p. 78; Terborg-Penn (1998) p. 154

[61] J. D. Smith (2002) pp. 58–59

[62] J. D. Smith (2002) p. 58

[63] Ibid., p. 252

[64] Ibid.; L. M. Smith (2001) p. 177

[65] J. D. Smith (2002) p. 252

[66] Ransby (2003) p. 106

[67] Ibid., pp. 114–115

[68] Ibid., p. 189

[69] SNCC; Crosby (2011) p. 374

[70] Thompson (2013)

[71] Height (2001) p. 90

[72] Armstrong (2012) p. 44

[73] Robnett (1997) p. 97

[74] Theoharis (2011) p. 408

[75] Ibid.

[76] Ibid.

[77] Knepler (2001a)

[78] "Third Force Women" (1970); "Voters Club Tours General Assembly" (1968)

[79] A. V. Green, personal communication (March 1, 2018)

[80] H. Johnson (1966)

[81] Robnett (1997) pp. 36, 40–44, 51, 59–60

[82] Swift (1993)

[83] A. V. Green, personal communication (March 1, 2018)

[84] Ibid.

[85] H. Smith, personal communication (February 20, 2018)

[86] Ligon 2017 pp. 86–87; "Many Witnesses Are Heard," 1960)

[87] "No Radical—Robertson" (1961)

[88] Ibid.

[89] "R. D. Robertson Mourned" (1969)

[90] "No Radical—Robertson" (1961)

[91] Ligon (2017) p. 88; "No Radical Leadership Wanted" (1961)

[92] Ligon (2017) pp. 89–90
[93] as quoted in Ligon (2017) p. 90–92
[94] "No Radical Leadership Wanted" (1961)
[95] Ligon (2017) p. 92
[96] as quoted in Ligon (2017) p. 920
[97] "Overwhelming Majority" 1961
[98] Ligon (2017) p. 93; "Three Buses To Washington" (1963)
[99] Ligon (2017) pp. 200–202
[100] Ibid., pp. 202–213
[101] Vegh (2009)
[102] Ligon (2017) p. 219
[103] "Candidates Attend First Gay-Sponsored Forum" (April 1984)
[104] Ibid.

## CHAPTER 7 Class—and No Class

[1] Keyssar (2009) pp. 218–219
[2] Tarter (2013) p. 17
[3] Global Nonviolent Action Database, n.d.; Grizzard & Smith (2007)
[4] Collier (1992) pp. 19–24; Rogers (1992) p. 7
[5] Rogers (1992) p. 7
[6] Collier (1992) p. 21
[7] Tarter (2013) p. 82
[8] Ibid., p. 85
[9] Ibid., p. 86
[10] Ibid.
[11] Lepore (2018) pp. 121–122
[12] Keyssar (2009) p. 21
[13] Ibid., pp. 22–24
[14] Waldman (2016) p. 25
[15] Lichtman (2018) pp. 2–3
[16] Ibid., p. 3
[17] Keyssar (2009) p. XXIV
[18] Walton, Puckett, & Deskins (2012) p. 92
[19] Ibid., p. 134
[20] Keyssar (2009) p. XXIV
[21] Keyssar (2009) pp. 89, 105, 218
[22] Foner (1992) pp. 55–58
[23] Ibid., p. 58
[24] Ibid.
[25] Ibid.
[26] Ibid.
[27] Pole (1958) p. 47; Keyssar (2009) p. 24
[28] Keyssar (2009) p. 30
[29] Pole (1958) p. 38
[30] Keyssar (2009) pp. 30–31
[31] Breitzer (2015)
[32] Keyssar (2009) p. 31
[33] Ibid., p. 84

34 Berman (2015) p. 11
35 Keyssar (2009) p. 85
36 Ibid.
37 Tarter (2013) pp. 250–251
38 Wynes (1961) p. 109
39 Ibid., p. 133
40 Wynes (1961) p. 132
41 Keyssar (2009) p. 89
42 Ibid.
43 Suggs (1988) p. 126
44 T. L. Jones (1982) p. 61
45 Ransby (2003) pp. 120–124
46 Ligon (2017) pp. 91–92

## CHAPTER 8 Voting Rights—and Wrongs—in Our Democracy

1 Komp (2016); Ligon (2017) p. 157
2 Keyssar (2009) pp. 88–89
3 Ibid., p. 89
4 Ibid., pp. 88–90
5 Ibid., pp. 85, 89
6 Ibid., pp. 90–91
7 Jackson (2016)
8 Lichtman (2018) p. 137; Parramore et al. (1994) p. 269
9 Buni (1967) p. 17; Keyssar (2009) p. 90; Lawson (1999) p. 12
10 Ogden (1958) p. 284
11 www.officialdata.org (n.d.)
12 Breitzer (2015); Buni (1967) p. 18
13 Tarter (2013) pp. 273–274
14 as quoted in Lewis (1991) p. 21
15 Lewis (1991) p. 21
16 Buni. (1967) p. 27
17 J. D. Smith (2002)
18 Ibid., p. 151
19 Ibid.
20 as quoted in Buni (1967) p. 19
21 Keyssar (2009) p. 91
22 Ibid., p. 92
23 Breitzer (2015); Tarter (2013) p. 270
24 Tarter (2013) pp. 271–272
25 Tarter (2013) p. 283
26 Sweeney (1994) p. 307
27 Tarter (2013) p. 282
28 Ibid., p. 283
29 "Voter Turnout in Presidential Elections" (n.d.)
30 Heinemann (1996) p. 273
31 Ibid.
32 Ibid., pp. 302–303
33 Ibid., p. 283

[34] Keyssar (2009) p. 138
[35] Klarman (2004) pp. 69–71
[36] Wynes (1961) p. 148
[37] Buni (1967) p. 108
[38] Edwards (1973) p. 95
[39] Dennis (2014)
[40] Edds (2018) pp. 104–105
[41] Ibid., p. 105
[42] Edwards (1973) pp. 61–60, 97
[43] Ogden (1958) pp. 52–54
[44] Lewis (1991) p. 117
[45] Ibid., p. 32; Tarter (2014)
[46] Ogden (1958) p. 65
[47] www.officialdata.org (n.d.)
[48] Lewis (1991) p. 178
[49] Ligon (2017) pp. 19–20
[50] Tacker (1970) p. 10
[51] Komp (2016)
[52] Ibid.
[53] Ligon (2017) p. 158

## CHAPTER 9 Massive Resistance

[1] Kluger (2004) p. 710; Sitkoff (2008) p. 22; Woodward (2002) p. 147
[2] Klarman (2004) p. 392
[3] Ibid., p. 389
[4] Ibid., p. 391
[5] Woodward (2002) p. 166
[6] Dailey (2004) p. 125
[7] Ibid., p. 130
[8] Woodward (2002) p. 147
[9] Ibid., pp. 152–155
[10] Lawson (1999) p. 135
[11] Klebau (1954)
[12] Huie (1956) para. 83
[13] Parramore et al. (1994) p. 364
[14] Littlejohn & Ford (2012) pp. 61–62
[15] Epps (1993) pp. 19–36; Maxwell (2010) pp. 14, 17; Parramore et al. (1994) p. 363; Sitkoff (2008) pp. 25–26; J. D. Smith (2002) p. 296; Woodward (2002) pp. 156–158
[16] as quoted in J. Williams (2013) p. 30
[17] Ibid.
[18] Buni (1967) p. 185
[19] Klarman (2004) pp. 395-396; Maxwell (2010) p. 27; J. D. Smith (2002) p. 295
[20] as quoted in White (2018) p. 52
[21] Littlejohn & Ford (2012) p. 70
[22] Ligon (2017) p. 61
[23] Ibid., p. 64
[24] Ibid., p. 66

[25] Littlejohn & Ford (2012) p. 93; Ligon (2017) pp. 68–71
[26] Littlejohn & Ford (2012) p. 77
[27] Ibid., pp. 78–79; Parramore et al. (1994) p. 363
[28] Littlejohn & Ford (2012) pp. 81–82
[29] Ibid., p. 82
[30] Ligon, (2017) p. 75
[31] Ibid., pp. 74–75
[32] Littlejohn & Ford (2012) p. 90
[33] Couteé (2008) para. 10
[34] Parramore et al. (1994) p. 366
[35] Sitkoff (2008) pp. 30–31
[36] Littlejohn & Ford (2012) p. 41; Parramore et al. (1994) p. 367
[37] Ligon (2017) pp. 78-79
[38] "Guide's Year-End Report" (1965); "Job, Housing Probe Due" (1964)
[39] White (1992) p. 292
[40] Ibid., p. 268
[41] Littlejohn & Ford (2012) pp. 116–118; Parramore et al. (1994) pp. 359–361

## CHAPTER 10 Evelyn Butts Joins the Flow

[1] Commonwealth of Virginia, State Board of Elections (1958)
[2] "Death of Democracy" (1958)
[3] National Register of Historic Places (2002)
[4] Bogger et al. (2018) p. 264
[5] Ligon (2017) p. 95
[6] Ibid., p. 96; "Norfolk Committees Push Drive" (1959)
[7] T. L. Bogger, personal communication with E. T. Butts (1989)
[8] "White Voters Suffering" (1961); S. W. Tucker (1965)
[9] as quoted in "White Voters Suffering" (1961)
[10] "Blank Sheet Law Dead" (1962)
[11] as quoted in Knepler (2001a)
[12] T. L. Bogger, personal communication with E. T. Butts, (1989); C. B. Ligon, personal communication (January 11, 2018)
[13] Dabney (1959); "Final Details Completed," (1959); Ligon, (2017) p. 97
[14] Ligon (2017) pp. 98, 166
[15] T. L. Bogger, personal communication with E. T. Butts (1989)
[16] C. B. Ligon, personal communication (January 11, 2018)
[17] A. V. Green, personal communication (March 1, 2018; June 1, 2018)
[18] Ligon (2017) p. 169
[19] "Over 100 Register" (1968) p. A-2
[20] "Third Force Women" (1970); Voters Club Tours General Assembly" (1968)

## CHAPTER 11 Deeds of the Ancestors

[1] as quoted in Crosby (2011) p. 374
[2] Moye (2011) p. 162
[3] as quoted in Robnett (1997) p. 112
[4] S. S. Hughes & Bogger, (2006) p. 81

[5] S. S. Hughes (1982) p. 46; S. S. Hughes & Bogger (2006) p. 90; Lewis (1991) p. 91
[6] Goggin (2014)
[7] Dennis (2014)
[8] Walton et al. (2012) p. 192
[9] Hogan (n.d.)
[10] S. S. Hughes & Bogger (2006) pp. 78, 90
[11] Olson (2001) p. 33
[12] Ibid., pp. 33–46
[13] Parramore et al. (1994) p. 255; Varon, and the Dictionary of Virginia Biography (2018)
[14] as quoted in C. S. Parker (2009) p 42
[15] Wolfe (2017)
[16] Law Library of Congress. (n.d.)
[17] Dunbar (2017)
[18] Nicholls (2016)
[19] Breen (2018)
[20] Glass (2018); M. S. Jones (2018) pp. 131–132; State Historical Society of Missouri (n.d.)
[21] Larson (2004)
[22] Newby-Alexander (2017)
[23] Ibid.
[24] Schley (2013) pp. 15–16
[25] Ibid., p. ii
[26] Ibid.
[27] Walton et al. (2012) p. 192
[28] M. S. Jones (2018) p. 23
[29] Lawson (1999) p. xviii
[30] Ibid.
[31] Parramore et al. (1994) p. 254
[32] Library of Virginia (n.d.)
[33] Jim Crow Lived Here (n.d.)
[34] Lewis (1991) p. 22
[35] Nation's Premier Civil Rights Organization (n.d.)
[36] Buni (1967) pp. 67–68
[37] Ibid., p. 67; Meacham (2018) pp. 171–175
[38] Edds (2018) pp. 37–40
[39] Suggs (1988) p. 160
[40] Littlejohn & Ford (2012) p. 36
[41] Ibid., p. 21
[42] Ibid., p. 49
[43] Edds (2018) pp. 78–80; Lewis (1991) pp. 157–161; Parramore et al. (1994) pp. 317–319; J. D. Smith (2002) pp. 256–258; Suggs (1988) pp. 160–162
[44] Littlejohn & Ford (2012) p. 9
[45] Edds (2018) p. 80; Lewis (1991) p.160; Parramore et al. (1994) p. 318; J. D. Smith (2002) p. 257; Suggs (1988) pp. 160–162
[46] Edds (2018) pp. 83-91; Lewis (1991) pp. 162–163; Littlejohn & Ford (2012) p. 21; Parramore et al. (1994) p. 329; J. D. Smith, (2002), pp. 271–272; Suggs (1988) pp. 160–162
[47] Kluger (2004) p. 215; J. D. Smith (2002) p. 272
[48] J. D. Smith (2002) p. 261

[49] Ibid., pp. 263–264

[50] Ibid., p. 264

[51] Ibid., pp. 264–266

[52] Edds (2018) p. 83; J. D. Smith (2002) pp. 267–270

[53] Lewis (1991) p. 26

[54] Ibid., p. 27

[55] "Flying to See" (1947); "Norfolkians Crowd Gotham" (1947)

[56] Nelson (1948); "Mr. and Mrs. Jackie Robinson" (1948); "Jackie Robinson's All-Stars" (1949); "10,000 Fans" (1949)

[57] Knepler (2017)

[58] Jacox (1954)

[59] D. M. Watson (2018)

[60] Virginia Department of Historic Resources (1982)

[61] Kachun (2017)

[62] Ibid.

[63] Parramore et al. (1994) pp. 370–371

[64] Moodie-Mills (2016); Nazaryan (2017)

[65] Lewis (1991) p. 3

[66] Parramore et al. (1994) p. 226

[67] Bogger et al. (2018) p. 96

[68] Tarter (2015)

[69] Bogger et al. (2018) p. 97

[70] Colored Monitor Union Club (1865) p. 4

[71] Lepore (2018) p. 317

[72] Dinnella-Borrego & the Dictionary of Virginia Biography (2018)

[73] Buni (1967) pp. 81–85; J. D. Smith (2002) pp. 60–67; Wynes (1961) p. 146

[74] Buni (1967) p. 108

[75] Ibid., p. 81; J. D. Smith (2002) pp. 60–67

[76] Buni (1967) p. 84

[77] Ibid., p. 88; Suggs (1988) p. 52

[78] Lewis (1991) p. 23

## CHAPTER 12 Double V on the Home Front

[1] Ligon (2017) p. 88

[2] Foner (1998) pp. 243–244; Lawson (1999) p. 65; C. S. Parker (2009) p. 42

[3] Ligon (2017) p. 87

[4] BlackPast (2007); Douglass, (1863); Douglass' Role in the Civil War (n.d.)

[5] Drury (2014) paras. 4, 5

[6] Lange (2017)

[7] West Point Monument (2014) Inscription, para. 2

[8] Newby-Alexander (n.d.) paras. 16, 18

[9] Hucles (2006) p. 50

[10] Bogger (2006)

[11] Ligon (2017) p. 25

[12] Biga (2018)

[13] Foner (1992) p. 59

[14] Ibid., pp. 58–59

[15] Walton et al. (2012) pp. 197–198

[16] Douglass' Role in the Civil War (n.d.)
[17] Bogger (2006)
[18] Ibid.
[19] C. S. Parker (2009) pp. 35–36
[20] as quoted in J. D. Smith (2002) pp. 44–45
[21] J. D. Smith (2002) p. 45
[22] C. S. Parker (2009) p. 38
[23] Ibid.
[24] Equal Justice Initiative (2018) para. 2
[25] C. S. Parker (2009) pp. 33–37
[26] Armstead (2009) p. 97; C. S. Parker (2009) p. 36
[27] as quoted in Armstead (2009)
[28] C. S. Parker (2009) p. 42
[29] Ibid.
[30] Ibid.
[31] Randolph (1942) "Why Should We March" para. 1
[32] Ibid., paras. 9, 10
[33] Armstead (2009); Baker (2016); T. Bell (2017); Morris (1984); Olson (2001); C. S. Parker (2009); Sitkoff (2008)
[34] Schlegel (1991) p. 194
[35] Lewis (1991) pp. 116–120; Suggs (1988) pp. 66–67, 89
[36] Suggs (1988) p. 120
[37] Lewis (1991) pp. 78–79
[38] Jones p. 56; Lewis, (1991) p. 177; Parramore et al. (1994) p. 337
[39] Lewis (1991) p. 189; Schlegel (1991) p. 226
[40] Lewis (1991) p. 191; Parramore et al. (1994) p. 339; Schlegel (1991) p. 193
[41] Lewis (1991) pp. 194–195; Schlegel (1991) pp. 73–74, 316; Bogger et al. (2018) p. 224
[42] Armstead (2009); T. Bell (2017); C. S. Parker (2009)
[43] Suggs (1988) pp. 132–136
[44] C. S. Parker (2009)
[45] Ibid., p. 10
[46] Ibid., p. 108
[47] Ibid., p. 107
[48] Ibid., pp. 110–111
[49] Hughes (1995) p. 281
[50] C. S. Parker (2009) p. 51
[51] T. Bell (2017); C. S. Parker (2009)
[52] T. Bell (2017) para. 12
[53] C. S. Parker (2009) p. xii
[54] Edds (2018) pp. 141–142; C. S. Parker (2009) pp. 47–48
[55] C. S. Parker (2009) p. 48
[56] Edds (2018) p. 154; C. S. Parker (2009) p. 48; J. D. Smith (2002) p. 291
[57] C. S. Parker (2009) p. 48
[58] Edds (2018) p. 154
[59] L. M. Smith (2001) p. 270
[60] Lawson (1999) p. xv
[61] Equal Justice Initiative (n.d.) Marching Toward a Movement section, para. 27
[62] Bloom (2019) p. 174
[63] Littlejohn & Ford (2012) p. 37

[64] Ibid., p. 36
[65] Ligon (2017) p. 59; F. R. White (2018) p. 40
[66] Littlejohn & Ford (2012) p. 71

## CHAPTER 13 Schooling the School Board

[1] Ligon (2017) p. 75
[2] C. B. Ligon, personal communication (January 11, 2018)
[3] Littlejohn & Ford (2012) p. 109; Ligon (2017) pp. 74–75
[4] Ligon (2017) pp. 74–75; "School Facilities Unequal" (1959); White (2018) pp.
        104–105, 174–175
[5] "What the Life of Martin Luther King, Jr. Has Meant to Me" (1986)
[6] Ligon (2017) pp. 15–16
[7] Ibid., p. 16
[8] Ligon (2017) p. 20; C. B. Ligon, personal communication (January 11, 2018)
[9] Littlejohn & Ford (2012) p. 250, fn. 47
[10] Ligon (2017) p. 53
[11] Ibid.
[12] Barnes & Proctor (1994) p. 90; Littlejohn & Ford (2012)
[13] Ligon (2017) p. 61
[14] McCollum (1963)
[15] Littlejohn & Ford (2012) pp. 129–131
[16] McCollum (1963)
[17] Littlejohn & Ford (2012) p. 129
[18] Ligon (2017) pp. 76–77; Littlejohn & Ford (2012) p. 129
[19] Littlejohn & Ford (2012) pp. 127-129; Roseberry (1963)
[20] Littlejohn & Ford (2012) pp. 129–131; Parramore et al. (1994) p. 379
[21] Scully (1963)
[22] Hollander (1963); Scully (1963)
[23] "No Let-Up In Protest" (1963)
[24] Ripley & Butts as quoted in Ligon (2017) pp. 77–78
[25] Ligon (2017) p. 100; "Three Buses to Washington" (1963)

## CHAPTER 14 A New Generation, A New Frontier

[1] Ligon (2017) pp. 17, 20
[2] White (2018) pp. 34–40
[3] Ibid.
[4] Ibid., pp. 39–40
[5] T. L. Bogger, personal communication with E. T. Butts (1989)
[6] White (2018) p. 40
[7] Ibid., pp. 78–79
[8] Colvin (1996); Knepler (2001a)
[9] Ligon (2017) p. 58
[10] Lewis (1991) p. 190; Parramore et al. (1994) p. 337; J. D. Smith (2002) p. 281
[11] Edds (2018) pp. 121–148
[12] Woodward (2002) p. 140
[13] Sitkoff (2008); J. Williams, 2013)

14 Ibid.
15 J. Williams (2013) pp. 126–127
16 D. M. Watson (2020)
17 Sitkoff (2008) pp. 61–77
18 Colvin (2003b)
19 Ligon (2017) p. 94
20 Ibid., p. 92
21 "Call For Voice" (1961)
22 as quoted in Knepler (2001a); Ligon (2017) p. 234
23 as quoted in Colvin (1995)
24 H. Smith, personal communication (February 20, 2018); R. Smith, personal communication (February 20, 2018)
25 "First Stop To Be In Area" (1964)
26 "Guide's Year-End Report" (1965); "Job, Housing Probe Due" (1964)
27 C. B. Ligon, personal communication (January 11, 2018)
28 Ligon (2017) pp. 171–172
29 Ibid., p. 170

## CHAPTER 15 Demanding Democracy

1 Ligon (2017) p. 100
2 Wallenstein (2004) p. 179
3 Ibid., p. 179–187
4 Ibid., p. 179
5 Lawson (1999) pp. 83–84
6 Heinemann (1996) pp. 230–231
7 Ibid.
8 Lawson (1999) pp. 58–63
9 Buni (1967) p. 146
10 Armstead (2009); Baker (2016); Morris (1984); Olson (2001); C. S. Parker (2009); Sitkoff (2008)
11 Buni (1967) p. 148
12 Buni (1967)
13 Ibid., pp. 148–149
14 Ibid., pp. 152–153
15 Ibid., pp. 155–157
16 U.S. Const. amend. XXIV
17 Walton et al. (2012) p. 476
18 Ibid., p. 479
19 Keyssar (2009) p. 210
20 Sweeney (1994) p. 334
21 Virginia Democrats hopeful (September 20, 1964)
22 Sweeney (1994) p. 346
23 Ibid., p. 334
24 Ibid., p. 347
25 Wallenstein (2004) p. 186; Heinemann (1996) p. 410
26 Tucker (2000) p. 59
27 Wallenstein (2004) p. 186
28 Ibid., p. 187

[29] A. V. Green, personal communication (June 1, 2018)
[30] Knepler (2001a)
[31] W. P. Johnson (2017)
[32] Bogger et al. (2018) pp. 260–262; Littlejohn (2011)
[33] Daugherity (2010) p. 89
[34] Littlejohn & Ford (2012) p. 127
[35] W. P. Johnson (2017)
[36] *Harper v. Virginia* (1966)
[37] McAllister (1966)
[38] Ibid.
[39] Bogger et al. (2018) pp. 262–266
[40] Ligon (2017) p. 163
[41] H. Smith, personal communication (February 20, 2018)
[42] "Legendary Local Activist" (1993); Ligon (2017) pp. 98, 166
[43] Colvin (2003b)
[44] Ligon (2017) p. 158
[45] "7 Va. Communities Pick Negro Councilmen" (1968)
[46] "A Worthy Celebration" (2006)
[47] Barnes & Proctor (1994) p. 91
[48] Ibid.; Ligon (2017) p. 167; Suggs (1988) p. 187
[49] Keyssar (2009) pp. 219–220
[50] Knepler (2001b)
[51] Podolefsky (1998) p. 887
[52] Tarter (2013) p. 329
[53] Ibid.
[54] Ibid.
[55] Ibid., pp. 329–330
[56] Ackerman & Nou (2009) p. 133
[57] Colvin (1996)
[58] Knepler (2001a)

## CHAPTER 16 The Evelyn Butts Way

[1] Couto (1995) p. 13
[2] Ibid.
[3] A. V. Green, personal communication (March 1, 2018)
[4] Isoke (2013) p. 81
[5] as quoted in Knepler (2001a)
[6] R. Smith, personal communication (February 20, 2018)
[7] Coit (1979)
[8] Knepler (1992)

## EPILOGUE Valorizing Leadership

[1] Bogger et al. (2018) p. 97
[2] Description of SRV Theory (n.d.)
[3] Ibid.
[4] Brown (2016)

[5] Ibid.
[6] Ibid.
[7] Campbell (2020)
[8] Duffin (Nov. 23, 2020)
[9] Wahba (Nov. 4, 2020)
[10] Khalid (September 13, 2020); Griswold (October 6, 2020)
[11] Khalid (2020)
[12] Gerber & Green (2015) p. 38
[13] Griswold (2020)
[14] Gerber & Green (2015) p. 21; Griswold (2020)
[15] Gerber & Green (2015) p. 21
[16] Griswold (2020), Johnson (2020); Tyler (2020)
[17] Tyler (2020)
[18] Khalid (2020)
[19] Bruner (November 6, 2020)
[20] Williams (November 13, 2020)
[21] North (November 11, 2020).
[22] Johnson (2020)
[23] King (November 12, 2020)
[24] Jones, M.S. (2020) p. 273
[25] Gafni (April 14, 2020)
[26] Onyenacho (March 30, 2020); Montgomery (March 24, 2020)
[27] Boone & Moore (2020) p. 57
[28] Murphy (2020)

# REFERENCES

A worthy celebration of Norfolk crusaders. (2006, March 30). *The Virginian-Pilot*, p. B-8.

Ackerman, B., & Nou, J. (2009, January 1). Canonizing the civil rights revolution: The people and the poll tax. *Faculty Scholarship Series*. Paper 3689. Retrieved from http://digitalcommons.law.yale.edu/fss_papers/3689

Adelson, B. (1999). *Brushing back Jim Crow: The integration of minor-league baseball in the American South*. Charlottesville, VA: University of Virginia Press.

Africans in America: Judgment Day (n.d.). *Public Broadcasting Service*. Retrieved from https://www.pbs.org/wgbh/aia/part4/4h2933t.html

Alexander, K. C. (2017, January 8). End the archaic practice of gerrymandering. *The Virginian-Pilot*.

Alston, J. A., & McClellan, P. A. (2011). *Herstories: Leading with the lessons of the lives of black women activists*. New York, NY: Peter Lang Publishing.

Altman, A. (2017). Civil rights. *The Stanford Encyclopedia of Philosophy* (Winter 2017 Edition), Edward N. Zalta (ed.). Retrieved from https://plato.stanford.edu/archives/win2017/entries/civil-rights/

Ambrosius, L. E. (Ed.). (2004). *Writing biography: Historians and their craft*. Lincoln, NE: University of Nebraska Press.

Armstead, R. E. (2009). Veterans in the fight for equal rights: from the Civil War to today. *Trotter Review, 18*(1), 92–105. Retrieved from http://scholarworks.umb.edu/trotter_review/vol18/iss1/12.

Armstrong, T. E. (2012). *The hidden help: Black domestic workers in the civil rights movement*. (Master's thesis, University of Louisville). (Order No. 1523640). Retrieved from Electronic Theses and Dissertations. Paper 46. (1430931200). https://doi.org/10.18297/etd/46

Baker, P. C. (2016, November 27). The tragic, forgotten history of black military veterans. *The New Yorker*. Retrieved from https://www.newyorker.com/news/news-desk/the-tragic-forgotten-history-of-black-military-veterans

Barnes, E. M., & Proctor, R. E. (1994). Black politics in Tidewater, Virginia. In H. Walton Jr. (Ed.), *Black politics and black political behavior: A linkage analysis* (pp. 83–96). Westport, CT: Praeger.

Barritt, L. (1986). Human sciences and the human image. *Phenomenology and Pedagogy, 4*(3), 14–22. https://doi.org/10.29173/pandp15028

Bayless, J. D. III. (2011). *An iron catalyst: Virginia's roadside historical markers and the shaping of a historical consciousness*. (Master's thesis, Virginia Commonwealth University). Retrieved from http://scholarscompass.vcu.edu/etd/2339. (OCLC No. 713671796)

Bell, J. D. (2015). *African American women leaders in the civil rights movement: A narrative inquiry*. (Doctoral dissertation, Antioch University). Retrieved from ProQuest Dissertations & Theses Global. (Order No. 3726866)

Bell, J. D. (2018). *Lighting the fires of freedom: African American women in the civil rights movement*. New York, NY: The New Press.

Bell, T. (2017, February 24). *How war veterans impacted the civil rights movement*. Retrieved from https://www.army.mil/article/183153/how_war_veterans_impacted_the_civil_rights_movement

Bennett, L. Jr. (1967). *Black Power U.S.A.: The human side of Reconstruction, 1867—1877*, p. 83. Chicago, IL: Johnson Publishing Co.

Berman, A. (2015). *Give us the ballot: The modern struggle for voting rights in America*. New York, NY: Picador.

Biga, L. A. (2018, January, 28). *Her mother's daughter: Charlene Butts Ligon carries on civil rights legacy of her late mother Evelyn Thomas Butts*. Retrieved from https://evelyntbutts.com/1484-2/

BlackPast, B. (2007, January 28). *(1863) Frederick Douglass, Men of Color, To Arms!* Retrieved from https://blackpast.org/african-american history/1863-frederick-douglass-men-color-arms/

Blank sheet law dead: Smart Va. Negro voters outsmarted politicians. (1962, December 1). *Journal and Guide*, pp. C1, C2.

Bloom, J. M. (2019). *Class, race, and the civil rights movement (2nd edition)*. Bloomington, IN: Indiana University Press.

Bloomberg, L. D., & Volpe, M. (2008). *Completing your qualitative dissertation: A roadmap from beginning to end*. Thousand Oaks, CA: Sage.

Bly, A. T. (2019, June 24). Slave literacy and education in Virginia. In *Encyclopedia Virginia*. Retrieved from http://www.EncyclopediaVirginia.org/Slave_Literacy_and_Education_in_Virginia.

Bogger, T. L. (1982). The colonization movement in lower Tidewater. In Jane H. Kobelski (Ed.), *Readings in black and white: Lower Tidewater Virginia* (pp. 9–15). Portsmouth, VA: Portsmouth Public Library.

Bogger, T. L. (2006, August 10). *West Point Cemetery, DHR File #122-5181.* (National Register of Historic Places Nomination Form).

Bogger, T. L., Hucles, M. E., Newby-Alexander, C., & Jackson, J. (2018). *I, too, am Norfolk: A history of African Americans in Norfolk, Virginia*. Manuscript in preparation.

Boone, L. D. & Moore, A. (2020, August). Building social capital: Youth engagement in "at opportunity" communities. *Police Chief Magazine*. Retrieved from policechiefmagazine.com

Breen, P. H. (2018, April 3). Nat Turner's revolt (1831). In *Encyclopedia Virginia*. Retrieved from http://www.EncyclopediaVirginia.org/Revolt_Nat_Turner_s_1831

Breitzer, S. (2015, May 20). Virginia Constitutional Convention (1901–1902). In *Encyclopedia Virginia*. Retrieved from http://www.EncyclopediaVirginia.org/Constitutional_Convention_Virginia_1901-1902

Brokaw, T. (2004). *The greatest generation*. New York, NY: Random House.

Brooks, J. I. (1966, January 27). Norfolkian tells court of tax "ills." *The Virginian-Pilot*, pp. A-1, A-10. F234.N8.V4, Perry Library Microforms, Old Dominion University.

Brooks, M. P., and Houck, D. W. (2011) *Speeches of Fannie Lou Hamer, To Tell It Like It Is*, edited by Maegan Parker Brooks and Davis W. Houck. Jackson, MS: University Press of Mississippi.

Brown, A. (2016, June 16). American opportunity: Getting Compton's young men to trade gang life for working life. *CNN Money*. Retrieved from https://money.cnn.com/2016/06/14/news/economy/aja-brown compton-gangs/index.html)

Bruner, R. (2020, November 6). 'Civic engagement doesn't have to be corny.' How Georgia pulled off unprecedented youth voter turnout. *Time*. Retrieved from https://time.com/5908483/georgia-youth-vote/

Buni, A. (1967). *The Negro in Virginia politics 1902–1965*. Charlottesville, VA: The University Press of Virginia.

Buzard-Boyett, P. M. (2011), *Race and Justice in Mississippi's Central Piney Woods, 1940, 2010*. Dissertations. 740. https://aquila.usm.edu/dissertations/740

Call for voice. (1961, February 18). *Journal and Guide*, p. B15.

Campbell, V. (2020, August 25). Aja Brown: community-oriented leader. *The Urban Media Lab*. Retrieved from https://labgov.city/theurbanmedialab/aja-brown-community-oriented-leader/)

Candidates attend first gay-sponsored forum. (1984, April). *Our Own Community Press*, 8(6), pp. 1–2.

Capps, K. (2016). In the U.S., almost no one votes in local elections. *CityLab*. Retrieved November 1, 2016, from https://www.citylab.com/equity/2016/11/in-the-us-almost-no-one-votes-in-local-elections/505766/

Chadwick, J. Q. A. (1969, February 22). Name 'man-in-street' to city boards— Jordan. *Journal and Guide*, p. B-1.

Clandinin, D. J., & Connelly, F. M. (2000). *Narrative inquiry: Experience and story in qualitative research*. San Francisco, CA: Jossey-Bass.

Coit, J. (1979, November 7). She's on party line and likes it fine. *The Virginian-Pilot*, p. A-3.

Coley, R. J., & Sum, A. (2012). *Fault lines in our democracy: Civic knowledge, voting behavior, and civic engagement in the United States*. Princeton, NJ: Educational Testing Service.

Collier, C. (1992). The American People as Christian white men of property: Suffrage and elections in Colonial and early national America. In D. W. Rogers with C. Scriabine (Eds.), *Voting and the spirit of American democracy: Essays on the history of voting and voting rights in America* (pp. 19–30). Urbana and Chicago, IL: University of Illinois Press.

Collier-Thomas, B., & Franklin, V. P. (Eds.). (2001). *Sisters in the struggle: African American women in the civil rights-black power movement*. New York, NY: New York University Press.

Colored Monitor Union Club (1865). Equal suffrage address. In *Encyclopedia Virginia*. Retrieved from _to_the_People_of_the_United_States_Also_an_Account_of_the_Agitation_among_the_Colored_People_of_Virginia_for_Equal_Rights_With_an_Appendix_Conce

Colvin, L. E. (1993, March 17). Area mourns for Evelyn Butts: She fought for, won case to end poll tax. *New Journal and Guide*, pp. 1, 7.

Colvin, L. E. (1995, August 9). Collins gets council to re-name Elm St. for Mrs. Evelyn Butts. *New Journal and Guide*, pp. 1, 7.

Colvin, L. E. (1996, March 27). 30 years after Butts' fight to end poll tax for voting, signing up new voters still challenges poll workers. *New Journal and Guide*, pp. 1, 8, 13.

Colvin, L. E. (2003a, July 9). The road to Washington 1963—A series: Youthful fervor had valuable role in civil rights movement. *New Journal and Guide*, pp. 1, 8, 11.

Colvin, L. E. (2003b, August 13). '63 march set stage for getting blacks in office: Learning to strategize was critical in electing first black to Norfolk council. *New Journal and Guide*, pp. 1, 8, 9.

Commonwealth of Virginia, State Board of Elections (1958, May 22). Virginia State Board of Elections Bulletin No. 29. *Social Welfare History Image Portal*. Retrieved from https://images.socialwelfare.library.vcu.edu

Couteé, A. (2008, February 25). Woman vividly recalls school desegregation as part of Norfolk 17. *The Virginian-Pilot*. Retrieved from pilotonline.com

Couto, R. A. (1995). Defining a citizen leader. In J. T. Wren (Ed.), *The leader's companion: Insights on leadership through the ages* (pp. 11–17). New York, NY: The Free Press.

Creswell, J. W. (2003). *Research design: Qualitative, quantitative, and mixed methods approaches* (2nd ed.). Thousand Oaks, CA: Sage.

Creswell, J. W. (2007). *Qualitative inquiry & research design: Choosing among five approaches* (2nd ed.). Thousand Oaks, CA: Sage.

Crosby, E. (2011). That movement responsibility: An interview with Judy Richardson on movement values and movement history. In E. Crosby (Ed.), *Civil rights history from the ground up: Local struggles, a national movement* (pp. 366–384). Athens, GA: The University of Georgia Press.

Crowley, R. M. (2013). "The goddamndest, toughest voting rights bill": Critical race theory and the Voting Rights Act of 1965. *Race Ethnicity and Education*, 16(5), 696–724. http://dx.doi.org/10.1080/13613324.2012.725037

Dabney, T. L. (1959, May 2). Voters rally in Norfolk: Use ballot for freedom; Rep. Powell, Rev. Borders, Judge Delany speakers. *Journal and Guide*, p. B17.

Dailey, J. (2004, June). Sex, segregation, and the sacred after Brown. *The Journal of American History*, 91(1), 119–144. https://doi.org/10.2307/3659617

Daugherity, B. J. (2010), *Keep on keeping on: The NAACP and the implementation of Brown v. Board of Education in Virginia*. Dissertations, Theses, and Masters Projects. Paper 1539791828. https://doi.org/10.21220/e80s-xd52

Davis, A. (1983). *Women, race & class*. New York, NY: Vintage Books.

Death of democracy. (1958, February 8). *Journal and Guide*, p. C9.

Dennis, M. (2005, May). The idea of citizenship in the early civil rights movement. *Citizenship Studies*, 9(2), 181–203. https://doi.org/10.1080/13621020500049135

Dennis, M. (2014). Luther Porter Jackson (1892–1950). In *Encyclopedia Virginia*. Retrieved from http://www.EncyclopediaVirginia.org/Jackson_Luther_Porter_1892-1950

Denzin, N. K., & Lincoln, Y. S. (2005). *The Sage handbook of qualitative research* (3rd ed.). Thousand Oaks, CA: Sage.

Description of SRV Theory (N.D.) SRV theory. *International Social Role Valorization Association*, https://socialrolevalorization.com/srv-theory/

DeSilver, D. (2018). *US trails most developed countries in voter turnout*. Washington, DC: Pew Research Center. Retrieved from https://www.pewresearch.org/fact-tank/2018/05/21/u-s-voter-turnout-trails-most-developed-countries/

Dinnella-Borrego, L., & the Dictionary of Virginia Biography. (2018). John Mercer Langston (1829–1897). In *Encyclopedia Virginia*. Retrieved from http://www.EncyclopediaVirginia.org/Langston_John_Mercer_1829-1897

Douglass, F. (1863, April) *Why should a colored man enlist?* Retrieved from http://www.frederick-douglass-heritage.org/why-should-a-colored-man-enlist/

Douglass' role in the Civil War. (n.d.). Retrieved from http://www.frederick-douglass-heritage.org/role-in-civil-war/

Drury, D. (2014, January 18). Called to arms in Civil War, Connecticut's black soldiers respond. *The Hartford Courant*. Retrieved from www.courant.com

Duffin, E. (2020, November 23). Voter turnout in U.S. presidential election, by state 2020. Retrieved from https://www.statista.com/statistics/1184621/presidential-election-voter-turnout-rate-state/#statisticContainer

Dunbar, E. A. (2017). *Never caught: The Washingtons' relentless pursuit of their runaway slave, Ona Judge*. New York, NY: Atria Publishing Group.

Eichelman, F. (1976). The Government as Textbook Writer: A Case History. *The Phi Delta Kappan, 57*(7), 456-458. Retrieved September 20, 2020, from http://www.jstor.org/stable/20298323

Edds, M. (2018). *We face the dawn: Oliver Hill, Spottswood Robinson, and the legal team that dismantled Jim Crow*. Charlottesville, VA: University of Virginia Press.

Edwards, C. L. (1973). *A political history of the poll tax in Virginia, 1900–1950*. (Master's thesis, University of Richmond). Retrieved from http://scholarship.richmond.edu/masters-theses

Enter Evelyn Butts. (1980, February 20). *The Virginian-Pilot*, p. A14. F234. N8.V4, Perry Library Microforms, Old Dominion University.

Epps, G. (1993, Winter). The littlest rebel: James J. Kilpatrick and the second Civil War. *Constitutional Commentary, 10*(1), 19–36. http://hdl.handle.net/11299/166879

Epps-Robertson, R. C. (2013). *"We're Still Here!": The Rhetorical Education of the Prince Edward County Free School Association, 1963-1964."* Writing Program–Dissertations. 36. https://surface.syr.edu/wp_etd/36

Epps-Robertson, C. (2016). The race to erase Brown v. Board of Education: The Virginia Way and the rhetoric of Massive Resistance. *Rhetoric Review, 35*(2), 108–120. https://doi.org/10.1080/07350198.2016.1142812

Equal Justice Initiative. (n.d.). *Lynching in America: Targeting black veterans*. Retrieved from https://eji.org/reports/online/lynching-in-america-targeting-black-veterans

Equal Justice Initiative. (2017). *Lynching in America: Confronting the legacy of racial terror* (3rd edition). Retrieved from https://lynchinginamerica.eji.org/report/

Equal Justice Initiative. (2018, November 12). *The struggle of black veterans*. Retrieved from https://eji.org/news/struggle-of-black-veterans

Ertmer, P. A., & Newby, T. J. (1993). Behaviorism, cognitivism, constructivism: Comparing critical features from an instructional design perspective. *Performance Improvement Quarterly, 6*(4), 50–72. https://doi:10.1111/j.1937-8327.1993.tb00605.x

Essed, P. (1996). *Diversity: gender, color, and culture*. Amherst, MA: University of Massachusetts Press.

Evelyn T. Butts. (1993, March 17). *The Virginian-Pilot*, p. D-2.

Fein, R. (2018, March 24). Harper v. Virginia and the wealth primary as a new poll tax. *Free Speech for People*. Retrieved from https://freespeechforpeople.org/harper-v-virginia-and-the-wealth-primary-as-a-new-poll-tax/

Ferguson, J. Y. (2015). *Anna Julia Cooper: a quintessential leader* (Doctoral dissertation, Antioch University). Retrieved from ProQuest Dissertations & Theses Global. (Order No. 3680525)

Final details completed: Capacity audience seen for arena voting rally. (1959, April 25). *Journal and Guide*, pp. B1, B2.

Fineout, G. (2020a, May 24). Federal judge strikes down restrictions on Florida felon voting. *Politico*. Retrieved from www.politico.com

Fineout, G. (2020b, July 16). Supreme Court allows limits on felon voting in Florida. *Politico*. Retrieved from www.politico.com

First stop to be in area: Dr. King to check on Rosemont school case. (1964, June 27). *Journal and Guide*, pp. 1–2.

Flying to See Jackie Robinson. (1947, July 19), *Journal and Guide*, p. A-15.

Foner, E. (1992). From slavery to citizenship: Blacks and the right to vote. In D. W. Rogers with C. Scriabine (Eds.), *Voting and the spirit of American democracy: Essays on the history of voting and voting rights in America* (pp. 55–66). Urbana and Chicago, IL: University of Illinois Press.

Foner, E. (1998). *The story of American freedom*. New York, NY: W.W. Norton & Company.

Fontana, A., & Frey, J. H. (2005). The interview: from neutral stance to political involvement. In N. K. Denzin, & Y. S. Lincoln (Eds.), *The Sage handbook of qualitative research* (3rd ed.). Thousand Oaks, CA: Sage.

Funeral on Saturday: Joseph Jordan, Norfolk lawyer's father, dies. (1966, December 31). *Journal and Guide*, p. A1.

Gafni, N. (2020, April 14). COVID and the grassroots: lessons on resilience. Retrieved from https://www.business.rutgers.edu/business-insights/covid-and-grassroots-lessons-resilience

Garrow, D. J. (2005). Grassroots organizers played the most important role in the civil rights movement. In J. Karson (Ed.), *The civil rights movement* (pp. 195–200). Farmington Hills, MI: Greenhaven Press.

Gilkes, C. T. (1994). "If it wasn't for the women..."; African American women, community work, and social change. In M. B. Zinn & B. T. Dill (Eds.), *Women of color in U.S. society* (pp. 229–246). Philadelphia, PA: Temple University Press.

Glass, A. (2018). Supreme Court decides Dred Scott case, March 6, 1857. *Politico*. Retrieved from https://www.politico.com/story/2018/03/06/supreme-court-decides-dred-scott-case-march-6-1857-435658

Global Nonviolent Action Database. (n.d.). *Polish artisans strike for the right to vote, Jamestown, Virginia, 1619*. Retrieved from https://nvdatabase.swarthmore.edu/content/polish-artisans-strike-right-vote-jamestown-virginia-1619

Goggin, J. (2014, May 27). Carter G. Woodson (1875–1950). In *Encyclopedia Virginia*. Retrieved from http://www.EncyclopediaVirginia.org/Woodson_Carter_G_1875-1950

Gottlieb, M. S. (2018, July 24). House of Burgesses. In *Encyclopedia Virginia*. Retrieved from http://www.EncyclopediaVirginia.org/House_of_Burgesses

Green, D. P., & Gerber, A. S. (2015). *Get out the vote: How to increase voter turnout*. 3rd Ed. Washington, DC: The Brookings Institution.

Griswold, E. (2020, October 6). Campaign chronicles: Does door-knocking matter? Republicans have been going door to door for months; Democrats start this week. Will it affect the election? *The New Yorker.* Retrieved from https://www.newyorker.com/news/campaign chronicles/does-door-knocking-matter

Grizzard, F. E. Jr., & Smith, D. B. (2007). *Jamestown Colony: A political, social, and cultural history.* Santa Barbara, CA: ABC-CLIO.

Guelzo, A. C. (2018, August 24). Robert E. Lee and slavery. In *Encyclopedia Virginia.* Retrieved from http://www.EncyclopediaVirginia.org/Lee_Robert_E_and_Slavery

Guide's year-end report: The year Negro voters made history. (1965, January 9). *Journal and Guide,* p. 9.

Hale, G. E. (1998). *Making whiteness: The culture of segregation in the South, 1890–1940.* New York, NY: Pantheon Books.

Hall, J. E. (2001). *Black and White: A Historical Examination of Lynching Coverage and Editorial Impact in Select Virginia Newspapers.* (Master's thesis, Virginia Commonwealth University). https://doi.org/10.25772/2JS9-MM26. Retrieved from https://scholarscompass.vcu.edu/etd/3937

Hansen, L. (2002, February 4). Miller's quiet strength—Almost two decades ago, Yvonne Miller broke into politics as the first black woman elected to the Virginia House. Today, she is South Hampton Roads' senior senator. *The Virginian-Pilot,* p. B-1.

Harper et al. v. Virginia State Board of Elections et al. 386 U.S. 663. (1966). Retrieved from https://supreme.justia.com/cases/federal/us/383/663/

Hate mail floods Norfolk: Chain letters threaten city's colored citizens (1958, November 22). *Journal and Guide,* p. 2.

Hayter, J. M. (2017, August 9). Commentary: Confederate monuments about maintaining white supremacy. *The Palm Beach Post.* www.palmbeachpost.com

Height, D. I. (2001). "We wanted the voice of a woman to be heard": Black women and the 1963 March on Washington. In B. Collier-Thomas & V. P. Franklin (Eds.), *Sisters in the struggle: African American women in the civil rights-black power movement* (pp. 83–91). New York, NY: New York University Press.

Heinemann, R. L. (1996). *Harry Byrd of Virginia.* Charlottesville, VA: University Press of Virginia.

Heinemann, R. L., & the Dictionary of Virginia Biography. Colgate W. Darden (1897–1981). (2015, November 9). In *Encyclopedia Virginia.* Retrieved from http://www.EncyclopediaVirginia.org/Darden_Colgate_W_1897-1981

Hogan, L. C. (n.d.). Associated Negro press. In *Encyclopedia of Chicago.* Retrieved from http://www.encyclopedia.chicagohistory.org/pages/1734.html

Hollander, R. A. (1963, September 20). Classes grow: School empty, but not for long. *The Virginian-Pilot,* p. 1. F234.N8.V4, Perry Library Microforms, Old Dominion University.

Horn, J. (2018). *1619: Jamestown and the Forging of American Democracy.* New York, NY: Basic Books.

Huberman, A. M., & Miles, M. B. (Eds.). (2002). *The qualitative researcher's companion.* Thousand Oaks, CA: Sage.

Hucles, M. (2006). The nineteenth century. In C. S. Draper (Ed.), *Don't grieve after me: The black experience in Virginia 1619–2005* (pp. 29–64). Richmond and Hampton, VA: The Virginia Foundation for the Humanities and Hampton University.

Huffman, G. (2019, April 10). Twisted sources: How Confederate propaganda ended up in the South's schoolbooks. *Facing South*. Retrieved from https://www.facingsouth.org/2019/04/twisted-sources-how-confederate-propaganda-ended-souths-schoolbooks

Hughes, L. (1995). *The collected poems of Langston Hughes*. New York, NY: Vintage Books.

Hughes, S. S. (1982). Social organization in the black community. In J. H. Kobelski (Ed.), *Readings in black and white: Lower Tidewater Virginia* (pp. 55–62). Portsmouth, VA: Portsmouth Public Library.

Hughes, S. S., & Bogger, T. (2006). The twentieth century. In C. S. Draper (Ed.), *Don't grieve after me: The black experience in Virginia 1619-2005* (pp. 65–104). Richmond and Hampton, VA: The Virginia Foundation for the Humanities and Hampton University.

Huie, W. B. (1956, January 24). The shocking story of approved killing in Mississippi. From *Look* magazine. Republished as Killer's Confession on PBS *American Experience*. Retrieved from https://www.pbs.org/wgbh/americanexperience/features/till-killers-confession/

In Norfolk, from plaintiff to political force: Evelyn Butts' gift to her city. (1993, March 15). *The Virginian-Pilot*, p. A-8

Isoke, Z. (2013). *Urban black women and the politics of resistance*. New York, NY: Palgrave Macmillan.

Jackie Robinson's All-Stars say "hello" to Peninsula folks. (1949, October 22). *Journal and Guide*, p. C-8.

Jackson, H. H. (2016, October 17). Alabama Bourbons. In *Encyclopedia of Alabama*. Retrieved from http://www.encyclopediaofalabama.org/article/h-1900

Jackson, J. & Daley, D. (2020, June 12). Voter suppression is still one of the greatest obstacles to a more just America. *Time*. Retrieved from https://time.com/5852837/voter-suppression-obstacles-just-america/

Jacox, C. (1954, April 17). From the press box. *Journal and Guide*, p. 18.

James, J. (1997). *Transcending the talented tenth: Black leaders and American intellectuals*. New York, NY: Routledge.

Jim Crow lived here. (n.d.). *1904 Richmond streetcar boycott*. Retrieved from http://jimcrowlivedhere.org/exhibits/show/streetcar

Job, housing probe due: School bias found by U.S.—Jordan. (1964, July 4). *Journal and Guide*, p. C1.

Johnson, H., Jr. (1966, April 23). The lawyer and the housewife. *Journal and Guide*, p. B4.

Johnson, M. (2020, November 12, 2020). Stacey Abrams puts muscle into Georgia runoffs. *The Hill*. Retrieved from https://thehill.com/homenews/state-watch/525594-stacey-abrams puts-muscle-into-georgia-runoffs

Johnson, W. P. II. (2017, Winter). The dying breath of Jim Crow: Harper v. Virginia Board of Elections. *The Fare Facs Gazette*, 14(1), 1, 6, 8–11.

Jones, M. S. (2018). *Birthright citizens: A history of race and rights in antebellum America*. New York, NY: Cambridge University Press.

Jones, M. S. (2019, March 8). Jones, M. S. (2019). How the daughters and granddaughters of former slaves secured voting rights for all. *Smithsonian Magazine.* www.smithsonianmag.com.

Jones, M. S. (2020). *Vanguard: How Black women broke barriers, won the vote, and insisted on equality for all.* New York, NY: Basic Books.

Jones, T. L. (1982). Race relations in Portsmouth during World War II. In J. H. Kobelski (Ed.), *Readings in black and white: Lower Tidewater Virginia.* (pp. 55–62). Portsmouth, VA: Portsmouth Public Library.

Kachun, M. (2017). *First martyr of liberty: Crispus Attucks in American memory.* New York, NY: Oxford University Press.

Keyssar, A. (2009). *The right to vote: The contested history of democracy in the United States* (Rev. Ed.). New York, NY: Basic Books.

Khalid, A. (2020, September 13). Elections: Republicans are knocking on doors. Democrats aren't. Biden's campaign says that's OK. *NPR.* Retrieved from https://www.npr.org/2020/09/13/911460651/republicans-are-knocking-on-doors democrats-arent-biden-s-campaign-says-that-s-o

King, M. (2020, November 8). 2020 elections: How Stacey Abrams and her band of believers turned Georgia blue: She and voting rights advocates saw 2020 as the perfect time to make a play for Georgia. The battle was getting the Democratic Party to believe it. *Politico.* Retrieved from https://www.politico.com/news/2020/11/08/stacey-abrams believers-georgia-blue-434985

King, M. L., Jr. (1957, May 17). *Give Us the Ballot.* Address delivered at the Prayer Pilgrimage for Freedom, Washington, D.C. The Martin Luther King, Jr. Papers Project. Retrieved from https://kinginstitute.stanford.edu/king-papers/documents/give-us-ballot-address-delivered-prayer-pilgrimage-freedom

Klarman, M. J. (2004). *From Jim Crow to civil rights: The Supreme Court and the struggle for racial equality.* New York, NY: Oxford University Press.

Klebau, J. D. (1954, September 20). Coronado Home Attacked. *The Norfolk Ledger-Dispatch.* Retrieved from http://cdm15987.contentdm.oclc.org/cdm/ref/collection/p15987coll9/id/2319

Kluger, R. (2004). *Simple justice: The history of Brown v. board of education and black America's struggle for equality.* New York, NY: Vintage Books.

Kneebone, J. T. (2016, November 4). Ku Klux Klan in Virginia. In Encyclopedia Virginia. Retrieved from http://www.EncyclopediaVirginia.org/Ku_Klux_Klan_in_Virginia.

Knepler, M. (1992, March 29). Ranks of registered voters decline as deadline nears, civic leaders are perplexed. *The Virginian-Pilot,* Compass community news section, p. 3.

Knepler, M. (2001a, February 26). Reforming democracy: anti-poll tax legacy lives on today/Butts' fight part of campaign. *The Virginian-Pilot.*

Knepler, M. (2001b, February 26). Poll-tax suit has far-reaching effects. *The Virginian-Pilot.*

Knepler, M. (2017, April 7). Today in local history: Norfolk Tars and the New York Yankees host a civil rights breakthrough. *AltDaily.com.* Retrieved from https://altdaily.com/today-in-local-history-norfolk-tars-and-the-new-york-yankees-host-a-civil-rights-breakthrough/

Komp, C. (2016, March 17). Patriotism, perseverance and the end of the poll tax. VPM public broadcasting. Retrieved from https://vpm.org/news/articles/2306/patriotism-perseverance-and-the-end-of-the-poll-tax

Kvale, S., & Brinkmann, S. (2009). *InterViews: Learning the craft of qualitative research interviewing.* (2nd ed.) Los Angeles, CA: Sage.

Lange, K. (2017, February 7). *Meet Sgt. William Carney: The first African-American Medal of Honor recipient.* U.S. Army. Retrieved from https://www.army.mil/article/181896/meet_sgt_william_carney_the_first_african_amerian_medal_of_honor_recipient

Larson, K. C. (2004). *Bound for the promised land: Harriet Tubman, portrait of an American hero.* New York: Ballantine Books.

Law Library of Congress. (n.d.) Slavery and indentured servants. Retrieved from https://memory.loc.gov/ammem/awhhtml/awlaw3/slavery.html

Lawless, J. & Casert, R. (2019, April 17). Rebuilding will be long, fraught—and pricey. The Virginian-Pilot. Retrieved from pilotonline.com

Lawson, S. F. (1991). Freedom then, freedom now: The historiography of the civil rights movement. *The American Historical Review, 96*(2), 456–471. https://doi.org/10.1086/ahr/96.2.456

Lawson, S. F. (1999). *Black ballots: Voting rights in the South, 1944–1969.* Lanham, MD: Lexington Books.

Lee, H. (2009). *Biography: A very short introduction.* New York, NY: Oxford University Press.

Legendary local activist Evelyn Butts dies at 68: She helped beat the poll tax and registered many black voters. (1993, March 12). *The Virginian-Pilot,* p. A-1.

Lepore, J. (2018). *These truths: A history of the United States.* New York, NY: W. W. Norton & Company.

Lewis, E. (1991). *In their own interests: Race, class, and power in twentieth century Norfolk, Virginia.* Berkeley and Los Angeles, CA: University of California Press.

Library of Virginia (n.d.). Richmond streetcar boycott, 1904. Retrieved from http://edu.lva.virginia.gov/online_classroom/shaping_the_constitution/doc/streetcar

Lichtman, A. J. (2018). *The embattled vote in America: From the founding to the present.* Cambridge, MA: Harvard University Press.

Ligon, C. B. (2017). *FEARLESS: How a poor Virginia seamstress took on Jim Crow, beat the poll tax and changed her city forever.* Hampton, VA: Smallwood Charlotte Press.

Lin, J. (2013). A greedy institution: Domestic workers and a legacy of legislative exclusion. *Fordham International Law Journal, (36)*3, 706–741.

Lindgren, J. M. (1993). *Preserving the Old Dominion: Historic preservation and Virginia traditionalism.* Charlottesville, VA: University of Virginia Press.

Littlejohn, J. L. (2011, March 25). "In the best American tradition of freedom, we defy you": The radical partnership of Joseph Jordan, Leonard Holt, and Edward Dawley. In *The Virginia Forum.* Conference conducted at Washington and Lee University, Lexington, VA.

Littlejohn, J. L., & Ford, C. H. (2012). *Elusive equality: desegregation and resegregation in Norfolk's public schools.* Charlottesville, VA: University of Virginia Press.

Maciag, M. (2014, October). Voter turnout plummeting in local elections. *Governing.com.* Retrieved from https://www.governing.com/topics/politics/gov-voter-turnout-municipal-elections.html

Many witnesses are heard: Pickets curbed at Norfolk market. (1960, March 19). *Journal and Guide*, p. A13.

Marshall, C., & Rossman, G. B. (2006). *Designing qualitative research* (4th ed.). Thousand Oaks, CA: Sage Publications.

Marshall, T. H. (1964). *Class, citizenship, and social development: Essays by T. H. Marshall.* Westport, CT: Greenwood Press.

Martin, R. B. (1958, November 29). The guide post: The ballot was loaded. *Journal and Guide*, p. 8.

Martin, J., & Shear, M. D. (2014, January 23). With 'Virginia Way,' state thought it didn't need rules. *The New York Times*. Retrieved from www.nytimes.com

Martinot, Steve (n.d.). *The question of fascism in the U.S.* Retrieved from https://www.ocf.berkeley.edu/~marto/fascism.htm

Maxwell, A. (2010, January). *The doctrine of interposition: James J. Kilpatrick and the radicalization of Virginia and the South.* Paper presented at the 124th Annual Meeting of the American Historical Association, San Diego, CA. Retrieved from https://aha.confex.com/aha/2010/webprogram/Paper4404.html

McAllister, B. (1966, March 25). Victor expects another fight. *The Virginian-Pilot*, pp. A-1, A-10. F234.N8.V4, Perry Library Microforms, Old Dominion University.

McCartney, M. Virginia's first Africans. (2018, June 26). *In Encyclopedia Virginia*. Retrieved from http://www.EncyclopediaVirginia.org/Virginia_s_First_Africans

McCollum, O. (1963, July 13). Rights demands urgent: Advisers set to survey hotels on racial policy. *Journal and Guide*, pp. C1–C2.

McDaid, J. D. (2018, October 26). Woman suffrage in Virginia. *Encyclopedia Virginia*. Retrieved from http://www.EncyclopediaVirginia.org/Woman_Suffrage_in_Virginia

McGuire, D. L. (2011). *At the dark end of the street: Black women, rape, and resistance—A new history of the civil rights movement from Rosa Parks to the rise of black power.* New York, NY: Alfred A. Knopf.

McKenna, D. (2011, September 2). Fight for new Dixie: Fifty years ago, a Washington Baltimore preseason game sparked protests over the Redskins' segregation policy. *Washington City Paper*. Retrieved from https://www.washingtoncitypaper.com/arts/theater/article/13041347/why-a-washingtonbaltimore-game-sparked-redskins-segregation-policy-protests

Meacham, J. (2018). *The soul of America: The battle for our better angels.* New York, NY: Random House Large Print.

Minton, B. (2020, July 31). The lies our textbooks told my generation of Virginians about slavery: State leaders went to great lengths to instill their gauzy version of the Lost Cause in young minds. *The Washington Post*. Retrieved from *www.washingtonpost.com*

Modern History Sourcebook: Sojourner Truth: "Ain't I a woman?", December 1851. (n.d.). Retrieved from https://sourcebooks.fordham.edu/mod/sojtruth-woman.asp

Montgomery, A. (2020, March 24). Grassroots support for local businesses shines through during COVID-19 disruption. *Beloit Daily News*. Retrieved from https://www.beloitdailynews.com/news/covid-19/grassroots-support-

for-local-businesses shines-through-during-covid-19-disruption/article_
f713db97-30cd-5260-8714 f1f6778c462c.html

Moodie-Mills, D. (2016, October, 11). The "Green Book" was a travel guide
just for black motorists. Retrieved from https://www.nbcnews.com/news/
nbcblk/green-book-was-travel-guide-just-black-motorists-n649081

More than 800 attend: Women crusaders stage Humphrey-Muskie rally. (1968,
November 2). *Journal and Guide*, pp. B1–B2.

Morris, A. D. (1984). *The origins of the civil rights movement: Black
communities organizing for change*. New York, NY: The Free Press.

Moye, J. T. (2011). Focusing our eyes on the prize: How community studies are
reframing and rewriting the history of the civil rights movement. In E. Crosby
(Ed.), *Civil rights history from the ground up: Local struggles, a national
movement* (pp. 147–171). Athens, GA: The University of Georgia Press.

Mr. and Mrs. Jackie Robinson visit Newport News. (1948, February 14). *Journal
and Guide*, p. A-4.

Murphy, R. (2020, June 2). As protests continue, Norfolk mayor is starting a
commission on racial disparities and criminal justice reform. *The Virginian-
Pilot*. Retrieved from www.pilotonline.com

Nasstrom, K. L. (1999, April). Down to now: Memory narrative, and women's
leadership in the civil rights movement in Atlanta, Georgia. *Gender &
History*, 11(1), 113–144.

National Register of Historic Places Registration Form. (2002, June 17). *Jackson
Ward Historic District (Additional Documentation)*, p. 15. United States
Department of the Interior National Park Service. Retrieved from https://
www.dhr.virginia.gov/wp-content/uploads/2018/04/127-0237_Jackson_
Ward_HD_2002_AdditionalDocumentation_Final_Nomination.pdf

Nation's Premier Civil Rights Organization. (n.d.). Retrieved from https://www.
naacp.org/nations-premier-civil-rights-organization/

Nazaryan, A. (2017, March 9). How the "Green Book" saved black lives on the
road. *Newsweek*. Retrieved from  https://www.newsweek.com/2017/03/17/
green-book-jim-crow-era-travel guide-saved-black-lives-565430.html

Nelson, C. (1948, February 14). Jackie and Mrs. Robinson see Hampton cagers
down Delaware. Journal and Guide, p. 2.

Newby-Alexander, C. L. (n.d.). Remembering Norfolk's African
American cemeteries. Retrieved from http://www.racetimeplace.com/
cemeteryhistory.htm

Newby-Alexander, C. L. (2017). *Virginia waterways and the Underground
Railroad*. Cheltenham, UK: The History Press.

Newby-Alexander, C. L. (2018, January 29). Underground Railroad in
Virginia. In *Encyclopedia Virginia*. Retrieved from http://www.
EncyclopediaVirginia.org/Underground_Railroad_in_Virginia

Nicholls, M. L. (2016, April 21). Gabriel's conspiracy (1800). In Encyclopedia
Virginia. Retrieved from http://www.EncyclopediaVirginia.org/Gabriel_s_
Conspiracy_1800

No let-up in protest. (1963, September 21). *Journal and Guide*, p. B23 (Part of a
package with photo captions, "A family affair ...," p. B9, and "Ignores rain
to 'March,'" p. B23).

No radical—Robertson: Norfolk NAACP branch sets election March 13. (1961,
March 4). *Journal and Guide*, pp. 1–2.

No radical leadership wanted: Norfolk NAACP to vote on 2 slates Monday evening. (1961, March 11). *Journal and Guide*, pp. 1, 2.

Norfolk committees push drive to increase number of votes. (1959, January 10). *Journal and Guide*, p. 4.

Norfolkians crowd Gotham for series play. (1947, October 11). *Journal and Guide*, p. 17.

North, A. (2020, November 11). 6 Black women organizers on what happened in Georgia—and what comes next. One lesson: "Do not take Black women for granted." *Vox*. Retrieved from https://www.vox.com/21556742/georgia-votes-election-organizers-stacey-abrams

O'Connor, L. (2020, July 24). LeBron James helping Florida ex-felons pay fees so they can vote: His campaign is partnering with a Florida voting rights group to help formerly incarcerated people pay fines that block them from casting votes. *HuffPost*. Retrieved from https://www.huffpost.com

Odum, H. W. (1943). *Race and rumors of race: Challenge to American crisis*. Chapel Hill, NC: The University of North Carolina Press.

Officers, purposes listed: Norfolk SCLC receives praises of Dr. King. (1963, November 16). *Journal and Guide*, p. B17.

Ogden, F. D. (1958). *The poll tax in the South*. Tuscaloosa, AL: University of Alabama Press.

Olson, L. (2001). *Freedom's daughters: The unsung heroines of the civil rights movement from 1830 to 1970*. New York, NY: Touchstone.

Online inflation calculator (n.d.). Retrieved from www.officialdata.org

Onyenacho, T. (2020, March 30). Power to the people: 50+ grassroots activists step up during the COVID 19 crisis. *Colorlines*. Retrieved from https://www.colorlines.com/articles/power-people-50-grassroots-activists-step-during covid-19-crisis-updated

Over 100 register on March 25: Requests extend night registration to May 6 (1968, March 30). *Journal and Guide*, p. A-2.

Overwhelming majority: Contested election won by Robert D. Robertson. (1961, March 18). *Journal and Guide*, pp. 1, 2.

Parramore, T. C., Stewart, P. C., & Bogger, T. L. (1994). *Norfolk: The first four centuries*. Charlottesville, VA: University Press of Virginia.

Parker, C. S. (2009). *Fighting for democracy: Black veterans and the struggle against white supremacy in the postwar South*. Princeton, NJ: Princeton University Press.

Parker, S. (2012, February 1). Memorial story reflects King's vision. *The Virginian-Pilot*, African American Today supplement. Retrieved from https://pilotonline.com/guides/africanamerican-today/article_f447b59b-b20e-53b8-9ab6-4d3124640fb4.html

Patton, M. Q. (2002). *Qualitative research and evaluation methods*. Thousand Oaks, CA: Sage.

People express desire for change: Jordan community choice in City Council election. (1968, June 22). *Journal and Guide*, p. 2.

Pittman, A. (2018, November 23). Hyde-Smith attended all-white "seg academy" to avoid integration. *Jackson Free Press*. Retrieved from http://www.jacksonfreepress.com

Podolefsky, (1998, January). Illusion of suffrage: Female voting rights and the women's poll tax repeal movement after the Nineteenth Amendment. *Notre Dame Law Review*, 73(3), 839–888. Retrieved from http://scholarship.law.nd.edu/ndlr/vol73/iss3/16

Pole, J. R. (1958, February). Representation and authority in Virginia from the Revolution to reform. *The Journal of Southern History*, 24(1), 16-50. Retrieved from https://www.jstor.org/stable/2955284.

Portland State University. (2016). Who votes for mayor. Retrieved from http://www.whovotesformayor.org/compare

Randolph, A. P. (1942, November). Why should we march? *Survey Graphic*, 488–489. Retrieved from http://web.mit.edu/21h.102/www/Primary%20source%20collections/World%20War%20II/Randolph,%20Why%20Should%20We%20March.htm

Ransby, B. (2003). *Ella Baker and the black freedom movement: A radical democratic vision*. Chapel Hill, NC: The University of North Carolina Press.

R. D. Robertson mourned: Funeral services for vet NAACP leader. (1969, June 28). *Journal and Guide*, p. 1.

Referendum post mortem (1958, November 29). *Journal and Guide*, p. 1.

Riessman, C. K. (1993). *Narrative analysis*. Qualitative research methods (series 30). Newbury Park, CA: Sage.

Robnett, B. (1997). *How long? How long? African-American women in the struggle for civil rights*. New York, NY: Oxford University Press.

Rogers, D. W. (1992). Introduction. In D. W. Rogers with C. Scriabine (Eds.), *Voting and the spirit of American democracy: Essays on the history of voting and voting rights in America* (pp. 3–18). Urbana and Chicago, IL: University of Illinois Press.

Rose, L. A. (2008). *Explorer: The life of Richard E. Byrd*. Columbia, MO: University of Missouri Press.

Rozsa, L. (2020, October 5). Most Florida felons kept from registering to vote by fines, fees or fears, activists say: The hurdle erected by Republican lawmakers proved consequential to this year's massive re-enfranchisement effort. *The Washington Post*. Retrieved from www.washingtonpost.com

Roseberry, J. R. (1963, July 16). Advisers vote for Negro on School Board. *The Virginian-Pilot*, p. 1. F234.N8.V4, Perry Library Microforms, Old Dominion University.

Schlegel, M. W. (1991). *Conscripted city: Norfolk in World War II*. Norfolk, VA: Hampton Roads Publishing.

Schley, M. M. (2013). *The United Order of Tents and 73 Cannon Street: A study of identity and place*. (Doctoral dissertation, Clemson University). Available from ProQuest Dissertations & Theses Global. (Order No. 1539441)

School facilities unequal: No halting of Coronado plans, board tells PTA. (1959, July 25). *Journal and Guide*, p. A20.

Schwandt, T. A. (2007). *The SAGE dictionary of qualitative inquiry* (3rd ed.). Thousand Oaks, CA: Sage.

Scully, M. (1963, September 20). Negro students march with list of grievances. *The Virginian-Pilot*, p. 1. F234.N8.V4, Perry Library Microforms, Old Dominion University.

Senate Clerk's Office. (n.d.). *Your guide to the Virginia General Assembly*. Retrieved from https://publications.virginiageneralassembly.gov/download_publication/121

7 Va. communities pick Negro councilmen: Portsmouth elects 2, Norfolk 1 Richmond drops 2; Joseph Owens loses seat in Petersburg. (1968, June 22). *Journal and Guide*, p. 3.

Shafer, J. (2010, August 30). Who said it first? Journalism is the first rough draft of history. *Slate*. Retrieved from https://slate.com/news-and-politics/2010/08/on-the-trail-of-the-question-who-first-said-or-wrote-that-journalism-is-the-first-rough-draft-of-history.html

Sitkoff, H. (2008). *The struggle for black equality*. (25th-anniversary ed.). New York, NY: Hill and Wang.

Smith, J. D. (2002). *Managing white supremacy: Race, politics, and citizenship in Jim Crow Virginia*. Chapel Hill, NC: The University of North Carolina Press.

Smith, L. M. (2001). *Where the South begins: Black politics and civil rights activism in Virginia, 1930–1951*. (Doctoral dissertation). Available from ProQuest Dissertations and Theses database. (Order No. 3018831).

Springston, R. (2014, April 14). Happy slaves? The peculiar story of three Virginia school textbooks. *Richmond Times-Dispatch*. Retrieved from www.richmond.com

Standley, A. (1993). The role of black women in the civil rights movement. In V. L. Crawford, J. C. Rouse, & B. Woods (Eds.), *Women in the civil rights movement: Trailblazers and torchbearers 1941–1965* (pp. 183–202). Bloomington, IN: Indiana University Press.

State Historical Society of Missouri. (n.d.). *Historic Missourians: Dred Scott, 1800?–1858*. Retrieved from https://shsmo.org/historicmissourians/name/s/scottd/

Suggs, H. L. (1988). *P. B. Young newspaperman: Race, politics, and journalism in the new South, 1910–62*. Charlottesville, VA: University of Virginia Press.

Support grows for 'our man Joe ...': Jordan gets backing in council bid (1968, June 8). *Journal and Guide*, pp. A1-2.

Sweeney, J. R. (1994). A new day in the old Dominion. *Virginia Magazine of History and Biography*, 102(3), 307-348. Retrieved from https://digitalcommons.odu.edu/history_fac_pubs/8

Swift, E. (1993, March 12). For all that she meant to Norfolk, Butts deserved better. *The Virginian-Pilot*, p. D-1.

Swim, J. K., & Hyers, L. L. (2009). Sexism. In T. D. Nelson (Ed.), *Handbook of prejudice, stereotyping, and discrimination* (pp. 407–430). New York, NY: Psychology Press.

Tacker, H. R. (1970, June). Household employment under OASDHI, 1951-66. *Social Security Bulletin* (p. 10). Retrieved from https://www.ssa.gov/policy/docs/ssb/v33n6/v33n6p10.pdf

Tarter, B. (2013). *The grandees of government: The origins and persistence of undemocratic politics in Virginia*. Charlottesville, VA: University of Virginia Press.

Tarter, B. Poll tax. (2014, July 2). In *Encyclopedia Virginia*. Retrieved from https://www.encyclopediavirginia.org/Poll_Tax

Tarter, B. (2015, October 21). African Americans and politics in Virginia (1865–1902). In *Encyclopedia Virginia*. Retrieved from https://www.encyclopediavirginia.org/African_Americans_and_Politics_in_Virginia_1865-1902

Tarter, B. (2019) *Gerrymanders: How redistricting has protected slavery, white supremacy, and partisan minorities in Virginia*. Charlottesville, VA: University of Virginia Press.

Taylor, J. M. (2002, July 27). Lee's biographer is a story himself. *The Washington Times*. Retrieved from https://www.washingtontimes.com/ news/2002/jul/27/20020727-034955-2321r/

10,000 fans see Robinson All-Stars at Norfolk. (1948, October 22). *Journal and Guide*, p. 15.

Terborg-Penn, R. (1998). *African American women in the struggle for the vote, 1850–1920*. Bloomington, IN: Indiana University Press.

The referendum and next steps. (1958, November 22). *Journal and Guide*, p. B14.

Theoharis, J. (2011). Accidental matriarchs and beautiful helpmates: Rosa Parks, Coretta Scott King, and the memorialization of the civil rights movement. In E. Crosby (Ed.), *Civil rights history from the ground up: Local struggles, a national movement* (pp. 385–418). Athens, GA: The University of Georgia Press.

Thomas, J. (2019). *The Virginia way: Democracy and power after 2016*. Charleston, SC: The History Press.

Third Force women make annual visit to the Capitol. (1970, February 28). *Journal and Guide*, p. B17.

Three buses to Washington: These Norfolkians went with NAACP caravan. (1963, August 31). *Journal and Guide*, pp. 1, 2.

Titus, J. O. (2011). *Brown's battleground: Students, segregationists, and the struggle for justice in Prince Edward County, Virginia*. Chapel Hill, NC: University of North Carolina Press.

Tucker, R. B. (2000). *Affirmative action, the Supreme Court, and political power in the old Confederacy*. Lanham, MD: University Press of America.

Tucker, S. W. (1965, March 31). Testimony, *Congressional Record*, p. 722.

Turner, D. W., III (2010). Qualitative interview design: A practical guide for novice investigators. *The Qualitative Report, 15*(3), 754–760. Retrieved from http://nsuworks.nova.edu/tqr/vol15/iss3/19

Tyler, J. (2020, October 17). Elections: Campaigns aim to reach new voters through mutual friends. *NPR*. Retrieved from https://www.npr. org/2020/10/17/924868621/campaigns aim-to-reach-new-voters-through-mutual-friends

United States Department of the Interior, National Park Service. (n.d.) *Jackson Ward Historic District (additional documentation), City of Richmond, Virginia*. National Register of Historic Places.

Varon, E., & the Dictionary of Virginia Biography. (2018, May 7). Joseph T. Wilson (1837–1890). In *Encyclopedia Virginia*. Retrieved from http://www. EncyclopediaVirginia.org/Wilson_Joseph_T_1837-1890

Vaismoradi, I., Jones, J., Turunen, H., & Snelgrove, S. (2016). Theme development in qualitative content analysis and thematic analysis. *Journal of Nursing Education and Practice, 6*(5), 100–110. doi:10.5430/jnep. v6n5p100

Vegh, S. G. (2009, February 20). Influential Hampton Roads Bishop L.E. Willis Sr. dies. *The Virginian-Pilot*. Retrieved from https://pilotonline.com/news/ article_df710afa-c411-50aa-9ac4-96f842941115.html

Virginia Democrats hopeful as Negro registration grows (1964, September 20). *The New York Times*.

Virginia Department of Historic Resources. (1982). *Attucks Theatre. National Register of Historic Places Inventory—Nomination Form*, United States Department of the Interior Heritage Conservation and Recreation Service. Retrieved from https://www.dhr.virginia.gov/historic-registers/122-0074/

Virginia Historical Society. (n.d.). *Becoming Virginians*. Retrieved from https://www.virginiahistory.org/sites/default/files/uploads/sov_virginians.pdf

Virginia Museum of History & Culture. (n.d.). *Affidavit, 1693*. Retrieved from https://www.virginiahistory.org/node/2290

Voter turnout in presidential elections: 1828—2016 (n.d.). *The American Presidency Project*. Retrieved from https://www.presidency.ucsb.edu/statistics/data/voter-turnout-in-presidential-elections

Voters club tours General Assembly in Richmond. (1968, March 9). *Journal and Guide*, p. A8.

Wahba, P. (2020, November 4). This nail-biter election generated the highest U.S. voter turnout rate in 120 years. *Fortune*. Retrieved from https://fortune.com/2020/11/04/record-voter turnout-2020-election-youth-vote-vote-by-mail/

Waldman, M. (2016). *The fight to vote*. New York, NY: Simon & Schuster.

Walker, A. (2012). "A horrible fascination": Sex, segregation, and the lost politics of obscenity, *Washington University Law Review, 89*(5), 1017. Retrieved from https://openscholarship.wustl.edu/law_lawreview/vol89/iss5/2

Wallace-Sanders, K. (2008). *Mammy: A century of race, gender, and southern memory*. Ann Arbor, MI: University of Michigan Press.

Wallenstein, P. (2004). *Blue laws and black codes: Conflict, courts, and change in twentieth century Virginia*. Charlottesville, VA: University of Virginia Press.

Walton, H., Jr., Puckett, S. C., & Deskins, D. R., Jr. (2012). *The African American electorate: A statistical history* (Vols. 1 & 2). Thousand Oaks, CA: Sage Publications.

Watson, D. M. (2017, February 19). Long road. *The Virginian-Pilot*, African American Today supplement, p. T-6.

Watson, D. M. (2018, July 8). More than a "little place for coloreds." Locals remember the fun and frustration of the area's old segregated beaches. *The Virginian-Pilot*, pp. 1, 10.

Watson, D. M. (2020, March 8). 'I guess that was our little protest.' The 1960 sit-in movement of the South spurred ongoing protests throughout the 1960s against racial inequality. *The Virginian-Pilot*, The Sunday Break section, pp. 1,3.

Welch, A. W. (2004). Law and the making of slavery in Colonial Virginia, *Explorations in Ethnic Studies, 27*(1), 1–22. https://doi.org/10.1525/esr.2004.27.1.1

West Point Monument (HM1ECQ). (2014). Norfolk's Civil War African American heritage. *Historical Marker Project*. Retrieved from https://www.historicalmarkerproject.com/markers/HM1ECQ_west-point-monument_Norfolk-VA.html

What the life of Martin Luther King, Jr. has meant to me ... (1986, January 15). *Journal and Guide MLK Supplement*, pp. 3–4.

White, F. R. (1992). *Pride and prejudice: School desegregation and urban renewal in Norfolk, 1950–1959*. Westport, CT: Praeger Publishers.

White, F. R. (2018). *Black, white and brown: The battle for progress in 1950s Norfolk*. Norfolk, VA: Parke Press.

Williams, J. (2013). *Eyes on the prize: America's civil rights years, 1954–1965* (30th anniversary ed.). New York, NY: Penguin Books.

Williams, J. P. (2020, November 13). Stacey Abrams' legacy: A Democratic South? The Georgia Democrat has spent the last few years registering voters and that might help Democrats gain a foothold in the South. *U.S. News & World Report*. Retrieved from https://www.usnews.com/news/elections/articles/2020-11-13/stacey-abrams-work-could bring-about-a-democratic-south

Williams, L. E. (1998). *Servants of the people: The 1960s legacy of African American leadership*. New York, NY: St. Martin's Griffin.

Winter, M. (2010, April 30). A nannies' bill of rights: A New York bill protecting domestic workers that would be the first of its kind. *Slate*. Retrieved from https://slate.com/humaninterest/2010/04/a-bill-of-rights-for-domestic-workers-in-new-york.html

Wolcott, H. F. (2001). *Writing up qualitative research* (2nd ed.). Thousand Oaks, CA: Sage Publications.

Wolfe, B. Colonial Virginia. (2017, August 11). In *Encyclopedia Virginia*. Retrieved from http://www.EncyclopediaVirginia.org/Colonial_Virginia

Women group gets name, plans July public meeting. (1969, June 21). *New Journal and Guide*, p. B10.

Woodward, C. V. (2002). *The strange career of Jim Crow* (commemorative ed.). New York, NY: Oxford University Press.

Wynes, C. E. (1961). *Race relations in Virginia 1870–1902*. Charlottesville, VA: University of Virginia Press.

You've got it...USE IT! (n.d.) Richmond Crusade for Voters flyer. *Social Welfare History Image Portal*. Retrieved from http://images.socialwelfare.library.vcu.edu

Zeitz, J. (2017, March 12). Lessons from the fake news pandemic of 1942: The South couldn't stop the rumors. Can we? *Politico*. Retrieved from https://www.politico.com/magazine/story/2017/03/lessons-from-the-fake-news pandemic-of-1942-214898

Zinn, M. B., & Dill, B. T. (Eds.). (1994). *Women of color in U.S. society*. Philadelphia, PA: Temple University Press.

# INDEX